Sherri Schoenborn Murray

The *Viola* Girl

Counterfeit Princess Series

Book Two

Sherri Schoenborn Murray

Visit Sherri's website:
www.christianromances.com

The Viola Girl

Cover photo of Wren by Clari Noel Photography
Cover design by Steve Novak Illustrations
Edited by: Cori Murray, Ethel Schoenborn, Jean Hall, Patty Slack, and final editor Kristi Weber.

Dedication

To my brother Brad,
who has been a romantic
since the day he was born,
and one of the best storytellers I know.

ΦΦΦ

I know the plans I have for you, declares the LORD...

JEREMIAH 29:11 – NIV

Prologue

Blue Sky Kingdom — 1869

To listen well can be a gift.

For the second time that evening, Maid Kimberlee tucked me into bed. I folded my arms behind my head while she smoothed the covers around me.

"Say your prayers, Miss Wren," she said.

"I already said them."

"Say them again, and ask our dear Lord to give you the self-control to stay in bed." She kissed my head to soften her reprimand. "If I catch you up one more time, I will have Herbert stand guard outside your door."

Herbert, one of our most formidable guards, held my utmost respect.

I closed my eyes, folding my hands together in prayer. "Father in Heaven, help me to be an obedient child." I peered out one eye at my governess, who'd also closed her eyes. "Grant me patience, for I can barely sleep with the music of Heaven drifting up to me." I peeked again at Maid Kimberlee. She had still not opened her eyes. "And I am so excited to hear all the stories that my sister will tell me in the morning." My eyelids were dancing and would not settle. "Amen."

"When one prays, Wren, it is not supposed to be a one-sided conversation with God. Did you allow yourself to listen to Him, as well?"

"I forgot." I smirked up at her.

Her eyes warmed. She bent and kissed my cheek once more.

But I was not ready to sleep. "Maid Kimberlee, what does *ally* mean?"

"Where did you hear that?" One stiff white brow lifted. "Have you been hiding in your father's study again?"

I tried not to squirm under her stern gaze. I'd heard *ally* several places this evening—twice when I'd hidden behind the drapery in Father's study, and once while I'd been hiding under the dessert table in the ballroom.

The matronly woman's large chest rose like the bow of a ship in high seas, or so I imagined since I had never seen the ocean outside of picture books.

"An *ally* is someone who will protect you, who'll always be on your side."

"Because they love you?" I asked.

"No, not necessarily. Because the two of you, for whatever reason, have decided to be on the same side."

"Like Blue Sky and Corra?" I said slowly, recalling some of the snippets I'd overheard tonight.

"Yes, and no." She sighed and sat down on the bed, near my hip. "Your father loves Edwin and, yes, he has made an oath to defend Edwin's homeland of Corra, but love is not always the basis for an alliance—ally," she amended at my puzzled look. "For considering someone an ally, that is."

I nodded, even though at my tender age of seven, I didn't completely understand.

She swept her fingertips gently across my forehead. "Sometimes the reasons are purely political. Sometimes there is no love at all. Now, no more questions." She rose. "And no more eavesdropping. It is a nasty habit and will only create enemies for you. Not allies."

I smiled softly up at her. She was such a tender-hearted woman that I knew she would not stay annoyed with me for long.

"Goodnight, Maid Kimberlee." I rolled to my side facing the door and clasped my hands beneath my cheek. "You are an ally of love," I said as she dimmed the gas lamps on the far wall.

"Shhh! You silly girl."

Despite her words, I heard a faint chuckle in her voice, all the same.

ΦΦΦ

I laid awake listening to the orchestra music that drifted up the stairwell and under my door and through the heat vents. My eyelids danced. Open and closed. I knew that I could not wait until morning to hear my sister's stories of her sixteenth birthday party, nor could I wait to tell her the joyous news I'd overheard: Mother was pregnant. I flipped back the covers, hitched up my green silk pajamas, and inched my door open to survey the hallway.

The noise of the people and the music was suddenly much louder. Herbert stood near the balustrade, watching the foyer full of people below.

I tiptoed quickly across the marble corridor, opened Alia's door and quietly closed it behind me. Hurrying, I climbed the steps to my older sister's bed and hid under a deluge of covers. She'd be annoyed with me at first, but then she'd welcome having someone to talk to, no matter how tired she was.

Hours later, I sat up. Orchestra music no longer floated in the air; only Alia's voice drew closer in the hallway. Was Maid Kimberlee with her? If she found me up again, she'd grab me by my earlobe and show no mercy.

I hurriedly smoothed the covers behind me, tumbled my way down the steps of the bed, and darted into the closet. Though I'd slid the door closed, I did not feel safe. I crouched low, pulled one of Alia's floor-length evening gowns over my head and stood up inside. While the garment remained intact above me on the hanger, I feared my bare feet might show beneath.

My heart pounded in my ears while I strained to listen. Alia was speaking to someone in her room. Her voice sounded tired.

The closet door slid open and someone—probably Maid Kimberlee—hung Alia's beautiful blue gown on a hanger next to mine.

Closing my eyes, I tried to silence my breathing.

The door was left open and, through the side opening of the gown, I had a view of the room.

"Your parents desire to say goodnight, dear," Maid Kimberlee said.

Oh, I just had to see, so I parted the button area of the gown until I had a decent one-eyed view.

Father and Mother entered and kissed Alia good night. For some reason, Dr. Krawl stood near her bedside holding a glass of milk.

"It's warm, Alia. It will help you sleep," the doctor said.

What a sweet gesture. I hoped they would do the same for me when I turned sixteen.

Alia yawned. "I will have no trouble sleeping." She curled her arms above her head and yawned some more.

In the silence that followed, I quietly unfastened more buttons and parted the chiffon for a better view.

"After what happened with Prince Dell, Alia, you are to drink this." Father took the glass from Dr. Krawl's hand, passing it to her. He looked at her tenderly.

Alia took a gulp of the milk and wrinkled her nose before setting the glass aside.

"Finish it, Alia," Father said in his stern voice.

As she attempted to obey him, my sister's arm dropped to her side, and she slumped back into the pillow—eyes closed, limbs lifeless by her side.

I sank my teeth down hard into my lower lip. What was happening?

"Thank you, Doctor." Father escorted him from the room.

Had something happened? Something they wanted Alia to forget?

Maid Kimberlee returned to the closet. This time, I could smell her rosewater scented soap as she retrieved the gown she'd just hung up. She rolled the garment into a tight ball and disappeared from my narrow vision of the room. Mother, in her wide-hooped ball gown, rustled past me into the closet and out again with an outfit over her arm.

With my heart in my throat, I watched as they flung back the sheets and changed Alia from her silk nightgown into the oddest of clothing. They guided her limp limbs into a shapeless, dirty-looking top, an old tattered skirt, leggings, and the ugliest shoes.

My teeth remained clamped down inside my mouth. Perhaps it was some clever joke. Alia was such a ninny about shoes. She would hate them.

"There is no time to cry, Maid Kimberlee," Mother sniffed. "There's no time."

Mother was crying. What were they doing with my sister? I wanted to know, but if they caught me out of bed, I might be next.

Father soon returned and carried Alia's limp body through the doorway. Mother followed. I wanted to, too, but Maid Kimberlee had stayed behind to tidy the room.

"Father in Heaven, watch over her all the days of her life." She wiped aside tears and pulled the bed coverings into place. "Precious, precious child." She mumbled more prayers before finally pulling the door closed behind her.

What was happening? I did not understand.

I tiptoed from the closet and waited near the top of the balcony until Maid Kimberlee's plump figure reached the main floor. I tried to hear past the wild beating of my heart. Far away, I heard a thud—downstairs from the direction of the kitchen, perhaps, the delivery door. I would never get there in time.

I raced down the marble hallway to Father's study, where there was a view of the road. I flung open the door, leaped on top of the settee onto the deep sill of the closed window. I caught myself; arms spread wide on the molding. Only the tip of my nose grazed the thick plate of glass.

Below, a wagon with a lone driver and a bunch of cages headed out the long, moonlit driveway. It resembled the wagon that delivered our eggs and milk each morning, but it was usually here at dawn, not midnight.

Down below in the courtyard, Father was holding Mother. They were watching, too.

In the marrow of my seven-year-old bones, I knew that the wagon was taking my sister somewhere. But where? And why had my parents given their permission? After several minutes of staring at the empty drive, I became aware of my silhouette in the window. Afraid of being caught, I hurried back to my room and slipped into bed before anyone would find me. I hugged my pillow to me and stared wide-eyed into the black of night.

Where had they taken Alia? Had she behaved badly at the ball? Were they trying to teach her a lesson? My heart stretched with the news I so longed to share with her. Mother was pregnant. We were going to have a little sister at last!

Chapter One

Five months and a birthday later . . .

After dinner, Father wanted to speak with me. He never spoke with me. Did he know that I'd hidden beneath his desk last night when the men had smoked cigars? I'd heard everything—Father was determined to defend a small coastal town named Corra, even if meant going to war with Davenport, the wealthiest country in all of Northend.

His advisors had argued with him. We'd only been at peace for five months. We needed time to rebuild our army and our allegiance.

There had been an onslaught of arguments and then Wilhelm, Father's top advisor, cleared his throat and the noise in the study dimmed. "Sons are for making kings and daughters are for making allies."

A pensive silence followed and then mumbles of agreement.

Surely, Father wouldn't marry me off at eight. He'd wait until I was older with hips and bumps like Alia.

Wouldn't he?

I gulped at the conversation before us and followed him up the stairs to the velvet settee in the hallway outside of his study.

We sat together. I clasped my trembling hands in my lap and like Father studied the life-sized oil painting of my sister.

She'd been fifteen when she stood for her portrait. In the ballroom, she'd faced north toward the veranda windows, and turned ever so slightly to look at the artist who'd captured a happy—hadn't a care—look in her hazel eyes.

"Your mother spoke with me recently." Father's voice was low, the same tone he used when he played chess with Wilhelm. "She said that you no longer desire to play the piano."

Like Alia, I played by ear and memory. But playing the Beast, as she'd called it, always reminded me of her. I missed her so. Mother told me she was now married to the future king of Yonder.

Sadly, I knew there was more to the story.

"I no longer enjoy playing... piano." Our time alone together was such a rarity that I tried to be brave.

"Wren," Father cleared his throat, "when you play, it fills our home not only with beautiful music but wonderful memories."

"Ye-s," I croaked. "But . . . Piano music—happy *or* sad—always reminds me of Alia. I miss her so terribly"—tears pooled as my gaze lingered on my sister's face—"that I feel it would be best if I didn't remember her so often." I knew I would weep if he told me I must continue playing.

"May I visit her?" I whispered, and just the thought of it lightened my spirit.

"No. It takes a month to get to Yonder, and it's a very difficult journey."

My gaze fell to the carpet as I tried to come to grips with the news.

"Have I ever told you about the battle that has no name?"

"No-oo." Although I'd overheard him retell numerous war stories, I'd never heard this particular one.

"It was horrific." Father's chest slowly deflated. "So horrific that I've seen no good in remembering it. You see, my remaining men and I decided never to speak of it or dwell on it again."

He had my attention now.

"What was so terrible about it, Father?" This tactical maneuver of emotion was new for me, and I didn't fully trust him.

He drew in a deep breath. "Somehow they knew that we'd had a brief reprieve at home. They'd planned their attack in a valley just north of here and caught us unaware." While he droned on and on, I was afraid to listen too deeply for there was pain in his voice.

"It was the battle in which young Edwin was maimed."

"Maimed?" The word was unfamiliar to me.

"Yes, his legs are permanently damaged. He will never walk again. Edwin Hew was a fine soldier, one of Blue Sky's best." Father blinked back the memories that filled his eyes. "Those of us who survived vowed to live a life worthy."

"Edwin's battle deserves a name, Father."

"I think so, too." He inhaled deeply. "Misery Hill," he whispered, lifting his gaze to Alia's, perfectly captured in the oil. "We were wrong not to remember. For in remembering, we heal; and when we are able to talk about it, Wren, we heal more. Have courage, little one, and remember whatever it is that has broken you."

He'd so quickly turned his story on me that I forcibly shook my head. I did not want to remember what haunted me night and day.

"If I can remember Misery Hill, you can remember yours."

I didn't like the game he played: A wound for a wound.

I lifted my gaze from the tall vase of coral-pink roses on the sideboard to Alia's. From there, I forced my memory up Misery Hill when I'd seen too much for my seven-year-old heart to bear.

Why had Father drugged her, sent her off in the middle of the night, not even let her say goodbye? His actions made me afraid of my future.

Tears dripped off the edge of my jaw onto my gown.

"You were brave, Wren." He held me stiffly with one arm. "We will find you your own instrument to play. Now, no more tears."

ΦΦΦ

Over the course of several days, the finest musicians in Blue Sky performed for Mother and me in the blue drawing room. It was on day three that I heard the viola.

While the dark-haired, middle-aged man played, I remembered watching my sister float about the ballroom with Pierre. After her lessons from the short Frenchman, I was often her partner, and we'd waltz, giggling and smiling at one another.

I'd heard music can transport a person to memories they've long forgotten. I now found it to be true, and I felt taller for it.

"I want to learn this one." I gazed up into Mother's sparkling eyes.

"Wait until he's done, dear." She nodded to the musician, smiling.

"I don't need to." I curled my finger for her to lean, so her ear was nearer to me. "This one has pulled at the strings of my heart."

Later that day, she arranged for my first lesson with the violist.

Sir Lambert fluffed his coat tails behind him and sat down across from me in a tufted Queen Anne chair. He went into great detail, explaining the length of the bow, and how the frog weighted it down, how tree sap was applied to the bow's strings as a resin for tone quality. His voice was like the bassoonist—so monotone and low that by the time he'd moved from the anatomy of the bow to the viola, my chaperone, Maid Kimberlee had fallen asleep. But I listened well, for the viola was to be my companion.

I liked that it was small enough to tote around, so unlike a piano. I would be able to take it with me on picnics, and even my hikes. I pictured myself at the foot of a waterfall, playing something dramatic.

My mind had wandered. "I'm sorry, Sir Lambert, can you repeat the name and purpose of the last part?"

"It is the bridge, a support for the strings." In the tiniest of whispers, he added, "imbecile child."

Maid Kimberlee's hearing was not as keen as mine, and her bowed head did not even bob.

For the next hour, Lambert droned on and on about the parts of a viola, adding every boring detail he could remember.

I cleared my throat. "Please teach me how to play." Once Mother heard of his name calling, this would most likely be his only session with me, and I wanted to learn all of his secrets.

"I *am* teaching you how to play." One dark brow arched.

He was not teaching me. He was dilly-dallying.

"I would like to watch you play again." He was a great musician, but not a great teacher.

With an arrogance that I had not detected earlier, he positioned his chin on the rest. He held the viola parallel to the floor, and keeping his wrist relaxed, turned the viola slightly toward me. Pulling the bow, he soon lost himself in a lovely piece. In the end, his music was so entrancing that I found myself willing to give Sir Lambert another chance.

"May I try?" I sat on my hands in case he said no.

"No. You need a child-sized viola."

"I would still like to try."

He rolled his eyes and handed me the instrument. I nestled my chin on the rest as he had done, and with good posture, I stretched my left hand toward the scroll piece on the end, but the breadth of me was much smaller, and my hand rested at the end of the belly instead. Determined to at least try, I held the viola parallel to the floor. He had not mentioned anything about chords, so in a way, trying without any instruction was comparable to learning to joust in the dark. I carefully positioned the bow on the strings and gently pulled down.

The beautiful viola emitted the ugliest, most piercing sound imaginable.

Lambert's deep, throaty laugh awakened Maid Kimberlee.

"Was that you, Wren?" Bottling a yawn, she clutched her hands in her lap.

"Yes, it sounded like you often do when you are snoring," I teased.

Her wide cheeks bunched.

I continued to experiment, and when the viola sound was unpleasant, Lambert laughed. When it was pleasant, he flushed.

Near the end of our lesson, I attempted something I'd seen Lambert do in Mother's presence. I bounced the bow against the strings and made the same pleasing sound that he'd made with the instrument.

An icy cold entered his eyes.

"Herbert," I called to the imposing guard who stood near the door, "Please get Mother."

In his absence, another guard stepped inside the room to take his place.

When Maid Kimberlee looked at me, a light shone in her eyes. She was going to let me handle today's lesson.

Mother arrived. Though her hair had turned gray at an early age, she was the loveliest of women. In her pink gown, I felt confident that the baby she carried was a girl.

"Mother, do you think it is appropriate that my new teacher has called me *imbecile child* beneath his breath?"

"Absolutely not." Her eyes flashed wide.

I took Maid Kimberlee's hand and escorted the middle-aged woman out of the room.

Mother would handle it from here.

Chapter Two

Mother soon found another teacher for me, and I was to spend an entire month in the country, learning the viola. Maid Kimberlee rolled one of my everyday dresses into a bundle and set it inside my trunk, which lay open on the floor.

"Who is Crauley?" I asked Mother, who sat beside me on my bed.

"He was Lambert's teacher."

"He must be very old." Lambert was at least Father's age.

"Yes, he is retired, but he has agreed to take you on as his last pupil."

I didn't like the sound of spending a month in the country with an elderly man, and I didn't like his name—Crauley. I imagined a growly old man keeling over in the middle of our lesson.

"I don't want to learn from him." I lifted my chin.

"He taught Lambert how to make the viola sing." Mother raised one brow at me. "He is the finest of teachers, Wren, and he is kind."

"Can you go with me?" My gaze lowered to the curved hemisphere of my baby sister inside her.

"No, sweetheart." She patted my arm. "My ankles are swollen. The doctor wants me to rest. In the morning, I will see you off, and then I am to go to bed for the next two months."

"Two months?" That was a long time to be in bed.

"Yes, while you're away, I will have the pleasure of reading books." She kissed my forehead. Mother loved to read. The image of a dozen books settled near her hip soothed me.

"Maid Kimberlee will be the one to accompany you." She glanced over her shoulder at our beloved companion. "We are to pack soft foods for Crauley. Oh, and he is fond of fruit butter."

"Why soft foods?" I asked.

"Crauley doesn't have very many teeth." Mother patted my hand and then stepped down from the bed.

She'd tweaked my imagination. Had Crauley lost his front teeth like me? With my tongue, I felt the wide gap between my teeth. At least I wasn't going alone to learn the viola from a growly old man. Maid Kimberlee would be with me.

ΦΦΦ

For our excursion, Maid Kimberlee and I traveled west by carriage through pleasant countryside. Our destination was a mere dot on the map, a tiny village called Hampershire.

"Why are Mother's ankles swelling?" Secretly, I had begun to worry that my baby sister would be born while I was away. I loved the stories Alia used to tell me of my first moments in life, and I wanted to be able to tell my little sister such stories, too.

"When a pregnant woman's ankles swell, it is a sign that she needs to rest and take up knitting." Maid Kimberlee patted my arm with her soft, plump hand.

"I thought God was knitting the baby."

She laughed softly under her breath. "He is, but now He needs your mother to rest so He can put in all the finishing touches."

"That's good. I don't think Mother knows how to knit."

My governess's cheeks bunched. "Reading is like knitting to your mother. It helps her put the rows of her life in order."

Hours later, Maid Kimberlee gently shook my knee to wake me. Our carriage had come to a complete stop. Stifling a yawn, I peered out the window on my side at a rustic cabin that wasn't even painted. Little wood shingles had been used for siding, and the roof was a bed of clover-green moss sprinkled with miniature white flowers. The grounds were knee-high grass with a stand of large, leafy umbrella-shaped trees behind the house.

The guard opened the carriage door and assisted me outside first, and then Maid Kimberlee joined me. Across from the cabin, an empty meadow rolled off into hills of distant blue. I could not even see the turrets of Blue Sky. Never had I been so far away from Mother.

Maid Kimberlee took my hand and led me inside the one-room home. Two common chairs sat in front of the fireplace; a grand piano sat near a wall of tiny windows, and some stringed instruments and piles of sheet music lay atop a low, dusty round table. One narrow bed sat against the far wall.

Where would Maid Kimberlee and I sleep? A ladder-like stairwell gave me hope that we would have a room in the attic.

"Put their things upstairs." To our left, an elderly man with wispy, white hair flicked his hand toward Herbert, the guard who'd carried in our cases.

I tried to be polite and not stare at Crauley, but I was curious as to how many teeth he had. His back and shoulders were curved like an owl's. Leaning on his cane, he gawked at me in return. His mouth bunched thoughtfully as he regarded my red hair—braided tight into one long plait, the waifishness of my eight-year-old form, and my brand-new lace-up leather shoes, purchased specifically for my trip to the country.

"We . . . we've brought you a crock of fruit butter," was the only thing I could think of to say.

"You have?" Using his cane, he rounded the side of the kitchen table, where the guard had set the box of food.

The guards finished delivering our things, and the door was pulled closed behind them. Paned glass windows lined all sides of the room, and I saw our uniformed men take their stations around the perimeter of the cabin.

Maid Kimberlee sat down in a large padded rocker and took out her needlepoint.

"Sit down, Wren." The elderly man patted the table at which he now sat. Perhaps it was because I was to be his pupil that he'd dropped my title.

"What am I to call you?" I asked.

He cleared his raspy throat. "Distinguished Sir Crauley is fine." Up close, his glasses were unlike any I had ever seen. The frames were like one finely twisted piece of wood that had been highly polished to bring out the burgundy and cream tones.

"Where did you get your glasses, Distinguished Sir Crauley?"

While he chuckled, I was able to count his teeth inside. There were only a dozen in all. And like I'd imagined, he was missing his two front teeth like me.

"My glasses are from Corra, a seaside town along the coast."

"Corra?" I'd heard of Corra.

"Yes, they are famous for their windblown trees." He reached for my nearest hand and, holding it in his, pressed his thumb across the length of my fingers as if he were counting. "Did they measure you for your new viola?"

"Yes. From here"—I pointed to the middle of my ribcage—"to here." I patted the middle of my left hand.

"You need a thirteen-inch viola," he said.

I nodded. "That's what they said, too."

"Why did you pick the viola?" He lifted the lid off the crock and dipped a spoonful of deep purple plum butter, which was my favorite.

I shook my head. "There are nice *soft* rolls to go with the butter." I handed him a fresh baked roll leftover from our morning breakfast and patted the tea towel back into place over the basket.

"Thank you, Wren." His bushy gray brows gathered, and he peered at Maid Kimberlee.

"She has always been a helpful child," she said, giving into a yawn.

Crauley slathered a roll with the purple butter and studied me while he chewed. He pressed on the side of my face and had me peer over one shoulder and then the other. I believe he was studying my ears.

I looked over at Maid Kimberlee. Mid-stitch, she'd already fallen asleep.

"Play something on the piano for me," Crauley said.

Was he kidding? I glanced toward my shiny new viola case on the side table.

"I no longer play the piano." Lowering my chin, I stared at him.

Behind his glasses, his round green eyes narrowed. "I heard that you have an exceptional ear, and I would like to hear what kind of ear that is."

"I dislike playing by ear." I was like my sister in that way. "I prefer to play from memory."

"And once you learn the viola that is how you will play it, also." He blinked softly. "But for now, I would like to hear you play the piano from memory."

"I play from my memories," I said. Music teachers often misunderstood Alia's and my gift. "I play from the memories inside my head and put them to melody."

"I'm familiar with the gift," he said and nodded toward Maid Kimberlee. "What is her name?"

With her hands folded over her wide, soft belly, my governess' snoring was only the slightest bit annoying.

"She is Maid Kimberlee, my constant companion."

"Wake her and tell her to nap upstairs. Her snoring is distracting."

Sir Crauley's ears were perhaps even more sensitive than mine. I gently shook Maid Kimberlee's shoulder until she was awake and assisted her across the room. With her hand on the wall, she carefully made her way up the ladder-like stairwell.

"I am tired from our travels. I will be down shortly," she said.

"Do not worry." Mother never allowed her to nap in the middle of the day, but I would. I returned to stand in front of Crauley.

"I want to hear your ear, Wren." He licked at the sticky purple on his fingers. "Play something on the piano."

My mother had found an odd, elderly man with only a dozen teeth and atrocious manners to be my instructor. I crossed the room to the piano. He was a viola teacher who let a dusty grand piano take up a quarter of his tiny home. Frowning, I stood between the piano and bench and smoothed the back of my skirt. I didn't want to remember Alia or Father right now.

"Why does the piano trouble you so?" he asked after I'd sat down.

"Some memories I do not wish to remember." I clasped my hands in my lap, and over my shoulder regarded him.

With a lift of those bushy brows of his, he curled his finger and bade my return.

What now?

Shoulders heavy, I crossed the room to stand within arm's reach of him. Behind his twisted frame glasses, his eyes were keen with many good years of life in them.

"Lesson number one . . . You did not choose the viola. The viola chose you."

"What do you mean?" It sounded like a riddle.

He flicked his wrist for me to return to the piano.

I wished Maid Kimberlee had not been so quick to nap. Perhaps I needed her. Perhaps Lambert had learned his rude behavior from his viola teacher—the Distinguished Sir Crauley.

I most certainly had been the one to choose the viola. I smoothed my dress behind me, sat down, and set the pads of my fingers lightly on the keys.

I thought about what I would play. My mind always returned to Alia and the night of her sixteenth party. I could not rid myself of the horrific memory. So I began with that evening and our last walk up the stairwell together. The chords were light as I recalled my exuberance and all that I'd wanted to share with her. She'd kissed the top of my head before returning to the party. I did not want to remember what lay ahead, but the tightness in my chest would not let me forget.

Driving my fingers deep into the keys, I recalled my view from Alia's closet: Father's tender gaze as he handed her the tainted milk, his betrayal, and even Mother's and Maid Kimberlee's. Melancholy chords were my refrain as the wagon pulled away in the moonlight, taking my childhood innocence with it.

I knew that now.

I pulled the piano lid closed and crossed the dusty sunlit room to stand in front of the elderly man. The skin on top of his head was freckled, and only sparse, wispy hairs grew.

Crauley leaned forward on his cane to get a better look at me.

"What was that memory?" He tilted his head to one side, a glassy sheen in his eyes. "What has happened to you, child?"

Everyone had always been happy enough to hear me play. No one had ever asked me *why* before. Not even Mother. My throat burned with emotion.

Maid Kimberlee's snoring was audible upstairs. Only the old man and I were awake in the cabin. He bid me closer and took my nearest hand in his. His tear-brimmed eyes led me to believe that he already knew the memories of my heart. So, I told him the unthinkable. The unsaid.

"The night of my sister's sixteenth birthday . . ." My voice trembled, and my hands began to shake with the emotion that was still in their fingertips. "My parents drugged Alia and changed her into peasant clothes. I think they hid her body in a wagon. I think that's how she traveled to Yonder. I was hiding in her closet, and I saw everything." Tears slid down my cheeks. "All I know, Sir Distin-guished…" I could not remember the rest of his title. "I loved her with all of my heart, and we never got to say goodbye."

He lifted a corner of the faded yellow tablecloth to dab at his eyes, nudged his windblown glasses higher up the bridge of his nose, and gazed at me.

"Where there is sadness, the viola's music uproots it. Where there is joy, it finds it. That is why I told you that the viola chose you."

I remembered the joy that Lambert's music had first surfaced in me: a memory of Alia and I waltzing together in an empty ballroom. I smiled at the old man's method of teaching, and I hugged his wisdom to me.

The viola had chosen me.

Chapter Three

"**O**ur first lesson today will be the sound of the oriole," Crauley said during breakfast.

"Oriole?" I knew an oriole was a bird, but I didn't know it had anything to do with the viola.

He spooned another dollop of fruit butter onto his plate and then handed the plate to me. "Carry this for me."

I followed his hunched frame as he hobbled out the back door. In the knee-high grass, two chairs faced a grove of tall elm trees with silvery-gray bark.

"Put it on top of that feeder over there." He pointed his free hand toward a wooden post with a flat platform on top of it.

On tippy-toe, I set the plate upon it and then sat down beside Crauley in the other wooden chair. The seats slanted up, our bottoms were lower than our knees, but I was comfortable all the same.

"The male oriole has a bright orange breast. Do you see it at the top up there?" Crauley pointed his cane toward the tree's upper green foliage.

"I see a bird, but I can't tell what color it is from here."

"Orioles like the top branches. From this distance, I hope to recognize it by its song." Lifting his chin, he studied the treetops.

"Do orioles like viola music, Sir Crauley?" I dropped the long title and was grateful that he didn't complain. I set my hand over my eyes, studying the sun-dappled foliage.

"Only if it is well played. The viola concerto in D is their favorite." Lowering his voice to a whisper, he added, "This morning is your first lesson in listening."

I'd been listening all of my life, but perhaps not keenly enough for Sir Crauley.

"To be a great viola player, you must listen for the tiniest of notes." Eyes averted, he paused. "Did you hear that?"

"Hear what?" I narrowed my gaze. Some birds were chattering back and forth; one might even be playing the flute.

"The rich whistling song of the oriole."

"No, but I heard a flute."

"Listen for the oriole's whistle—it is a short series of paired notes."

I closed my eyes. Off to my left, a crow cawed. Low in the brush out in front of us, I detected remnants of a warbled song. Then, I heard a distinct whistle. "Was that it, just now?" I whispered.

"Yes. Focus on where you heard it. Next time, count how many notes you hear."

I wanted to but was distracted by the inch-long hair that grew out of Sir Crauley's nearest ear. The swath of gray appeared to sway in the breeze. Suppressing a giggle, I closed my eyes and listened for the oriole's short song.

"I heard three!" I whispered.

"No, they're in pairs," he reminded me.

In the mottled sunlight, I closed my eyes and waited. There it was again, this time equally fast.

"Four," I said, correcting myself.

"Good." A smile flitted across his profile. "He's being unusually shy this morning, taking so long to come down; and for our fruit butter, at that." Crauley set both hands atop his cane.

At last, the oriole swooped down our side of the trees and with his wings spread, landed lightly upon the feeder. The bird's cap was a vibrant black while its lower plumage was as bright an orange as the wild poppies lining the roadside. The bird dipped its beak onto the plate, feasting on the dark purple butter.

"Next, I want you to listen for the wood thrush's flute-like song."

Crauley taught me the notes of many birds, and by mid-morning, my face hurt from smiling so much. "What is the other bird?" I felt quite positive there was a voice unaccounted for.

"What does it sound like to you?"

I listened to the bird's mixed and tumbled notes. "There are no distinct syllables like the wood thrush. This one's a busybody, zipping about, not minding its own business at all."

His smile lines deepened, and I could not help but feel pleased.

"That's a very good description. Describe the bird's song in *one* word." Sir Crauley's voice was soft, and I liked to think grandfatherly, though I'd not known either of my grandfathers.

Eyes closed, I pictured black and detected a jumbled, yet happy melody. "Happy," is the word I chose for the busy, little bird.

"Yes. This plain little brown bird has a *happy* voice, much like your own." He looked proud of himself as he peered at me.

"What type of bird is it?" I watched the brush for signs of the little bird. Then, in his silence, I turned to meet his gaze.

"It is a wren." His eyes twinkled.

"Oh-hh . . ." Sir Crauley had just given me a gift. I had never knowingly heard a wren before.

"Is there a story behind why your parents named you *Wren*?"

"Not that I know of." I glanced toward the house. Maybe Maid Kimberlee knew why I was named after a plain, little brown bird. She didn't appear to be watching through the windows.

"Perhaps just hearing the name made them feel *happy*," he said.

I loved listening to the birds with Sir Crauley. I felt a sense of belonging that had been missing for a very long time. I gazed over my shoulder at the dear elderly man and wondered if it was too early in my stay to tell him how much I already loved him.

Chin lifted, he studied the trees, and with a smile evident in his lean cheek, he reached over and patted my hand.

I think he already knew.

ΦΦΦ

"Do you think Mother and Father would allow me to live here?" I asked Maid Kimberlee on the third night while we lay in the soft, lumpy bed in the upstairs loft.

"No-oo." Her voice held humor. "Your parents would miss you far too much. And, Princess Wren, you will soon have a new baby brother or sister—someone else to love."

"I have Sir Crauley now, and I love it here." The elderly man's lessons and my eagerness to learn had bonded us.

"They will be pleased that you adore him, but no, Princess Wren, they will not allow you to stay."

ΦΦΦ

As our month together drew to a close, Distinguished Sir Crauley and I played duets in the evenings. We would play our particular memories of the day, and because Crauley could also play by memory, our music sounded like two souls remembering the same beautiful sunset.

Maid Kimberlee was our audience, and she would often dab at her eyes with her handkerchief or immerse her entire face in it.

"Posture, Wren," Crauley whispered, so gentle in his teaching.

This one simple word reminded me to set my shoulders back, breathe in, and relax while my third appendage, the bow, took over for my soul.

Our last evening together by the fire, I could no longer contain my heavy heart. "Do you think that you could go home and live with me?" I asked Crauley.

"Do you mean to live in your castle instead of mine?" He chuckled softly under his breath.

"Yes, you could have Alia's old room." I could picture the two of us sitting out on the terrace listening to the music of morning together.

He shook his head. "I would miss my birds and my little home too much. I have penned a letter to your parents. Hereafter, I want to see you each February, June and October until I am too old to listen, or until . . . Heaven forbid, you no longer desire to play viola."

"That will never happen," I said with all sincerity.

"Good."

Chapter Four

During the carriage ride home, I remembered to ask Maid Kimberlee about the meaning of a word that had bothered me off and on for quite some time.

"What does *artifice* mean?" I asked.

"Oh, dear, dear, dear . . ." Her tongue seemed to bounce in her mouth. "That's a question you will have to ask your father."

I couldn't ask Father; he'd know I'd been spying.

"Are you sure you don't know what artifice means?"

"Oh, I know, but that is a question for you to ask your father."

Hours later, when we reached home, I raced up the stairwell, carrying my viola case. I was so excited to tell Mother all about Crauley. I would play for her while she was in bed.

In the wide corridor outside their room, Father sat on a settee, staring at the opposite wall. I approached tentatively at first, and then Mother's screams reached my ears.

"What's happening? Is she all right?" I knocked on their door.

"Your mother is in early labor." Father bid me to him and then took my free hand in his. "We are to wait here until the doctor calls me in."

"May I please see her?" I glanced toward the large paneled door. Mother would want to see me. Never had we been apart for so long. "Just for a moment?" I asked.

He rubbed at his tired eyes. "After her next wave of pain, you'll enter, tell her hello, and then you must leave. I do not want you to see her in pain."

Shoulders hunched, I sat down beside him and waited through the heavy silence.

"Childbirth is very hard on fathers," he said. "Yours was the easiest for me, for when you were born, Wren, I was in a battle of my own."

"The Battle of Stockford." I knew the story all too well.

Father nodded.

Mother's next wail was a godsend, saving me from what would inevitably be another one of his long-winded war stories.

After she quieted, I entered their bedchamber. Their tri-fold room divider stood between the door and the bed. I maneuvered around it and strode to Mother's side. Beneath the sheets, her belly looked like an immense tortoise shell.

I suppressed a giggle.

"Wren, you're home!" She lifted her head from the pillow. Her face was flushed, other than that she appeared to be in no pain at all. She held her arms out, hugging me to her.

"Oh, Mother, I loved Crauley! I have so much to tell you." I beamed with happiness.

"I can't wait to hear all about it and to hear you—Uhhhh!" Mother's face scrunched up, and she gritted her teeth.

"Princess Wren, you are to leave." Dr. Duggan, our new family physician, flicked his hand.

"I love you, Mother." I kissed her forehead and did not look back. I hurried toward the door and remembered to close it behind me.

Father held out his hand for me, desiring my company. I sat down beside him and prepared myself to listen to the telling of the Battle of Stockford.

"Half their army had been wiped out, or so we'd been told. We picked evening, which most often is the best time to attack the enemy and begin battle. But no-oo." A painful sigh escaped him. "Our spies had been misinformed. Not only was their battalion ready for us, but they also had a very precise plan." Father placed his hands on his knees and heaved a heavy sigh. "Instead of an easy skirmish, we lost half of our men in the battle. But… we gained a country."

"Half victory, half heartbreak," I said, remembering the conclusion from his prior telling.

"Yes." He nodded.

Mother was in their room crying and moaning, and Father was remembering the war.

"How old was I, Father, when you first held me in your arms?"

"Two, I believe. No . . ." He rubbed his forehead. "You were three years old. Your red hair is like your mother's and also like my Grandmother Odessa's—a fine woman from across the ocean. When I first saw you, I knew you were like her. She always claimed that saltwater was in her blood. She was never happy with the mainland."

I didn't remember my father's first embrace. Oftentimes, he was this stranger who spoke of war to convey emotion.

"You wanted nothing to do with me, Wren." He sighed. "As a father, you expect your child to know you. You expect a bond, even if they are a toddler when you first meet. You wanted nothing to do with me. Flailing in my arms, you whimpered for your mother."

"I'm sorry, Father." Though I didn't remember back that far, I felt the same way now and yearned for my mother's comfort.

"How are they going to get the baby out?" I asked, worried about her well-being.

His mouth opened briefly and then he swallowed. "That is a question you will have to ask your mother."

"Ohh." His response reminded me of Maid Kimberlee's earlier in the day. "Father, what does artifice mean?" I asked.

"Where did you hear that?" He eyed me. "Never mind," he said because he already knew.

I clasped my hands and staring straight ahead recalled the night in his study when I'd heard the mysterious word for the first time. *Though you've mastered artifice, King Francis, we need a West Coast ally larger than Corra.*

Father cleared his throat. "Artifice means clever tricks to deceive."

The word had nothing to do with art and was not at all as it sounded. Father had mastered clever tricks of deception. I remembered only too clearly the look of a loving father as he'd served Alia the tainted milk.

ΦΦΦ

The door to their bedchamber swung open. "She's getting closer," Dr. Duggan said, rolling up his shirt sleeves.

"Wren, you are to go to your room and not come out until you are told." Father's gaze locked on mine. "You need to obey."

"What if Mother needs me?" I stared up at him.

"I will be here for her. You are to go to your room and wait until you are called."

I retreated down the corridor toward my chamber. Childbirth wasn't only difficult for fathers, but daughters as well.

A new silk nightgown had been laid out for me on my bed. Lace trim encompassed the neckline and the cuff of the half sleeves. Maid Kimberlee was not present to help me, so I changed into my new nightie all by myself. I climbed into my bed and said a prayer that God would keep my mother and baby sister safe. Then, I hugged my pillow and waited through Mother's wails. Tonight was a time when I wished I didn't have the gift of listening.

After what felt like hours, I heard the faintest wee baby's cry and my heart soared.

I tumbled down the steps of my bed, swung open the door, and raced down the dimly lit corridor to my parents' room. I saw the back of Maid Kimberlee as she slipped inside. Ever so quietly, I nudged the door open to the sounds of great excitement. The tri-fold room divider still stood near the foot of the bed, and Maid Kimberlee stood behind it, with her back to me. The divider blocked my view of Mother and Father, but I heard them. Mother was breathing with small painful gasps, and Father was trying to comfort her.

She was in great anguish, and it took everything that was in me not to announce myself. *Where was the baby?*

I hurried behind a nearby planter and parted the flax leaves for a better view.

"Push!" Dr. Duggan ordered, standing at the foot of the four-poster bed. "Now! Push!"

Guided by the doctor's hands, my little sister was squeezed out from Mother's world into ours. It was a wonder I did not faint at the education I received.

"You have a son," Dr. Duggan said, cutting the long, waxy looking cord.

No! Was he blind? My baby sister was a girl! I'd seen her precious, gooey, little body emerge.

Maid Kimberlee, still positioned behind the divider, knelt down and leaned forward toward the doctor with something in her arms—an equally tiny, naked infant.

Near the foot of the bed, Father watched with downcast eyes as the doctor smeared my baby sister's gooiness onto the baby in Maid Kimberlee's arms. All this occurred below Mother's scope of vision.

Whatever was going on was with Father's permission.

"How is he? Is he alive?" Mother asked, weakly.

"Irene, we have our son," Father said.

Dr. Duggan smacked the infant firmly between the shoulder blades and held up the crying baby boy.

All eyes were focused on either Mother or the foot of the bed when I crept back to the hallway. Feeling sick and shaky, I huddled down against the granite side table. I'd heard the cry before the babe was even born because Maid Kimberlee had carried someone else's baby down the hallway. Someone else's little boy.

Father had found a way to have a son—the future king. His artifice, his tricks of deception were not limited to the enemy. I felt sick to the core of my being.

What would become of my baby sister? Would they keep her, too?

I wanted Crauley. I wanted to go home.

ΦΦΦ

My parents' door creaked open. Maid Kimberlee slipped into the hallway and carried a bundle toward the stairs. "Breathe, child, breathe." She smacked the baby. "Breathe, baby girl. Breathe!" She smacked her again, and at last the infant cried.

In my royal nightmare, I followed them down the stairs and across the wide marble entry into the kitchen where copper skillets hung from the ceiling. I hid behind the pantry door while my governess paused. She spread a soft cream-colored blanket on top of the wide counter and laid the baby in the upper corner. Its little legs kicked with life as Maid Kimberlee swaddled her tiny little body tightly.

"Oh, precious baby, Jesus loves you. He'll watch over you all the days of your life. Precious, precious child." She mumbled more prayers as I followed her out the side door to a carriage that waited in the gray moonlit night.

Father was sending my baby sister away because she wasn't a boy.

While Maid Kimberlee took a seat inside, I stepped onto the back rungs of the carriage and held on to the overhead baggage rack. In my new silk nightie, I held on for dear life. The gas lamp-lit streets changed to moonlit country roads. I tried to memorize the way, but I quickly lost track of all the twists and turns.

Miles from home, the carriage slowed to a stop in front of a cottage. Pears hung golden in the moonlight, within my reach. A white picket fence surrounded a lovely little garden. A young woman with golden hair strolled toward the carriage. She wore a dark cloak. The door creaked open, and Maid Kimberlee's arms transferred the little bundle—my baby sister—whose hand I might never hold.

I could stay here, step off and remain behind. I could help take care of her. But then I thought of Mother. My sweet mother had no idea that my father had traded their daughter for someone else's son.

If only I'd obeyed Father and waited in my room until they came for me, I would never have known his secrets. Secrets too painful for my heart to bear.

ΦΦΦ

I slept late the next morning.

"Little Dove, you have good reason to get up and greet this beautiful day," Maid Kimberlee's voice awakened me.

I flung back the blue velvet bedspread, and groggily remembered last night.

"Come see, child, a most beautiful sight." My dear governess waited in the doorway while I shrugged my house robe on over my nightgown. "Cheer up, baby girl. You are still their shining star. You will simply have to share the galaxy a little." Her warm, plump hand gripped my shoulder as we moved down the hallway toward my parents' room.

The room divider had returned to its usual place beside Mother's vanity table. Sunlight dappled through the slightly parted drapes. Mother lay in their large bed, her countenance radiant. With her arms stretched out, she cuddled babies, one on each side of her.

"You have a brother," she breathed. Pure happiness exuded from her.

"Twins?" I found my voice.

"Yes. Odessa . . ." she said, looking to the baby on her left side, "took her own sweet time."

Twin sisters. I gazed lovingly at the dewy auburn-haired infant.

"And Edwin, of course, was first," she said, to the towheaded baby on her right. "It's only fitting that he should be the strongest and most handsome." She smiled over at Father.

"They look nothing alike," I dared to breathe.

"Yes, I think so, too. They're fraternal twins. Not identical."

"Time will tell," Father said.

His countenance, which I openly studied, was bittersweet. There was a glaze to his eyes. Half heartbreak. Half victory. Like the Battle of Stockford, when he'd lost half his men, but gained a country.

ΦΦΦ

I found myself not wanting to get too close to the babies because someday I would turn sixteen, and my father would drug me and ship me off in the middle of the night to my future husband. The bond intended for a lifetime would be ripped in two.

In spite of my misgivings, I inched past Father, closer to the right side of the bed. One cannot help but love a baby, a bundle of helplessness and longing. I did not want to love Odessa too much as I'd done with Alia. Still, I inched my index finger to hers, and her long, slim fingers curled around it, gripping my heart.

"Do you think twins hug in the womb?" I asked mother while Maid Kimberlee drew open the drapes for morning light.

"What a lovely thought. I would think so. Don't you?" Mother smiled. I'd never seen her so happy.

I nodded. "I would think that hugging would make their tight quarters cozier," I said, and my spirits lifted despite Father's presence.

"There is no doubt that these two got along in the womb, for there was very little fighting," Maid Kimberlee said. Stopping on baby Edwin's side of the bed, she clasped her hands and stared at the trio with loving adoration. "When the mother does not know that she is bearing twins, it is a sign of great love."

I studied my old governess's countenance. Did it hurt her to say this? No one had known Mother carried twins. Not even mother. My baby sisters loved each other very much. Yet outside of Mother's womb, they might never know one another.

Too afraid of my father, I bottled it all inside.

ΦΦΦ

Later that evening when everyone believed me to be in bed, I went to Father's study and unrolled his map. I began to chart a map of my own from Blue Sky to Yonder. Father had not sent Alia away until her sixteenth birthday, so I would run away when I was fifteen. It would give me seven years to plan. A year should give me time to make it there and back. Or would I come back?

Yes, I would come back for Mother.

Chapter Five

Six years later, late June . . .

The morning of my planned escape, I sat at the writing desk in my room at our Lake House near Brightwood, three hours east of home. I was two months shy of fifteen and a young woman with hips and lumps. I had coppery-red hair like my mother; and like Alia, I was also known for my clear complexion. I penned my goodbye letter to both of my parents, even though Father was away on business.

Mother and Father,

Though I love you both, each day I worry that it will be my last before you ship me off. Since I was a child, I've harbored an enormous heartbreaking secret. It is this: I was in Alia's closet the night Father gave her the tainted milk. I saw you and Maid Kimberlee change her into peasant clothes. Though you wept over her and prayed for her, I know very well that the same fate awaits me. You loved Alia as much as two parents can. If I had stayed, my future would be no different.

Father, if you come for me, I will inform Mother of a very large secret you have been keeping. And, if you do find me and manage to marry me off, I will make it my life pledge to inform Mother of it.

Your beloved daughter,

Wren

I would not tell them of my plans to see Alia, for that would make me too easy to track. After I saw her, I would be a dutiful daughter and return to marry, to create an alliance and fulfill my duty to my country. But in the meantime, I did not want anyone or anything to hamper my plans. I printed *Mother* across the face of the envelope and hid it out of plain view.

Shortly after lunch while Odessa practiced her violin, I informed Mother that I was going to my chamber for a much-needed nap.

"Are you well, Wren?" She glanced up from her embroidery.

"Yes, Mother. I didn't sleep well last night; that's all."

In my room, I tucked pillows and clothes beneath the covers of my bed to make it appear that I was indeed taking a nap. Then I braided my hair and tucked it up inside Edwin's gray cap. Next, I leaned the letter that I'd written for Mother against the hurricane lamp atop my bureau.

I had given my escape a great deal of thought. I'd drawn a map, saved money, sewn a backpack-of-sorts, which I now wore, collected food, and packed two extra sets of clothes.

Beginning my journey, I climbed out of my window and dropped below into the sword-shaped leaves of the deep purple irises. The first leg of getting past our guards would be the most difficult.

ΦΦΦ

Between my window and the woods lay an open meadow, spanning one hundred meters of waist-high green grass tipped with copper highlights and intermittent wild daisies. My brother Edwin, now seven, often played cricket with the guards, and I could hear them on the other side of the house in the east meadow. My timing was perfect. Not wanting to take any chances of being seen, I crouched to my knees and in my everyday frock crawled through the tall grass. I parted the blades in front of me and slithered through like I was doing the breaststroke on dry land. The sun beat down upon my back, and I longed for a glass of fresh lemonade to quench my thirst. I reminded myself of my goal: *to see Alia one last time before I was married.*

"Princess Wren . . . what are ya doing?"

"Aww-h!" I gasped, clutching at the grass in front of me as a shadow loomed overhead. I wasn't even to the road. Yet, right above me stood one of our young guards, a long rifle in his possession, and a raven tethered to his shoulder.

"I saw the daisies waving. I thought ya might be a predator." He had a West Coast accent.

"What kind of predator?" I tried to mask my shock and annoyance.

"A coyote, cougar, or . . . pig. Wild pigs do roam these parts, ya know."

"Do I look like a wild pig to you?" I eyed him, crossly.

He scanned the meadow. "Where are ya going?"

"I'm not going anywhere. I'm simply playing hide-and-go-seek with Odessa."

A smile curved his cheek. "Yer sister is practicing her violin."

So she was. Even from our fifty-meter distance from the house, Odessa's unpleasant music was heard. I should have taken more time with my answer.

"Yes, and she knows that as soon as she's done with this piece, she is to come find me."

I prayed the simpleton was as simple as I prayed he was.

"Tell me where yer hiding place will be, in case ya prove difficult to find?"

"That tall sycamore at the edge of the meadow." Without rising above the swells of the grass, I nodded toward the broccoli-shaped tree in the distance. "I shall hide behind that tree," I said, continuing my breaststroke through the grass.

"Princess Wren, if yer only playing hide-and-go-seek, why are ya wearing yer brother's cap and a knapsack?" With his thick auburn hair, strong jaw and ruddy complexion, the guard was good looking, and probably knew it, if he'd ever seen a mirror.

"I've brought milk and cookies to drink for when my sister finds me," I said over my shoulder. I had also brought the chalky milk plant if needed for my enemies. Milk and cookies were the only things I could steal away from the lunch table, without Maid Kimberlee thinking too much about it. "If you had red hair, you would wear a cap too, when playing hide-and-go-seek," I added.

"I believe ya, Princess Wren, but only because I see the jars of milk." The simpleton strolled away, whistling.

It was not the start I'd hoped for, but at least the guard had proved to be one of little brain.

I made it to the woods and hid behind the tall sycamore. Leaning away from the tree, I scanned the house and meadow for any signs that someone might have seen me.

In the woods to my right, a horse exhaled, which was odd. The horses were in the carriage house, and the guards were on the field playing cricket. Was the young guard here? With my heart in my throat, I studied the trees in my immediate vicinity. The sides of a white horse's belly and its rider's boots were visible as they attempted to hide behind an expansive tree.

I had not gone through years of planning to not even make it to the road!

My escape had to be today, and it had to be now.

I tiptoed to the next tree and hid behind it. Silencing my mind, I listened deeply. Only the low, soft notes of a wood thrush were audible. I crept to the next tree, and pushing the odds a bit, to the next, a wide-girthed cedar. After my heart stopped its loud gonging, I listened deeply as Crauley had taught me.

A bird foraged through leaf litter. There was a snap of a twig, and then the puff of breath as a horse exhaled. *It couldn't be.* I tiptoed between trees, peering around the side of them. I'd lost sight of the horse and rider, and hopefully, they'd lost sight of me. At last, I reached the road, where I stayed in the shin-high grass in the shade of the trees, and started toward the small town of Brightwood.

"Princess Wren." A man's voice startled me, but this time, I did not gasp.

To my left, near the edge of the trees, the young guard stood holding the reins of his horse, the bird steady on his shoulder.

I nodded and kept walking.

"Princess Wren . . ."

I ignored him.

"Where are ya going?" With a kick to the horse's sides, the rider and animal soon blocked my path. He frowned down at me. "Yer not to leave in the middle of the day. Alone. Yer father would have our throats."

I rubbed at my temple and eyed his thoroughbred. How could I get it away from him?

"Now, tell me what it is yer after in town?"

I smiled; this simpleton was God's way of providing me with a horse.

"Edwin got into my stash of candy," I said. Most everyone knew I had a weakness for lollies.

"Instead of tramping around, endangering yourself, all ya needed to do was ask. Any one of us would have ridden into town for ya."

I'd seen him before. He'd been one of the guards in attendance at Crauley's earlier in the month. He was younger than most of the guards that Father entrusted with our care. I was surprised that I hadn't heard the servant girls talking about him. Or maybe I had. He might very well be the young guard that they giggled incessantly about.

"Would you take me into town?" I asked though I knew Father would never approve of me being alone with any guard—young or old.

"No. We'll go back and get the carriage and a few more men."

How was I going to get the horse away from this do-gooder?

"Well, I'm sorry you don't agree with me, but I have every intention of buying candy for myself in Brightwood." I attempted to walk around the side of them, but rider and horse were quite gifted at zig-zagging backward in front of me.

"What is your name?" I asked in my most regal, condescending tone.

"Brody . . . Hew."

"Are you related to Edwin?" I cupped a hand over my eyes and peered up at him. Edwin Hew was my father's favorite soldier, maimed at the Battle of Misery Hill.

"Only by blood." A smile tweaked a corner of his mouth. "He's my older brother."

"Well, Brody Hew, we are at a crossroads. Will you accompany me to town to buy candy, or…" With a lift of my brow, I imitated my mother when she'd decided firmly on something.

"Princess Wren, why do ya have a knapsack on yer back and yer hair in a hat, if yer only going to buy candy?" He slid off his horse.

Mistake number one.

"Brody, do you have any rope?"

"Yes." He reached into his saddlebag, withdrew a coiled piece and handed it to me.

"Can you do me a favor?" We stood surprisingly close, and I attempted coyness as I lifted one brow.

"Yes." He held the reins of my future horse in one hand.

"I've been learning a few knots, and I would like to see if I am tying them correctly." Unfortunately, I knew no knots other than sewing knots and tying one's shoes, but I thought it a good line for the simple guard.

"Ya want to practice on me, aye?" He tied his horse to the limb of a nearby tree and patted his muzzle. "There ya go, Dilly." The simpleton sat down on a fallen log and with the raven still on his shoulder, glanced behind us.

Would the bird peck at me?

"Is the bird for sending messages?" I hoped not. I didn't want Father to receive information of my escape any earlier than necessary.

Brody nodded. "She's your father's experiment."

"What do you mean?"

"To see if a raven can be trained to deliver messages like a homing pigeon."

The shiny black bird and I eyed one another. It looked more intelligent than a pigeon.

"So you're a messenger boy?"

"For starters." He held his closed fists out in front of him.

"No, please, behind your back." I suppressed a smile as he swiveled and held his closed fists behind him. I worked the rope around his wrists, knotting it with simple knots here and there. Dirt grazed the knuckles of his strong hands.

"Did I hear you correctly? Did you call your horse *Dilly*?" This simpleton would not last long in Father's regime.

"Yes, ya heard right."

"Such a fine horse needs a strong name." Like many of our men's horses, the thoroughbred's coat and mane were white, and its skin beneath, a soft pink. Dilly was beautiful with dark eyes.

"Ya don't give a bossy horse a strong name," her owner said.

"But Dilly?" The name was ridiculous.

The horse neighed and glanced back at us.

"Yes, we're talking about ya, Dilly. Yer a good horse," he said.

The horse nickered.

"Okay, yer the best horse."

The horse's tail swished.

"See what I'm up against?" Brody glanced over his shoulder at me.

"Yes. But, *Dilly*?" I knotted a pile of knots, one on top of the other.

"Why are ya running away?"

"I'm not. I told you, I'm just craving lollies." Heat crept up my neck as I focused on my knot tying. Several months had passed since I'd poured my heart out to Crauley, and something was appealing about the simpleton. "Did you know my father has most assuredly arranged a marriage for me, without asking, and to a man I've never met?"

"And that makes ya crave lollies?"

"No." I frowned at him. "How would you like to be married off to someone you've never met for political gain?" I pulled the rope tighter about his wrists and tied it the best I could. Unfortunately, knots had not been a part of my princess training.

"Look at the bright side of yer arranged royal marriage: Ya will never know poverty or hunger, and neither will yer children."

To argue with him would only confirm that I was indeed running away. Holding back a rebuttal, I stepped away and dusted off my hands.

The guard rose to his feet, smiled at me, and dusted off his hands, as well.

How had he untied my knots so quickly?

"And, ya should honor yer father, so life goes well for ya," he continued.

"And, you are not in my shoes." I wanted empathy, not a lecture.

He glanced down at my lace-up boots and then met my gaze. "What kind of candy do ya like?"

"Chewy lollies," I shrugged. "I'm not fond of chocolate. How did you untie my knot?"

"I had a pocketknife in this hand." He smiled, holding up his right. "When ya are tying someone up, ya should always check their hands."

"Then I must try again." I smiled, trying to cover my frustration.

"Yer knot was very good. Without the knife, I would not have been able to free myself." One of his dark brows lifted as he regarded me.

"My life might someday depend on a knot, Brody Hew. Please give me the satisfaction of knowing that my workmanship works."

"No, Princess Wren. I am to guard ya with my life. I am to stay with ya where ever ya go. And if harm should befall ya, I am to die in yer place." I knew from the serious tone in his voice how seriously he'd taken this oath. "It would not be wise of me to allow you to tie my hands and watch ya ride away on my horse."

Warm tears of frustration gathered in the corners of my eyes.

If I wanted to escape Brody Hew, I would have to resort to the chalky milk, and so early in my journey. After I poisoned him, I would escape with his pocketknife and his horse.

"I'm a wee bit hungry." I returned to the log and sat down. From there, I wrestled the knapsack off my back and untied my bundle. I handed him a piece of shortbread.

While he studied the cookie and the road toward home, I discreetly rubbed the powdery plant into one of the jelly-sized jars of milk that I'd packed for my first day's travel. It had taken me hours of study in Father's war journals to come across his notes of the chalky milk plant. Several times, he'd employed the plant as a weapon in war, as well as the home front.

"I hope you like your milk frothy?" I shook both jars.

"Not really." His gaze narrowed for a moment.

I unscrewed the lids and set his jar of milk on the stump between us and took a sip out of mine.

"The bickie was good. May I have anotha?" he asked.

"Yes." I was familiar with *bickie,* the odd West Coast term for cookies. Even though my provisions were quickly dwindling, I untied the bandana of shortbread and handed him a second bickie. Suppressing a smile, I met his gaze.

"A toast." He held up his jar of milk.

"Yes, a toast." I lifted my glass to his and forced myself to focus on his eyes instead of his horse.

"May all the days of yer life be bonnie and blessed," he said.

"And may your days be bonnie and blessed, as well." I added a smile.

Our glasses touched, and then I tipped back my head and watched the simpleton swallow as I did the same. For some reason, my milk tasted odd . . . chalky.

Had he tricked me?

Though the trees began to sway, I managed to set down the glass. Then the young guard's arms reached behind me and caught me as everything faded to black.

Chapter Six

I dreamed of a young, handsome guard who smiled into my eyes. "May all of yer days be as blessed and bonnie as ya are."

I smiled back like I had no sense of self and no sense at all.

"May all of your days be—" my odd sentiments were interrupted.

Someone tapped twice upon my chamber door before the light from the hallway spilled into the room. "Wren, love, it's time for supper," Maid Kimberlee said.

"Supper?" I blinked myself awake. Why was I in bed if it was time for supper?

"Yes, love, you have slept the afternoon away. Are you all right, dear, or should I deliver your meal to you?"

What in the world! I flung back the covering and stepped down from the high bed. I immediately felt dizzy and had to hold onto the side of the mattress.

"Bed . . . please," I managed.

"All right, love." She pulled the door closed.

I glanced toward the window, with its white ruffled curtains. My head spun with memories of a young, handsome guard and frothy milk. Had it all been a dream? Why was I sleeping in the middle of the afternoon? And why did my throat feel lined with chalk?

The corner of my knapsack poked out from beneath the covers. My plans had failed on account of Brody Hew.

The letter! I moved slowly to the bureau. I had to get the letter before Mother or Maid Kimberlee spotted it. In its place was a small brown bag. I unfolded the top. Inside were Pinwheels and other chewy lollies.

The dream had been reality, and my letter was gone! Closing my eyes, I sank to the floor. Had Mother or Maid Kimberlee already read it? Did they know my plans? If they did, any hopes I had of seeing Alia were dashed.

My world spun in a kaleidoscope of gray. The side-effects of the chalky milk plant were not kind. I lay on my side until the room stopping spinning.

Later, Maid Kimberlee delivered dinner to me in bed. Roast beef with Yorkshire pudding, steamed baby peas, and another shortbread cookie for dessert.

"Has anyone been in my room this afternoon?" I asked.

"No. Edwin spent the entire day outside and Odessa, bless her sweet spirit, has been practicing her violin. She so wants to be like her big sister."

I leaned back into my pillow and closed my eyes. Poor Odessa had not been blessed with the gift of listening. Her violin music suffered greatly for it.

"No one at all?" I murmured.

"Just you, love." Maid Kimberlee set her cool hand to my forehead. "No fever."

After she exited the room, I studied every inch of my knapsack. The corner edge of an envelope stuck out of the top opening. I retrieved it and with a pounding heart recognized my handwriting across the front. It was my letter, unopened. Not even the slightest tear lined the sealed edge.

I rose from the bed and crept to the window. Stationed at the fringe of the meadow, the young guard sat atop his horse. He knew I'd tried to escape. When we returned home, he'd tell

Father, and for the rest of my days, there'd be little hope of my ever seeing Alia again.

I sank to my knees and gave into a pitiful sob.

ΦΦΦ

Shortly after I turned fifteen, my parents commissioned for a portrait to be painted of me in the ballroom. I was the same age Alia had been when she'd posed for hers. In a light blue gown, she'd stood beside the piano near the terrace windows, and faced north toward Yonder. At the time, she didn't know that she gazed toward her future kingdom.

For the portrait, Mother selected a floor-length, sage-green chiffon dress with a jeweled bodice. The dress was decisively more opulent than Alia's had been. I wondered why as I stood in front of the window.

With my feet apart, I stood in the playing position, gripped the shoulder of my viola with my left hand, and rested the side of my jaw on the chin rest. George, the artist, fiddled with the bow in my relaxed right hand and then he had me turn ever so slightly. If I swiveled my feet a bit, I, like Alia, would face Yonder. My dress felt tight about my rib cage as I tried to breathe deeply. Though numerous provinces lay between Alia and me, oh, how I longed to believe that my future kingdom would be close to hers.

While George strolled back to the canvas, I turned my feet to the left, so they faced Yonder. The painter, a gangly and quiet fellow, did not appear to notice. Over the course of the next few weeks, I stood idly in the same spot, facing northwest while my feet pointed northeast toward Alia. From this stance in front of the windows, I often saw Brody Hew ride by on his fine horse. I knew it was wrong to hate, but the young guard had ruined my plans.

"I have completed the painting from your feet to your shoulders. It is time for you to look over your shoulder at me," George said.

"I want your eyes to have a faraway happy look like you are thinking of the wonderful man you will someday marry," George said.

"Is that what you told Alia, my sister?" I asked. The pose was the same as hers had been.

"By George, I think it was."

I did not have enough imagination to picture the man assigned to my future. Instead, I thought of Alia and seeing her again. I imagined showing up on her doorstep and saying, "It's me, Wren, and I've missed you so very, very much."

"Oh, that's wonderful," George kissed his fingers and flung them into the air. "That's exactly the look I want. Exactly."

With a small smile and a heart full of memories, I thought of Alia and how wonderful our reunion would be. And then in my idleness, I began to map out the plan I'd been devising since childhood. I would escape and travel like Alia had, as a commoner—that much I'd pieced together.

I could not simply wait until my sixteenth birthday to be drugged and shipped off. With my gaze toward Yonder, I began to plan anew.

ΦΦΦ

One afternoon, Father paused beside George's easel on his way through the Great Hall.

"Have I not captured a faraway look in her eyes?" the painter asked.

Father expelled a heavy sigh. "What are you thinking about, Wren?" he asked from behind the canvas.

"What do you mean?" I remained in my stationary stance.

"While George has been painting you, what have you been thinking about?"

"I've thought of a great many things." In all honesty, I had.

"George has captured your look of devising."

I muffled a laugh. "I was merely musing . . . absorbed in thought, Father."

"I know what *musing* means."

Of course, he did, and I knew what *devising* meant. My heart pounded in my chest. I couldn't let him know that I was planning anything.

"This is the expression she has worn almost the entire time." The artist swirled his brush in a bottle of turpentine and then wiped it on a rag. "Are you not happy with my work?"

"No, George. Just like Alia, you have captured her well. Wren, what are you up to?"

Father must have been furious to ask it right in front of the painter. My expression for the portrait confirmed one of his greatest fears: I would not go easily.

"Well . . . I need to get more rosin for my bow, and Maid Kimberlee's sixtieth birthday is next month, and—"

"You know very well what I meant."

I turned my head slightly, meeting his gaze.

"What secrets are you keeping, Wren?" He'd hoped the artist would capture a serene faraway look, but I was not Alia. George had painted a schemer, not a dreamer.

"What are you hiding?" Father asked.

He was the one hiding. He was the one with secrets! On the night of my sixteenth birthday, after my coming of age party—which was already being planned—they would drug me and cart me off. The trick was either not to be home or not to turn sixteen.

"Wren, I demand that you tell me this instant." Father's voice quivered through the air.

"Or . . . ?" I waited. Would he ship me off before my party? His features froze.

George craned his skinny neck around the canvas to peer wide-eyed at me, also.

"What are you up to?" Father asked.

I longed for air, but my dress was too tight. I would tell my oldest secret in exchange for one of his. It would be a secret for a secret.

"I was in her closet, Father." My voice did not tremble as I tightly gripped my hands beneath the bodice of my gown. "I watched you serve Alia the warm milk." Hot tears burned my throat.

"Dear God!" he breathed. "All these years, that's what it's been."

"Why am I facing northeast? To whom am I betrothed?"

Without turning, Father glanced at George. The artist was flushed and fiddled with his paints.

"Please tell me *my* future."

One brow arched while he weighed the consequences. Then his mouth bunched and he shook his head once more. "Prince Vincent von Drake of Davenport."

Davenport!

"Davenport isn't even an ally. You traded me in lieu of war." Feeling sick to my stomach, I shook my head.

"Now, why do you say that?"

"I overheard. I was hiding under your desk years ago in your study. I heard everything…" I swallowed the bitter truth. "'Sons are for making kings and daughters are for making allies.'"

"You've been a most unhappy child, Wren; and I can't help but think it's due to all of your eavesdropping."

I had no rebuttal. I'd thought the same myself numerous times. There were many things I wished I'd never overheard, many things I wished I'd never learned about my father.

"Davenport is rich in sailing vessels, their steel industry, and imports from the Western Hemisphere. A railway system will be built, connecting two powerful countries. Trade and commerce will increase. Your marriage will prove a favorable merger for both."

Now that he'd had a few years off from the barbarism of war, my father was becoming a progressive. Alia and I were simply chattels, and most likely Odessa would be, too. Odessa's twin was lucky to be in her little pear orchard, far removed from Father's dealings. Edwin was the future of Blue Sky, even though he wasn't truly an heir. Would Father arrange his marriage as well?

Tell your father of your desires. Crauley's advice teased me at this inopportune time. *Seek his blessing. Let him know.*

"Father . . ." I felt the color drain from my face. "I have one request before I marry," my voice was clear and distinct.

"Yes, what is it?"

"Might I visit Alia, see her one more time?" Tears blurred my vision, but I held my posture upright.

"No, Wren." He chuckled softly under his breath. "The road is still several years away from completion."

"But . . . you've made the journey before?"

"It is too difficult."

I pulled my lip between my teeth and held it there for a moment before turning to the painter. "Start a new canvas, George."

His head snapped up.

I rocked back my shoulders and filled my lungs with air. "This is the pose that I want captured." Chin high, posture perfect, I stared toward Yonder while tears dripped down my cheeks.

I renewed my vow to self: Before my life was traded for a railway, I was going to see Alia. I would do everything in my power to make it happen.

Chapter Seven

"**W**hat is new?" I asked Crauley as we sat by the fire. It was the first evening of our February get-together, and it was stormy outside the cabin.

"I've lost another tooth."

"I'm so sorry." He was now down to seven.

Maid Kimberlee was not with me this time; she'd stayed behind to oversee Odessa's and Edwin's violin lessons. Out of the blue, he wanted to learn, too.

"What is new with you?" Crauley asked.

"I am betrothed to Prince Vincent von Drake of Davenport, whom I have never met. We will marry this September, a few weeks after I turn sixteen."

"Your Father told you." He smiled. "This is good news. There is hope for him yet."

"Yes. When there is hope for a king, there is hope for a country." A heavy sigh escaped me. "Father only told me because I demanded."

"He did not have to tell you. But I'm glad he did."

I met his gaze in the fire's light. "You're right. Father told me and I should be thankful for that."

How I would miss Crauley's tutelage and friendship when my future divided us. "My visit this June might very well be our last time together," I said. I would turn sixteen in August, and my parents would most likely ship me off in the middle of the night.

"It might be my last June, too." He cleared his raspy throat.

I studied him in the firelight. His face appeared thinner than I remembered. "Are you not well?" An uneasy knot formed in my gut.

"I'm well enough for a man as old as I." He added a dry chuckle.

I nodded, thoughtfully. "I have mapped out a plan to see my sister."

"On your own?" His bushy brows gathered.

"Yes, I will leave from here this June." I determined to tell him everything. "When Aggie and her husband deliver the cream, I'll trade clothes with her and pose as her on the way out. That means she'll have to stay here one night. This will give me time to get ahead of the guards on my way to Yonder." I told him now because I'd always told Crauley everything, and he had proven himself trustworthy.

"You will worry your parents and me." He studied me with wise old eyes.

"I will leave a letter for my father. No one else is to open it."

"You will need protection."

"I have prayer." Though I had not consulted with God yet, I would when the time arrived.

Crauley's eyelids fluttered as if he were already saying a prayer. "You will break your parents' hearts and give them kidney stones."

"Can they die from them?"

"They are so painful; they will want to die. Will you travel as a commoner?"

"Yes, just like Alia did."

"You should ask your father, first. Seek his blessing."

"I tried. You would have been proud of me." I swallowed and peered over my shoulder to the sheet music on the table. "He said it is too difficult of a journey and, the road to Yonder is taking longer than expected."

Crauley's eyes contemplated all that could go wrong. "Tell him how strongly you desire it. Seek his blessing."

"No, he has given me his answer. I don't want to draw attention now."

Shaking his head, Crauley chewed on his lower lip.

His response pained me. How could he take Father's side when he knew mine?

ΦΦΦ

Crauley and I spent the next morning sitting in the dappled sunlight together listening to the birds.

"Wren, I know how much you've longed to see Alia." He held his vein-riddled hand out for mine and clasped it warmly. "I'm worried about you leaving here all by yourself to see her, and at the same time, I worry that you might never see her again."

I gazed into his faded green eyes and wondered where his thoughts were headed.

He swallowed. "During the war years, my wife worried about a great many things. We even worried about our wee little castle being attacked." He chuckled briefly before his countenance sobered. "We dug a tunnel beneath our home as an escape route."

I listened keenly now.

"In the bottom right yellow cupboard in the kitchen, you'll find the floorboard to our tunnel. It's tall enough to walk upright in. We shoveled it many years ago when I was fit... as a fiddle." His eyes twinkled as he went into greater detail.

I would rather stick with my plan to pose as Aggie seated beside her husband in the wagon than escape through a dark tunnel. Still, I listened.

"If things should go wrong for you this June, there is a woman named Amy, who lives in Hampershire. She is an angel of mercy. Throughout the war years and since, she has placed a lit candle in her front window each night. Her home is open to those in need."

My beloved teacher was giving me his blessing.

"Thank you, Crauley."

For our evening meal, we made a soup of finely minced chicken and vegetables and enjoyed it with the soft rolls and fruit butter that I'd brought from home. Afterward, we sat by the fire and my dearest friend in all the world gazed softly at me.

"You won't be here very long on your next visit, so tonight we will practice our goodbyes." He reached for his bow on the dusty round table. "We'll begin with Misery Hill in C and get it over with, and then we'll remember our years together, beginning with your first visit when you were only eight." His face brightened into his six-toothed smile. "Do you remember your first words to me?"

"Of course." I breathed. The memory was as distinct as if it were yesterday. "We've brought you a crock of fruit butter."

"Yes." Crauley's features froze in a smile. "I didn't think I could love a little girl so much." He inhaled deeply before regaining his usual composure. "Like your father, Wren, I have never been very good at goodbyes, so we must practice."

I nodded and tried to prepare my heart as well.

That evening, we fiddled of our love for one another, an old man and a young woman who shared so many memories. In Crauley, God had given me the grandfather I'd never had, a sense of belonging, and a bond that I would cherish all of my days.

Reaching for his hand, I too, practiced my goodbye. "I will never forget you, Distinguished Sir Crauley."

"I know." He smiled, back to his normal stoic self. "I know."

ΦΦΦ

Time with Odessa, who was now seven, became more important to me, even precious. "Tell me *The Smiling Princess Story*," she said, pleading with her hazel eyes, so like Alia's and Father's.

I had grown up sitting beside Alia on this same settee, listening endlessly to handed-down stories. *The Smiling Princess Story* had been one of my favorites, too, a story in which some of our own experiences were added to help us come to grips with them.

"There was once a young princess who was raised to smile." I paused to smile at Odessa in the crook of my arm, and she beamed up at me. "Good news or bad news, blue sky or rain showers, the princess was told to smile. As she rode atop her fine, white horse through the streets, she would wave to her countrymen and smile."

Odessa leaned against me and sighed contentedly.

"When other children made fun of her, she was told to smile. Once, when the princess heard that war was only a few hours away, she was told to smile. And once when her father left for war, she was ordered to smile." I nudged Odessa. "Your turn."

"Once"—her gaze lingered on the bronze table statue of Father atop his favorite gelding—"when a boy said my hair was kinky and that I have the neck of a giraffe, I was told to smile."

"Who told you that?" I asked.

"Renald."

The scribe's ten-year-old son was a gifted apprentice and his father's constant companion.

"Renald's description is right. Your hair is very curly, and you've been blessed with an elegant, long neck. But, remember something very important." I suppressed a smile at my cheekiness, "Boys' opinions of us do not matter until we turn sixteen." I nudged her, teasingly. "That is the magic age when a girl can start thinking about boys, and only then."

She pursed her mouth, unhappily. "Your turn. One more *once*." She gazed up at me.

A country would someday separate us.

Maybe Father and Mother had been right not to tell Alia. She'd been happy till the end.

"Once . . ." I said, my voice guarded and unusually solemn, "a princess was married off to a man she'd never met, who lived in a country far away from her home. She was ordered to smile. Her younger sister missed her and wanted to see her more than anything in the world." My voice climbed past the tears. "But, before she could, she, too, was married off and ordered to smile." I paused on a stronger note.

"May it never be so." Odessa hugged my arm.

I nodded and returned to the main story. "So tiresome was the princess's smile that whenever she passed a mirror, she would frown and make the most contorted faces, simply to relieve her facial muscles."

My sister melted more against me.

"On one occasion, when she passed a royal mirror, she frowned horridly, and her reflection was observed by a handsome prince, who'd been invited to dine with her family that evening. It was his first impression of her, and though she smiled beautifully the remainder of the evening, he could not forget the face he'd first seen in the mirror."

Odessa sighed.

"What is the moral of the story?" I asked.

"The lesson of this story is even if you do not have the gift of listening…" Odessa smiled bravely, "you are to smile."

She was the first of us girls who had not received the gift, and I knew it was difficult for her. "God gives everyone a gift," I whispered. "Sometimes it just takes longer to discover what yours is."

ΦΦΦ

I returned to Hampershire that June. I planned to spend four days with Crauley before I'd escape and begin my journey to see Alia.

At dusk, the carriage rolled up to the mossy roofed cabin, and I remembered back to when I'd been a girl of eight, and my fear and fascination in meeting my new teacher.

My old governess had again stayed behind to help with Odessa and Edwin. Brody Hew was among the ten guards who'd accompanied me. I was glad that he and his black bird, which often sat on his shoulder, were here. When my escape came, it would mean that much more when I outwitted him.

Several guards carried my trunks upstairs. Another set a box containing Crauley's favorite foods upon the table.

I took off my cloak and laid it over the back of a chair. Some of my fondest childhood memories were in this cabin, and I loved that nothing about it had changed. The piles of sheet music, the dust on the round table, the woodsy smell of cedar branches in the fire. I lovingly turned my gaze to Crauley.

Seated upright in his padded chair, his complexion was a gray pallor, and his eyes were sunken into his face more than I remembered. He was very ill.

I strode over and knelt down in front of him.

He lifted a hand slightly and then it dropped to the arm of the chair. "I forgot"—he held up a finger—"you must tell Amy that you are a *lost soul*." Slowly, he moistened his lips.

"What was that?" I tucked the blanket around him, surprised by his odd greeting.

"You have to tell her . . . you are a lost soul." His head tipped back like he didn't have the energy to hold it upright.

Amy? My memory reeled back to his stories of the woman in the village who opened her home to those in need. "Thank you, Sir Crauley." I swallowed a knot in my throat and gripped his cool, bony hand.

He almost smiled. "Get my fiddle." One finger pointed toward the round, dusty table.

With my heart pounding in my chest, I fetched his viola. I knelt again in front of his chair, handing it to him.

I did not need experience with death to know that my Crauley was dying.

I had neither prepared, nor planned for this.

I unpacked my viola and sat down on the worn padded stool, my knees touching his. He wasn't holding his viola properly. I leaned forward and made sure he held his fingers correctly for C major on the fingerboard.

"We'll play of the years together." My voice was almost as craggy as his.

He mustered the energy to clear his throat.

"I waited for you." His words were barely a breath, but I'd heard them.

Though his fingers remained in the C major position, his bow lay motionless against the bridge. His chin wasn't even on the rest. He leaned his head to one side and simply watched me, barely blinking.

"I love you, Distinguished Sir Crauley." I inhaled deeply, holding the perfect posture he'd instilled in me, and played our first memory—beginning with the fruit butter. I played through our seven summers together; listening to the birds, his gentle mentoring, the precious bond we shared. I paused and leaning toward him, kissed his forehead.

"Play." His lips parted, but the word was air.

Music was more important to Crauley than words or actions, for music was both to him. But still, I needed to say them.

"I will never forget you. You have been the most wonderful teacher and the grandfather I never had." I stared in his dimly lit gaze.

The corner of his mouth twitched, and his eyes fluttered.

I drew the bow, and while I played of our memories together, Sir Crauley's face turned ashen. His dark pupils rolled up until only the whites of his eyes were visible, and his soul saw Heaven. My dear friend was no longer with me, but I had no doubt that he was in the best of company.

Though tears streamed down my face, I continued playing the chords of my broken heart. Crauley had hung on for me because he knew that it would have been very difficult for me if he'd left without saying goodbye.

Chapter Eight

I clutched Crauley's knees and cried as I had never cried for anyone, not even Alia. Amidst my sobs, I heard a knock on the door. I straightened, sniffled, and wiped my cheeks on the long sleeves of my dress. Our usual evening duet had been a solo, and the guards were more perceptive than I had foreseen. If I didn't pull myself together, my escape would soon be impossible.

Without my bidding, the door opened.

Still on my knees, I wiped my face again before I turned.

"Princess Wren, are ya all right?" The guard was Brody Hew.

I nodded and though I tried to lock eyes with him, he lifted his gaze to where Crauley sat above me.

"And Sir Crauley . . . is he all right?"

"We're well. Thank you. Please leave."

"Are you certain?" His gaze narrowed to the shell of my beloved Crauley.

"Please leave us. Our time together is precious." Tears slid down my cheeks.

"I'm sorry." He lowered his gaze then pulled the door closed behind him.

Though night had fallen, I had to leave now. The guards would not allow me to stay alone in the cabin, and Brody already knew I was not to be trusted. I spotted my cloak on the chair where I'd left it. I was just about to climb the stairs for my things when a knock on the door was followed by someone opening it again.

Two guards, Herbert and then Brody Hew stepped inside.

"I'm sorry to disturb you, Princess Wren, but I'm well trained in medical ways." Herbert made his way toward Crauley.

My hopes of riding out of here in Aggie's place had dissipated like a vapor before my eyes. Crauley had gone to Heaven and changed my plans.

"I . . ." I glanced ever so briefly toward the yellow cupboard. My cloak was on the back of the chair. My money, maps, and peasant attire were in my bag upstairs.

In front of these men, I couldn't very well take my bag and cloak and slip inside a cupboard.

"I need water," I said, feeling agitated.

"I'll get it for ya." Brody started for the pump at the sink.

"I'm, I'm cold," I said, gripping my arms in front of me.

"Yer in shock."

Perhaps I was. I tried to think clearly.

The young guard returned empty-handed to fetch my cloak for me and helped me slide it on over my long, blue dress that Mother had selected for me to wear only that morning. While Brody returned to the kitchen for a glass of water, I tried to get my wits about me.

My viola was on the chair. If I took it, its absence might be spotted before mine. If I left my most treasured possession behind, it might very well buy me a little time. Plus, running with a viola would only slow me down.

"I'm sorry to say, Princess Wren, but his soul is gone," Herbert said. "Tomorrow morning, we'll transport his body to Blue Sky."

"Blue Sky?" My voice teetered.

"Yes, your father wants your royal teacher buried there," Herbert said.

"Ohhh," a deep moan escaped me. Father had known Crauley was dying, and he hadn't informed me. My beloved Crauley would be buried at home. A fresh wave of tears flowed. "Crauley would want to be buried here, not in Blue Sky."

"Here, Princess Wren," Brody handed me a tin cup of water. "Is there anything else I can get for ya?" he asked, softly.

My gaze drifted to the cupboard. Instinct told me that Crauley's tunnel might very well be my only chance for seeing Alia.

"Yes, there is. In my trunk upstairs is a blue cloth bag. Only bring down the bag and my hairbrush, which is in the middle compartment of the smaller trunk." I purposefully told him the wrong trunk, hoping it would lengthen his search. "And a more comfortable pair of shoes, please." As I said it, I knew it was my first mistake, for Brody's gaze lowered to my white, button-up boots, the tips of which poked out the bottom of my dress.

Was now my only chance? Or should I wait until the guards were asleep? Knowing Brody Hew, he'd sleep with one eye open.

"I'll bring yer bag and shoes down for ya." He started for the staircase.

While Herbert went outside to inform the others, I took a lit candlestick over to the yellow cupboard and set it on the floor. I opened the doors, pried up the floorboard and shifted it to the left inside the base of the cabinet. I eased myself backward into the hole and thanked heaven that I wasn't wearing my crinolette with its steel hoop cage. My feet found the rungs of a wooden ladder. I descended several steps, holding the candlestick. Knowing that I had to be quick, I pulled the cupboard door closed and then shifted the floorboard back into place above me.

Step by step, I lowered my foot to each rung, descending into the pitch black hole—the bowels of Crauley's tunnel.

The cramped, musty-smelling hole was my deepest nightmare.

I cupped my hand around the candle—my lifeline—and stared straight ahead. The tunnel was tall enough for me to stand up in and wide enough that two people could squeeze through together. Crauley said that it ended near the woods, far enough away from the house that the guards shouldn't notice me. *Unless I danced like a banshee*, that is. In spite of his humor, I found myself afraid of the dark, tight space. Fear, teamed with grief, made my hands shake violently.

Determined to not lose the light, I pinned my arms against my sides, and lowered myself to my knees, cupping the tallow candle. The flame wavered. "Please, God. Please, God." In the end, it was my whispered prayer, my breath hovering over the flame that put it out.

Darkness followed.

The journey before me did not have my father's blessing or God's.

I groped forward. "You know. You know my heart's desire." Touching the walls, I tried to keep my sense of direction.

I was disobeying my upbringing. Yet, before I married and became the Queen of Davenport, I would die a thousand deaths to see Alia once more.

ΦΦΦ

I walked straight into a solid wall of hard-packed earth. Was it the end? Around me, I felt only dirt. There were no side tunnels. I patted my hands on the hard-packed earth above me. I continued patting until I found what felt like wood. I pushed up with all my strength, dislodging a somewhat rotten round of wood, covering the hole. The outside world was not much lighter than my present one. I grabbed onto tufts of grass, attempting to pull myself up. On my second try, I got a knee over the side and found success. I rolled the wood back over the hole and then established my bearings in the dark shadows of the tightly grouped trees.

Crauley's road was off to my right. I remembered his advice *not to dance like a banshee*, and oh, how I felt tempted. I stayed in the trees lining the roadside until I reached an open meadow. By this time, I was fully out of view from the cabin, so I ran on the pebbly dirt road in the gray sliver of moonlight. I ran until I was too winded to run another step. After walking for a spell, I caught my breath before running again. Never had I been alone in all of my life, and the experience was both exhilarating and frightening.

I ran until I reached the white-painted sign at the edge of the village. *Hampershire Population 91.* Unless a baby had been born this evening, the population was now 90. Two-story homes with tiny yards sat only a few feet off the road. A man sat dozing in front of one, a dark jug in one hand.

"Who goes there?" His hand wobbled as he pointed at me.

My pulse pounded in my chest as I hurried through the moonlit village. Homes were buckled up tight for the night and rightly so. I glanced over my shoulder at the empty dirt road. The man hadn't followed me.

A home with a flat front and no porch sat on the corner of one block near the center of town, a candle flickering in the first-floor window. Large, overgrown lilac bushes blocked the front door. I followed a narrow path of stones to the side entrance and rapped my knuckles thrice upon the door. Senses keen, I watched the road out front. I knocked once more before hearing movement inside.

The door creaked open, and the light of the candlestick she was holding illuminated a large-boned woman's face. Her gray hair hung in one long, thin braid down the front of her cotton house robe.

"I'm a lost soul." My mouth was so dry I could barely get the words out, so I repeated myself.

"What is your name, child?" She studied only my face, not my cloak or my long dress.

"Wr . . ." I paused, trying to clear my throat. "En . . . nie."

"Ennie, you look like you've been cryin' since the day you were born. Come 'ere, child, and we'll get you goin' where you're supposed to be goin'." Amy's warm hand pulled me in from the chilly night. Her arms wrapped around me as she walked me down a narrow hallway.

"The good Lord told me to set a new candle out tonight, that a very tender soul would be visitin'. Ennie, you are loved. We'll get you a glass of warm milk and then to bed."

"I don't drink warm milk before bed. Water is fine," I said.

"All right, water it 'tis. After you get a good night's rest, you'll share your troubles in the morning." We moved into a kitchen where crocheted potholders hung from wooden pegs.

I sat at the table and stared while the elderly woman puttered between the stove and a row of cupboards. Crauley was gone. My well-laid plans were in my blue bag for all of Father's guards to read. They'd be waiting for me in every town between here and Yonder. My plans could not have gone more wrong.

Yet . . . here I was. I'd made it to Amy's. If I could keep my wits about me, there was a chance, if God should deem it so, that I would see my sister once more.

Chapter Nine

"Ennie . . . Ennie, there is someone here for you," a matronly voice woke me from the heavy quilt of sleep.

I lifted my head, groggy.

The light in the hallway outlined a tall, large-boned woman, standing in the doorway.

"There is someone here for you," Amy said.

"Me?" I flipped back the covers. "You didn't tell him I was here, did you?"

"No."

"Who was he?" Adrenaline wobbled through my veins as I pulled on my boots. Fortunately, I had slept in my dress.

"I didn't get his name, but he was young, strong, with thick, auburn hair. Is he your—"

"Did he have a white horse?"

"Yes. Is he your husband?"

"No, I'm not married."

"What are you runnin' from, Ennie?" Her posture reminded me of Maid Kimberlee's as she waited with her long fingers entwined in front of her.

There was not time for anything but the truth, condensed. "I have not seen my sister for eight years, and now is my only chance."

"He said that you left without even leaving a note and that someone very dear to you just died. Ennie, have you given this proper thought?"

"Yes." I fought back tears, pushing the memories of Crauley aside. "I've planned for many years." I'd planned to leave the letter that was in my case back at Crauley's. I'd planned to take my map, money, and peasant clothes too. But, then he'd died, and I'd lost my scope of reason. I'd simply panicked.

I'd make a very poor soldier.

"I've sent the young man to the magistrate. When he returns with the proper papers, I have to let him in my home. If you still want to leave, it has to be now. She turned to leave.

"I do." I hurried after her down a short hallway and a white-painted stairwell.

"And I haven't fed you breakfast or lunch."

"Lunch?"

"Yes, Ennie. I let you sleep in." At the foot of the stairs, she opened a door onto the main floor hallway. "You'll be in cramped quarters during your ride. Your first stop is a farm where you'll work for your room and board for three full days before you head to Stockford."

Stockford was on my map to Yonder.

I followed her through the kitchen. She paused to open a cupboard, struck a match and lit the wick of a kerosene lantern. To the right of the icebox, she opened another door. It looked like it went to the cellar, it was so dark. She held the wire handle high as she led the way down the open wooden stairs.

"There will be two of you hidden away behind the bench seat. There is nothing to fear."

"Two of us?"

"Yes, you will have a traveling companion. Put this in your pocket." Amy turned and stuffed a small roll of paper into my hand.

"I don't have a pocket." It was then I realized I'd forgotten my cloak on the foot of the bed, but it was too late to go back for it.

"Hold onto it then. It will see you through your journey, love."

Was the dear old woman giving me money? I pushed the paper up inside the sleeve of my gown.

"I didn't get to write down the verse in its entirety before the young man arrived."

"Wait, child, another one has come to me." She paused again on the stairs and held the lantern between us. Her gray eyes were keen in its light. "The Lord's given me another verse for you, Ennie. *To knock and keep on knocking.* Repeat that for me," she said, continuing down the steps.

"To knock and keep on knocking," I said.

A lone wagon sat in the dirt-floored basement.

"Where are the horses?" I asked.

"Outside, he'll hitch them up when we're ready." Amy turned to study me, her eyes wide in the lantern light. "Repeat it again."

"To knock and keep on knocking." I didn't like our circumstances or how serious she was, but there was nothing I could do about it.

"Hurry up." A scrawny, middle-aged driver climbed into the bed of the wagon, waving at me.

"Thank you for everything, Amy." As I stepped onto a bale of hay, I lost the guidance of the light behind me. I moved past the driver to the box beneath the bench seat. I noted dark shoes on the left, so I entered with my right foot first and then lowering my head, shimmied back against the wall. The box was narrow, pressing into my shoulders, and the tips of my shoes touched my fellow traveler's.

As the man pounded the boards back into place, I tried to see the elderly woman one last time, but it was too dark. Mere slits of Amy's lantern light peeked through the cracks. I'd determined only last night that I didn't like small, dark places, and here I was again in the same predicament, this time with a stranger. However, for some reason, I did not feel afraid. Perhaps it was because of the elderly woman's prayers.

A large door was rolled open, and my companion and I sat in silence while the driver hitched the team and tossed the reins into the bench seat. The boards of the old wagon creaked as he climbed to his station. My shoulder pressed heavily into the side of the box as the wagon rolled forward out of the basement and onto the side street.

"Your hair is long," said a smooth, young woman's voice across from me. "I saw a swish of it."

"It is," I said into the darkness.

"And I smell the prettiest soap I've ever smelled, like lilac and French powder. My aunt wore French powder once, and I had the pleasure of its scent. My name is Pearl."

"Mine is Ennie." And though I tried, I could not discern what type of soap she used, or if there were any special scent that belonged to her, separate from the loose straw that we sat upon.

"Did Amy give you something for your pocket?" Pearl asked.

"Yes. I tucked it inside my sleeve."

"Don't you have a pocket?"

"No."

"Aw, you poor thing. So poor you don't even have a pocket. Lucky for us, I have a needle and thread."

The driver tapped his foot on the footboards.

"Shhh!" Though Pearl had been the only one speaking, she shushed me.

We had not traveled more than the length of the town before the wagon rolled to a complete stop.

"Why the long line?" our driver called out to someone.

"Blue Sky soldiers are here. Searching for something," volleyed a man.

"Or someone," said a gruff male voice.

I was thankful it had not been our driver who'd said it.

"On behalf of the King," Herbert repeated over and over in the distance. "On behalf of the King."

I tried to listen past the clamor of my heart.

"Blue Sky soldiers are here." People mumbled near our wagon. I couldn't tell if they were merely onlookers or travelers.

"It was not like this last time," Pearl whispered.

Had she escaped from Amy's before?

The driver tapped his foot on the floorboard.

"On behalf of King Francis. On behalf of the King." Herbert sounded so stern, not his usual jovial self.

What if our driver died suddenly in the middle of nowhere? Would Pearl and I be able to kick out the boards? The dark box began to feel warm and cramped like it was caving in on me. Was Amy's verse from God for a moment such as this: *To knock and keep on knocking?* My chest tightened into uncomfortable knots, and I could not draw a breath deeply into my lungs.

Pearl leaned forward and squeezed my hand. "We are in this together," she whispered. "Together."

I squeezed her hand in return. Taking slow deep breaths, I was able to slow my sprinting heart. My imagination had almost gotten the better of me.

Our wagon rolled forward to another stop.

"Where are you headed?" Herbert asked our driver.

"Farms, I'm a peddler."

"And what do you peddle?"

"I'm in the oil business. Castor Oil."

While the guards had a good laugh, the back of the wagon lurched as someone stepped inside.

"There are crates and crates of *Castor* Oil," a guard announced, rousing a second round of laughter.

"Might I ask what you're looking for?" our driver asked.

"Something of value to the king," Herbert said.

"Is there a reward?" our driver asked.

My heart sank at our ill fortune.

"There is the reward of serving yer King," Brody Hew said. His West Coast accent so distinct to the ear.

I closed my eyes. The guard's allegiance was annoying. Was another guard going to the magistrate for paperwork while he'd ridden on ahead? Would they find my cloak?

"Search the underside of this wagon, every nook, and cranny," Brody said.

What had drawn his suspicion? Now was not the time to be wearing a sky blue dress. Was any of it visible through the box's slats?

You have not let me come this far, I reasoned with God. *Eight years. I haven't seen Alia for eight years!* A voice inside my head or heart, I could not tell which, reasoned with me, also. *You should have* sought your father's blessing.

Crauley's voice joined in like he was seated in a rocking chair beside the Holy Spirit: *You will break your parents' hearts and give them kidney stones.*

Knees cracked, and gravel crunched as a guard searched beneath the wagon. The words: *I am here* teased my brain and tongue. I would go home, seek Father's forgiveness and tell him the longings of my heart. *But*, I reasoned, to surrender now meant I would expose Pearl. Was her running away honorable? Surely Amy asked the same questions of her.

"What we're looking for is not here," the guard said, rising to his feet.

I relaxed back into the barn wood.

The wagon jostled for several miles. Neither Pearl nor I dared to speak.

"What could it be? Something so valuable that they'd stop and search everyone. Something of the King's," she whispered.

"It could be a great many things."

"Do you still have your verse?"

"Do you mean what Amy gave me?" I'd been hoping there might also be money.

"Yes. Amy always gives a verse to those who leave her place."

"How do you know?"

"I ran away last year before my pa found me. Amy gave me a verse then, too. I did not like it much. I hope this one's better."

I didn't like the second verse she'd given me: *to knock and keep on knocking.* For the first leg of my travel, the verse didn't sound very reassuring.

There wasn't enough light to read our verses, so we'd have to wait.

"To pass the time, I'll work on your pocket," Pearl said.

"Now?"

"Yes, I can sew a straight stitch in the dark, never fear. My mum was a seamstress, and she taught me before she died." There was a sound of metal rubbing metal as she pried open a tin. "I'm going to cut off my extra pocket and sew it near the hem of your dress." Pearl's sentiments were followed by the squeak of scissors as she began cutting. "We don't want to make an ugly pocket on the outside for everyone to see. It should be one that doesn't show—a hidden pocket."

I couldn't even thread a needle in the dark, and Pearl was sewing pockets. "Have you ever embroidered?" I asked. Embroidery in my own mother's mind was a social art form, almost as important as conversation.

"Yes, but I never seem to have the time for it. This material feels so genteel," she murmured.

My long-sleeved dress was a sky blue color, but after my trip through Crauley's tunnel, it might be more of a dusty blue. My attire was a far cry from the peasant clothing I'd left back at Crauley's. I would stick out like a sore thumb, like a princess on the run.

"Last year when I traveled from Amy's, it was with a boy who smelled like fish," Pearl said.

"Oh, it sounds dreadful." I questioned if there was such a thing as the gift of smell?

"What are you running from, Ennie?"

"I'm not running away; I am running to."

"How romantic. What are you running to?" My gown lifted slightly as she took another stitch.

"My sister, who I haven't seen for over eight years."

"Awhhh . . . A noble quest. I hope you find her."

Noble quest. I was of nobility, but was my quest noble? Noble had been one of those words I'd been weaned on. *Honor*, *virtue*, *selflessness* came to mind. I would be blind to self if I believed mine a noble quest.

"Why are you running, Pearl?"

"My father wants to marry me off to the neighbor boy for his land. They'd be partners and raise cows." She sighed unhappily. "I'm not fond of manure. I'm going to do my best to marry myself off first."

"Is there no hope for the neighbor boy?" I was surprised to hear that commoners were also married off.

"None. He smells like old moldy cheese."

"Do you know where you're running to?" I asked.

"No. 'Tis my dream to have a string of pearls. I've always been told that I have the neck for them."

Pearl's voice was pleasantly smooth. I enjoyed listening to her. While she sewed a pocket on my dress, I wondered what my new friend looked like in the light of day.

Chapter Ten

"**W**hat are your greatest fears?" Pearl asked. We were still in the back of the wagon and in the dark. My fears were the last things I wanted to think about. "You tell me one, and then I'll tell you. Start with the greatest one."

"Hell," I heard the tremble in my voice when I said it and prayed God would forgive me for running away.

"Oh, mine too." She inhaled thoughtfully. "I'm scared of pain."

"Me, too. Um . . ." I searched the dark corners of my mind. "Marriage," I admitted.

"That's higher on your list than mine. I think I'm more afraid of dentures. When I was young, I had to get my grandfather's dentures from beneath the bed, and I know that it scarred me."

I prayed this conversation would not scar me.

Hours later, the wagon finally lurched to a stop. Our driver pried the boards off of the box. I blinked in the rays of evening light. Pearl climbed out first, and I glimpsed a swath of her long, wavy blond hair and a plain peasant dress of white cotton dimity.

She came from poverty.

We stood up in the wagon with our hands on our hips, stretching the kinks out of our backs and shoulders.

"Good, it's a different farm than last year." Pearl surveyed the landscape.

Off to my left sat a two-story tangerine-colored farmhouse with a front porch. There was a patch of lawn in front, the garden in back rolled into a sea of tall, green tasseled corn as far as the eye could see. As I turned, Pearl came into my view. Hands cupped over our eyes, we stared at one another.

"You're beautiful." She took in my long, wavy coppery-red hair, my fair complexion, and my blue-green eyes.

Pearl was magnificent. Her ivory skin was flawless, and her neck, long and elegant like she'd said, was made for pearls. Thick, golden hair rippled halfway down her back, and she was just a tad willowier than me.

"Your name is perfect for you," I said with all sincerity.

"Pearl buttons!" Mouth agape, she stared at my dress. "I've never seen pearl buttons before."

I peered down at the bodice of my gown. The buttons were indeed pearls. Beginning at the high collar, they trailed down in pairs past the fitted waist all the way to the floor.

"Wherever did you get it?" Pearl asked.

"Uh . . ." It was the perfect time in our conversation to follow our driver, who'd gone ahead to knock upon the door. I dropped from the bed of the wagon to the hard packed dirt and waved a hand for Pearl to follow.

The farmhouse's front windows were filled with the grimy faces of children, one in each of the lower panes. Not a good sign. I recalled Amy's words: *you'll work for your room and board for three full days before you head to Stockford.*

The door swung open and the woman of the house, skinny and stern, waved at us. "Come in and sit down," she said gruffly and then tucked two small coins into our driver's hand.

He climbed back into the wagon and left us there.

The front room was messy, littered with wooden blocks and piles of dirty clothes. A collection of grimy fingerprints marred the walls, and all of the furniture cushions were lumpy.

"Sit down for supper." The woman pointed to a long table full of children who hadn't washed their hands or faces before sitting down. They ranged in age from a toddler in a high chair to older teens—two heavy-set girls and a rough-and-tumbled teenage boy with a disheveled mop of sandy blond hair and twinkling eyes.

"Are those real pearl buttons?" The oldest girl stared at the bodice of my dress while the boy eyed Pearl.

"I believe so, yes." I nodded.

Pearl passed the warm cassoulet to me. I had not eaten all day and my mouth watered. Instead of slowly cooked duck and pork sausage in a savory broth, the earthenware bowl contained a mashed potato-topped peasant's dish, with very little meat.

"Yum! Shepherd's pie," said the youngest, girl.

"Where did you get your dress?" the older sister asked. Squinting one eye, she attempted to flick something out from between her lower molars with her tongue.

"Close your mouth, Clara Bell," her mother said, setting an elbow on the table. "If your future in-laws see your manners before the wedding, there won't be one."

"Where did you get it?" Clara Bell eyed me again.

"My mother purchased it for me," I said politely, meeting her gaze across the table.

With each chew of the potato pie, Clara Bell dropped her jaw, exposing mashed potatoes and the minuscule chunks of mutton. Her manners were worse than a cow's.

My stomach turned.

"Who's your mother?" Clara Bell asked.

I wanted to open my mouth and give her a taste of her own medicine, but I swallowed instead. "My mother is my

Uncle Teddy's sister." We were in a corn field in the middle of nowhere. Surely, this was safe enough to say.

The woman of the house regarded me with narrowed eyes. "Queen Irene has a brother named Teddy. I read it last week in the Stockford Times."

In the future, I would not be so flippant about my relations.

Had anyone guessed the truth? I glanced at Pearl. Was her mind galloping back to Hampershire and all the King's men? Instead, her gaze had narrowed to my pearl buttons. She couldn't take her eyes off them.

ΦΦΦ

Pearl and I washed the supper dishes and all the walls and windows in the front room before we joined the other girls upstairs. Plain, white night frocks were set out for us on the two full-sized beds.

"You won't dare take your dress off here, or it won't be yours in the morning," Pearl whispered. She was probably right.

While the other girls puttered about the room, we sat on the edge of our bed. The time had come to unfold our slips of paper from Amy. I retrieved her note from my new hidden pocket.

Pearl went first and held the slim strip toward the tallow candle's light. "I like this one so much better than last year's." She nudged me. "*For I know the plans I have for you, declares the Lord, plans for good and not for evil, to give you a future and a hope.*" She rolled the fingers of her right hand thoughtfully near the base of her neck. "I'd say pearls are in order."

I smiled at my new friend's determination and unrolled my slip of paper. It simply read: *God has a plan for you…*

Boy, didn't I know that.

"I like mine better." Pearl peered over my shoulder.

I liked hers better, too. I reminded myself that Amy had not had the time to write down all of my verse. Maybe the rest of the verse read: you will travel to distant lands, see your beloved sister, marry a wonderful man and live happily ever after, staring at the sea.

God has a plan for you did not have to sound so bleak. So final.

We said our prayers, slid into bed, and one of the younger girls, who was only four, squeezed between us. Similar to the night before, I again slept in my dress.

"You'll wrinkle your lovely dress, sleeping in it," Clara Bell voiced in the dark.

"It's already wrinkled," I yawned.

"It'll be much more comfortable for you to sleep in a nightgown," she continued.

"I'm comfortable enough." I needed peasant clothes, but my beautiful gown would be nice for me to wear in Yonder.

The candles were snuffed, and a sliver of moon shone through the slightly parted curtains. The youngest girls giggled for a spell, perhaps excited about our company, before they finally quieted.

I closed my eyes and felt like I was still swaying back and forth with the wagon's gentle jostle before I fell asleep.

I awoke in the middle of the night to what felt like a mouse scampering over my feet. On the verge of a scream, I kicked at it, then sat up, and scooted toward the headboard. Aided by the moonlight that shone through the slightly parted curtains, I watched the foot of the bed for several minutes. No little creature scurried beneath or across the covers.

My eyes soon grew heavy, and I drifted back to sleep. I found myself dreaming of Alia. My beautiful sister was playing the piano. Smiling softly, she'd just turned to look over her shoulder at me. Before our eyes had the chance to meet, I awoke.

I blinked several times in the dark. I wanted to return to the dream, to lock eyes and embrace one another—

"I want it for my ring pillow. Now, shush!" Clara Bell whispered.

"It ain't right," said Jane, the younger of the two.

"Shhh . . . both of you," Pearl whispered.

"I'll get rid of two on the list—something *borrowed*, something *blue*."

"It's not that, you dummy. It's something borrowed, something *new*."

"Oh, pooh."

Wasn't it both—something *new* and something *blue*? It was the middle of the night, and the girls were arguing about the old wedding rhyme.

I yawned.

The girls immediately quieted.

Then I closed my eyes, searching for my dream.

ΦΦΦ

When I awoke in the morning, I slipped my feet into my boots and noted that two pearl buttons of my gown were missing below the knee. Could Pearl have nabbed them in the night? Had she been the mouse I'd felt scamper across my feet?

Over a bowl of crunchy dry cereal, I felt sick as I thought about the missing buttons. A bond had quickly formed between Pearl and me, yet on account of the buttons, I began to question her character. Why had she run away? Was her father really wanting to marry her off to the neighbor boy, or was she was a button-stealing fugitive on the run?

"Hughie, close your mouth. You chew like a horse!" bellowed the woman of the house.

Oats flew out of the young man's mouth as he smacked his lips together, eyeing Pearl. I tried to remember what a horse looked like while chewing. I did not think a horse's manners were as poor as Hughie's.

With no verbal warning, his mother reached across the table and smacked him on the head with a wooden spoon.

"Ouch, you old witch!" he hissed.

"What'd you call me?" The woman's eyes were enormous as she lifted the spoon again.

Covering his head with both hands, he dashed for the door. In her faded yellow house robe, his mother chased after him waving the spoon. They ran over the threshold and down the porch steps.

I followed the children to the front windows, where we watched their mother chase Hughie back and forth across the yard before they disappeared down a row of corn. The tassels shook, making a maze-like ripple through the tall green foliage.

Pearl had stayed behind at the table to feed the toddler who was locked in his high chair. She was good with the infant, making little faces at him to get him to open his mouth for the spoon. If she'd indeed stolen my buttons, perhaps I could forgive her.

While the mother chased Hughie about the yard, waving her wooden spoon, the two older girls returned upstairs to their room. Pearl did the dishes while I sat on the sofa and read stories to the children. I'd glance up from time to time to see the young man sprint out of the corn, his mother not far behind. She'd pause, panting for a moment in the yard, hands on her hips and bun fallen, her house robe open at the lapels. The morning was a good lesson for me. If I ever had a teenage son, I would never have any more children. Teenage boys simply required too much energy.

ΦΦΦ

Pearl and I, hired help that we were, were sent to the back garden to hoe weeds. The woman of the house showed us what were weeds and what were turnip starts, and then left us alone in a large patch.

I worked the hoe while Pearl picked up the weeds and set them in a bucket behind me.

"What happened to your gown?" she gasped.

"What do you mean?"

"A chunk of it's missing in back. Hold still." She knelt to one knee and pulled the folds of my dress until they were smooth. "Someone's cut a tea towel-sized hole in the back. I can see your frock."

I recalled waking from my dream. "The older girls were whispering in the middle of the night about something borrowed, something blue." I eyed Pearl. "You don't think?"

"I'll go check right now." She rose to her feet and with a purpose in her stride, my avenger started toward the house.

"Don't get in trouble because of me," I called after her.

She waved a hand.

In her absence, I picked up weeds, dropping them inside the bucket. The sun climbed to a higher station in the sky. To protect my fair complexion, I returned to the house for an old straw hat that I'd seen near the back door. I asked the woman of the house if I might borrow it.

She frowned. "Yes, and wear one of my work aprons to protect that dress of yours. If you steal either of them, I'll have your hide."

"There'll be no worry of that." If for some reason she ever had to chase me through the corn, I knew she'd catch me. The woman had amazing lung power and, thanks to her teenage son, was in much better shape than I was.

Instead of returning out the back door, I snuck up the stairwell to check on Pearl. She was alone in the girls' room. Crouched on her knees near the far wall, Pearl hummed. I drew closer. Her sewing tin lay open on the bed, and she was cutting off the bottom section of the blue-and-white striped curtains.

Heaven forbid!

"What are you doing?" I asked, keeping my voice low.

"I'm returning a wrong for a wrong. Look in there and you'll see why." Pearl pointed toward an old cedar chest at the foot of the bed.

I knelt down in front of it and lifted back the lid. A heart-shaped, lace-trimmed pillow made of the same sky-blue material as my gown lay on top of the trunk full of keepsakes. A ring pillow! Despite all the girls' deceitful cleverness, I was *still* missing two pearl buttons.

"And, why are you cutting the curtains?" I asked.

"I'm going to fix your dress. You needn't worry; it's going to be beautiful." Pearl started cutting the second panel, probably so both curtains would match. "I have it all figured out. We'll swap dresses. I'll wear yours, and while I sit in the corn, I'll work on mending it. When I'm done, we'll swap back."

I stared at the remodeled curtains. I was never going to see Alia. We were going to die on this farm and be buried in the turnip patch.

"Now, get out of your dress." Pearl nodded at me.

"Are you certain?" I croaked. Surely, the woman of the house would notice the change to my dress, recognize the material.

"What are you girls doing up there? You're supposed to be weeding," the woman hollered up the stairwell.

"We'll be right down," I said, starting for the stairs.

Pearl took her own sweet time, putting her scissors away and folding the striped fabric into squares. She didn't appear to be afraid in the least of the woman's temper, or her spoon.

Outside, we hid deep in a row of corn. As I unbuttoned my dress, I tried to ignore the knot in my belly. Could I trust Pearl?

After we had swapped garments, she stayed in the shade, fixing my dress and humming while I weeded in the hot sun. Her white knee-length frock was much lighter in weight and far more comfortable than mine. I wore the missus' apron over the top, and, thanks to the straw hat, I didn't get heatstroke.

"It's done." Pearl stepped out of the corn and curtsied, holding the skirt of my dress in front of her. She turned slowly to show me the back. A block of the blue-and-white striped material was sewn on both sides, tying the two together beautifully.

"What will you do with the other block from my dress?" I asked, wondering if she'd make her own ring pillow.

"I've put it in your hidden pocket for now." She smiled. "I thought I might eventually make the sweetest little purse with it for you."

"Thank you, Pearl. You're ever so clever." The dress looked so exquisite on her that I felt torn about keeping it for myself.

"I'd love to see what it looks like on me. Do you mind?" Pearl nodded toward the house. "It's the closest I've ever been to wearing a string of pearls."

An uneasy feeling settled in my gut, and I tried to dismiss it. When she saw how beautiful the dress looked on her, she would never take it off. I'd be stuck with her old, loose-fitting, gunny sack of a dress. I leaned on my hoe. The ugly peasant dress that I wore was exactly what I needed, but my old one was beautiful.

Should I just give it to Pearl? Or should I see if she would return it first? I was still missing the two buttons. Was it wrong to test a friend?

She touched the pearls near the collar. "Would you mind if I go take a quick peek?" She glanced toward the house.

Were we supposed to finish weeding the garden by suppertime or just this row? While she'd sat in the shade humming, my back had begun to ache from all the stooping I'd done, and dirt had lodged beneath every one of my fingernails.

"Go ahead." I wiped a hand across my brow. After Pearl saw how the dress looked with her common shoes, she'd be asking to try on my lace-up, high-heeled boots next. I dismissed the unsettling thought and continued working.

Pearl did not hurry. In her absence, I began to feel parched and a tad lightheaded. What was taking her so long? Most likely, she was swishing and twirling in front of the mirror, admiring herself. She might even be celebrating her victory of possessing my dress. Did she sincerely plan to return it? Or would she come up with excuses to retain it?

I sighed.

While I picked up weeds, two men in a wagon half filled with hay rode up the long, dirt driveway and halted in front of the house. The skinny driver who strode to the door looked very similar to the one who'd driven us here yesterday. This time, he was not alone—a broad-shouldered man with a pot belly accompanied him to the door, and they went inside. If they were collecting us, they were two days early.

I strode halfway to the porch and peered around the pump house. Had they come for me, or was it simply routine for the men to stop by? I strained to listen and at first heard only the hammering of my heart.

"No, I'm not. Take your hands off me!" Pearl's voice traveled through the open windows upstairs.

They thought Pearl was me!

I ran into the nearest row of corn. No! I had to be smarter than that. Hiding in the corn would be expected. I had to take the most unexpected route, my life as a war strategist's daughter had taught me this much.

I raced to the wagon and climbed into the back. Bales of hay had replaced the crates of castor oil. I squeezed between the hay and planked wooden sides of the bed. Then, I shimmied a bale above me. Would they notice the shift of the hay? It was a chance I had to take.

Voices soon warned of the men's approach. Had they decided not to take Pearl? I didn't hear her. The back of the wagon creaked, and someone stepped up inside.

I didn't dare breathe.

"Put her in the boogey hole. We don't need anyone robbing us before Stockford." The boards were yanked out of the back of the wagon seat. Pearl must have been gagged, for she didn't make a peep as they pushed her and all of my finery inside. The boards were pounded back into place.

My only hope to free her now was to hide until Stockford.

"A runaway princess with a reward on her head," the driver's voice rose. "You were entertaining royalty last night and didn't even know it."

"We had our suspicions in that fancy dress of hers," said the woman of the house. "The other girl's around here, too, some a wheres."

"This is the one we want." The bench seat creaked as the henchman joined him up front.

"Where are you taking her? My husband will ask."

"Stockford. The King's men are in every town within 200 kilometers." The driver slapped the reins, and the wagon rolled forward.

I cringed. Heaven forbid! I was still wearing the woman of the household's hat and apron.

ΦΦΦ

A few hours later, the wagon came to a halt in the bustling town of Stockford. The rear of the wagon buckled as one of the men stepped inside. He removed the boards from the box. Pearl was most certainly gagged, for she didn't mumble a word as they descended from the wagon. I waited until I felt confident that they were out of sight before I shimmied the bale of hay above me off to one side. No passersby appeared to notice my sudden emergence. Using my legs, I pushed the bale to cover the hiding spot. It wouldn't be long before they discovered that Pearl was not me.

In the meantime, I wanted to be sure she was okay, and that no harm would come to her on my behalf.

Stockford was five times the size of Hampershire. On the left side of the crowded main square, a circus act was in parade. A choir of women, all dressed in the same gray garb, sung a gospel hymn, and a large pink and black mottled pig on a leash wore a straw hat similar to mine. A man with a top hat and a long black wand led the procession.

In their crisp blue and white uniforms, Blue Sky soldiers were everywhere on horseback. Despite my unease, I could not have asked for a better disguise. My common garb and the straw hat with my hair tucked up inside, helped me to blend in like any other commoner in the crowd. I still had to be careful and not do anything to draw attention to myself while I searched for Pearl.

My ear was drawn to the center of the square. Someone was playing terrible violin music. While I scanned the area, a long line of red-haired young women, three and four people wide, came into view. Never had I seen so many redheads in one place before. Either the town had very strong Celtic roots, or there was a redhead convention in full swing.

Chin lifted, I almost walked right into a sandwich board. As I went to sidestep it, a hand-printed poster caught my eye.

REWARD for the return of:
 Princess Wren Wells of Blue Sky
 15 years old with red hair and blue eyes
 Plays the violin.
 Ł100 pounds for her safe return.

My life was summarized in two short lines, and our guards had got it all wrong. My eyes were blue-green, my hair a coppery-red and I played the viola not the violin.

The redhead convention was on account of me.

Tucking my braids down the back of my frock, I turned to face the crowd. Near the end of the long line and no longer gagged stood Pearl—the prettiest girl of them all—wearing the prettiest dress of them all. Her captors, one on each side of her, had apparently not noticed that her hair was golden, not red.

Many of the young women stood alone in line, while the others, like Pearl, appeared to be held captive by bounty hunters.

The violin music drifted in the air from a woman who waited in the middle of the line. She was heavy-set and her teen years were at least two decades behind her.

"I'm not her; I tell you." Pearl elbowed one of the men. Other girls spoke out as well.

The reward for my return was set far too high.

Where could I wait for Pearl?

Up ahead, a narrow wooden stairwell marked the side of a brick building. I could sit up there with a grand view of the entire show—the street fair and the red-haired princess convention. As I squeezed my way through the crowd, I was suddenly blocked against the side of a large, white horse.

In the pit of my stomach, I knew the horse was Dilly.

I kept the brim of my straw hat to Brody while I stared down at the tips of my white boots. The swirly hand-stitching that curved around each button might very well expose my royal roots.

"Over here, guard," Pearl's captor, the middle-aged wagon driver, summoned Brody. "This line is far too long for Princess Wren to be kept waiting."

Perhaps it was on account of Pearl wearing my old dress that the guard turned Dilly in their direction. As the rider with the dark bird on his shoulder maneuvered his way through the crowd, I watched with bated breath.

Pearl would not be in line for long. This young guard knew only too well that my hair was not golden, or my neck like that of a swan's.

Wanting a better view, I held onto my hat and squished between people, making my way toward the brick building. A particularly large woman blocked my path and she laughed huskily when I tried to get around her. She had the dark stubble of a man who'd not shaved, and the hairiest of arms. Eyes wide, I realized that she was a man dressed up as a woman with three other people hiding beneath the skirt to expound her enormity. It was circus day in Stockford, and we were all stuck in the middle of it.

"After her!" Two men yelled, pushing their way through the crowd.

I froze. How could they possibly know it was me?

A girl brushed past wearing a straw hat very much like mine and then like a sitting duck, I watched her pursuers come into view.

"Trying to get away were ya?" A tall, rough looking man sneered at me as he clamped a steel bond onto my wrist.

"I'm not her." I pointed behind me. "See, see the hat." I could still see the bob of the straw hat behind us in the crowd as the girl fled.

The man grunted, pulling me forward.

"Tell them. Tell them it wasn't me," I called back to the enormous man dressed as a woman.

His head wobbled like a crazed doll that didn't have a brain.

"Enough of ya!" My captor jeered, exposing tobacco-stained teeth. Jerking me forward, he connected my chain to a middle-aged woman in the gray clothed women's choir. Then he batted at a woman's shin with his long stick as he proceeded to the front of the parade.

"Wait! You have the wrong girl!" I said, afraid to raise my voice too loud.

"Jesus knows." The women's choir sang. "He knows your trouble. He knows your name. Remember His blood. Remember the stain."

"What's happening?" I asked the woman whom I was chained to.

"We're going to auction." Her greasy dark hair was pulled flat against her head, and her bloodshot eyes looked like she hadn't slept. Two other women were chained to her left side.

"What do you mean *we?*" I almost laughed. She'd made it sound like we were the cattle, the livestock.

"Us." The woman nodded.

"Are we not in Blue Sky?" I asked in my most impertinent tone. Father did not allow his subjects to be traded as chattel, only his daughters.

"Eh? Where'd you think you were—La La Land?"

The other women around us laughed bitterly beneath their breath.

In the distance, Brody Hew sat atop his white horse talking with Pearl and her captors. I knew the question that he asked: *Where did you get your dress?*

What would become of Pearl in my dress?

What would become of me in hers?

Are you ready to go home yet, Wren? The inner voice again sounded like Crauley's.

Am I wrong? Is this all in vain? I asked Him. I remembered Maid Kimberlee's advice of days gone by—to listen for the Helper's counsel. But all that came to mind were Crauley's words: *You'll break your parents' hearts and give them kidney stones.*

While I loved my mother very much, I felt no allegiance to my father. I felt only the grief of his decisions: sending Alia away, sending my baby sister away, and trading my future for a railroad. Alia's fate had strengthened an alliance, not created one. Mine would be different. I was to marry the enemy in a political alliance to prevent war.

My future grieved me.

While Brody rode through the crowd following Pearl's captors, I lowered my head again. Would he follow them back to the farm? Or did he know better?

Where was Pearl? I saw no sign of her in the crowd.

"What will happen next?" I asked the greasy-haired woman beside me.

"We'll stand on the block, and the blokes will yell their bids."

"I'm not even supposed to be here. He grabbed the wrong girl. I—"

"Yet here you are like us, facing your tomorrows," said an elderly woman in front of us, over her shoulder.

"How'd you get picked?" I asked. Did the men just go around grabbing women out of the crowd?

"I ran out of money to pay for my lodging. They don't let you panhandle here in Stockford." The elderly woman's eyes were half sunk in her face, as Crauley's had been.

"What's panhandling?" I asked.

"Holding out a pan for change," the greasy-haired woman said.

"Begging," said another.

"My husband came home from war without a leg and without a hope." The elderly woman sighed. "He's gone now. Heaven only knows who'll bid on an old woman."

She was a widow. Father's mandate after the war had been that widows and orphans were supposed to be taken care of. There was no justice here in Stockford. The war had been over eight years. Why were Father's laws not enforced here?

"What happens if no one bids on me?" the elderly woman asked.

"The poor farm," said the greasy-haired woman.

Misery entered the old woman's eyes.

"If the people from the coast buy you, you'll work in a cannery from sunup to sundown. But, they're better than Blaird's. He buys a new cook each week for his giant farm, with no word on what happened to the last."

I didn't want to end up on a huge farm or a cannery. One cry could change my tomorrows. If I yelled *I am Wren,* one of our guards would save me from this cruel, cruel fate.

But . . . to go home now was the easy way out.

Because they were poor, these women were to become slaves. One cry could change my fate.

Though I didn't know what the next hour would bring, I knew this: I could not give up so easily on seeing Alia. And, like these women, I would face my fate.

The women began to sing another mournful tune, this time about God and Heaven, reminding me to pray.

You know, Lord, more than anyone. You know. I was wrong to leave, but You also know everything. Whatever hardships lie before me, please don't make them too hard. Allow me to see Alia before I marry.

I couldn't get on top of an auction block wearing these boots. Mother had paid 100 pounds for them. I better understood the value of money now. With the use of my free hand, I unfastened the buttons and left my boots behind in the crowd.

Chapter Eleven

Blaird, the scrawny man who'd paid five pounds for me, wore a pointed black beard and a scowl. Though I pleaded with him to also buy the elderly woman, neither he nor anyone else did. Her fate was the poor farm, and I felt ripped in two by the injustice going on in my kingdom.

In the back of the wagon, Blaird used a scratchy rope to fasten my hands to the bale of hay behind me.

"A . . . a man just grabbed me out of the crowd. Another girl wearing a straw hat escaped, and they grabbed me. They grabbed the wrong—"

"I paid for you. You're mine," Blaird hissed.

Seated beside me was the large, pink and black mottled pig that I'd seen earlier in the day. It sat upright and regal on its back haunches. Large calla lily ears poked through a frayed straw hat, secured to its head by a green-and-white checked ribbon.

A boy and a girl holding their father's hands strolled toward us. They halted in front of the pig while Blaird stacked supplies behind us in the wagon.

"Bye, Druscella," said the father.

"Bye, Druscella." The boy patted the pig's shoulder.

"Bye, Daisy." The girl, who looked about seven—the twins' age, threw her arms around the pig's neck and burst into tears. "You should never have gotten into Mother's flower garden. Never. Never. Never."

"It's time to go," the father said.

While the little family walked away, the girl peered sadly over her shoulder at the pig before her father tugged her forward.

As Blaird's wagon jostled along the bumpy dirt road, I watched the town of Stockford disappear from view. I'd had a chance to change my fate, and I'd chosen Blaird over going home.

The pig and I watched the scenery change from scattered houses to vast rolling prairie, wooden fence posts, and an occasional jersey cow. I tried to untie the rope, but my attempts only made my arms ache.

"Looks like we're facing our fate," I said, breaking the silence between the pig and me. Daisy continued staring at the rutted road behind us. "I shouldn't have run away. I could be home right now with a full belly, listening to Odessa's off-key violin practice." I inhaled deeply and peered at the pig's profile. She had the longest, wispiest lashes. They were even longer than Pearl's.

"Have you ever loved someone so much . . ." A warm rush of emotion flooded me. I tipped back my head and blinked at the deep blue sky.

The pig's whiskers twitched, and I took it as her silent *yes*.

"That's how it was for me with my sister." Tears flowed at my admittance, and there was no hope of wiping them away or stopping them for that matter. Blaird's farm might very well be the end of the road for me, and I might never see Alia.

"If I ever see my sister again, Daisy," I smiled bravely at the pig's profile, "I know what I'd do."

The pig gazed steadily at the empty road behind us.

"I'd weep. There would simply be too much happiness," I whispered and cleared my throat that she might hear me. "That's what people do when they're too happy. Their happiness is so deep that it comes out as tears." I swallowed and hung on to this thought for a long boring stretch of road.

The last time Alia and I had been together was the night of her sixteenth birthday party, almost nine years ago. At the top of the stairs, she'd transferred my hand to Maid Kimberlee's and said, *in the morning, I'll tell you all about tonight*. That was the last thing my sister had ever said to me. I still had the letter from her that Father had given me after her wedding, but my heart wanted more. I wanted to see her one last time.

Within two months I'd turn sixteen, and I still wasn't over being a little girl of seven.

I cast the pig a weak smile. Daisy was good about not filling the empty air between us with idle chatter.

Thereafter, I tried to be a better-traveling companion and not only focus on myself. "Daisy is an odd name for a pig. Perhaps it was not your first visit to the mother's flower garden." I tried to soften my observation. "I'm certain it was lovely and attracted your attention. My sister, Alia, who I was telling you about, had a nickname for me, too. It was *Ducky*."

I inhaled deeply. The low valley that we rode through matched my mood.

"Having a nickname means that we were loved. We can't forget that, Daisy. We were loved."

ΦΦΦ

"You'll do the cooking," Blair said over his shoulder, "and if you don't pull your weight, the giants will take care of you."

"Giants?" I asked over my shoulder. "What do you mean *giants*?"

"My giants," Blair said, waving an arm out to his side.

I craned my neck to see. Men of giant stature worked the fields on my left.

I blinked.

The largest men I had ever seen or imagined pushed cylinder-shaped bales of wheat that were as tall as they were while Men on horseback rode nearby, holding whips.

Blaird's was not a giant farm. It was a farm of giants.

Chapter Twelve

I watched the road behind us, hoping for a glimpse of Brody Hew and his white horse. Had he gone back with Pearl's captors looking for me? Would the woman tell him that I'd stolen her hat and apron? When he returned to Stockford, would he hear that I'd been sold to Blaird? Or had I so blended into the crowd that no one would remember the fair-skinned teenaged girl on the auction block?

I was in big trouble.

"I don't know how to cook," I said over my shoulder to Blaird.

"What? Why the devil are you wearing an apron?"

"I was protecting my dress when I was weeding."

"Argggh!" he groaned.

What was to become of me? I lifted my face toward heaven.

"I'll get a new cook at auction next week," he mumbled under his breath.

Never had I felt more motivated to learn cooking.

My father was not managing his own kingdom well enough when men like Blaird could also govern. Not that I, his own daughter, had been easy to govern.

Blaird passed a crude stone castle on his left and drove another hundred meters before taking a right. The bed of the wagon jostled as he careened over a deeply trenched road toward a large, stone building. Adjacent to it, no more than a stone's throw away, a stadium with no roof sat off in the field, blocking the view of the north.

"Helmer, tell the new cook what to make for breakfast," Blaird bellowed.

A very broad-shouldered giant with a horseshoe rim of dark hair lumbered over to the back of the wagon. Although he was huge, his clothes were a size too large on him—loose at the chest and gathered with a belt about his middle. He untied Daisy and then me, hoisted the sizeable pig over one shoulder and grunted for me to follow him. Barefoot, I carefully watched each step as I ran behind him on the rocky path.

"Do not look at Remford's finger," Helmer said.

"Who's Remford?"

"That *giant* giant." He nodded up ahead to a giant with brown, kinky curls. Holding a whip at his side, Remford stood guard in front of a large stone building.

He was so huge that I only dared to glance at him once.

"Don't look at his finger," Helmer whispered.

As we neared, I ever so briefly glanced at his hands. His wedding ring finger was completely missing. I diverted my attention to the craggy, rolling landscape, Blaird's crude castle, and the empty road.

Where was Brody Hew when a girl really needed him?

"Do you know how to make gruel cakes, Ennie?"

"No, I've never heard of them."

Helmer stopped near the giant and lifted a wooden slat from a very wide door. Chiseled into the upper panel were two words: Gruel Kitchen.

"Remford, this is the new cook," Helmer said.

"Hello." I tipped back my head to meet the giant's dark, broody gaze.

Maybe he had a sliver or an ingrown toenail, but never had I seen a more unfriendly giant.

"Three days," Remford mumbled, looking down at Helmer.

"Can you sing?" Helmer asked me. "Gid likes it when the cooks can sing."

"No-oo," my voice wobbled only slightly. Now didn't seem the appropriate time to tell them that I couldn't cook either.

"Two days." Remford patted at the handle of the whip.

Helmer led the way through the immense doorway into my future domain. I couldn't sing. I couldn't cook... The door was bolted closed behind us. I couldn't leave.

Torches lit the expansive, high-ceilinged room. On the left, massive bunks were built into the thick rock walls. A u-shaped kitchen lined the right side of the room. Between the kitchen and long, crude tables, two large stones supported a capstone—a grand piano-sized boulder. Perhaps, it was simply giant art, as it appeared to serve no real purpose.

"My mum used to be the cook," Helmer said. "Everyone called her Beulah. 'Cept for me, I just called her Mum."

"Oh." I continued peering around.

"She was a great cook, but you cannot work an old woman so hard."

"What happened to her?" My stomach knotted as I waited for his answer.

"She's buried outside in Cook's Cemetery."

Cook's Cemetery. They'd overworked the poor old woman, and she'd died.

"I'm so sorry…" I said, glad that he didn't provide more details. I liked to think that in the midst of his mother's last recipe, she'd hummed softly and died mid-stir of old age.

"I don't know how to cook," I admitted. "No one's ever taught me."

"You won't last long." Helmer expelled a heavy breath.

God was getting back at me.

I followed Helmer to the far side of the kitchen where he swung open a heavy door. He lowered Daisy to the mud, shooing her inside. I felt sorry for my new friend. The dark stone pen had high, tiny windows permitting only slivers of daylight to enter.

Helmer dropped a large wooden bolt into place. "Make mush. There's not time for anything else," he said.

A chipped white sink and a hand pump sat beneath a barred window in the kitchen—the only one in the enormous room. To the left of the sink, sat a wide cook stove, saddled with a large chopping block.

"The ratio of water to oats is two cups to one." The giant pointed to a bag of oats at the foot of the counter. "You're feeding ten giants. One cup is a normal serving, quadruple it for giants."

"Stay and help me, Helmer," I pleaded. Surely, the son of a cook knew more than I.

"I have to get back to work. You don't want me to get in trouble."

I shook my head, remembering Remford's whip.

"Start the mush and don't forget the salt."

Helmer exited the kitchen. Outside, the bolt dropped into place. "You are too dumb; you cannot flee. Your work is Blaird's for eternity," Remford bellowed.

I hoped that wasn't his usual speech. I didn't find it very encouraging.

ΦΦΦ

"Two cups to one, and there are ten giants. Quadrupled," I mumbled over and over as I wrestled a humongous pot from one of the open shelves to the wooden counter. From a gunny sack, I scooped forty cupfuls of rolled oats into the pot. I shook the salt shaker over the oats like I was lightly salting my dinner. After stirring in twenty cups of water, I set the thick mixture on the stove that was heated by a fire that someone had kindled.

There wasn't much to making mush. Cooking was easier than I'd expected. I set the table with ten giant-sized bowls and spoons, familiarized myself with the kitchen a bit more, and stirred the clumpy mush.

"Hurry and dish up," Helmer yelled while he strode past the window. "The giants are hungry."

A bucket of fresh milk sat nearby on the counter. I poured it into several pitchers and set them on the tables. Back home, Cook always served winter porridge with currants, brown sugar, honey, and cream. If you doctored it enough, mush could taste like dessert. I prayed the mush was done, grabbed the pot from the stove, and walked around the tables, ladling a helping into each bowl. Though I had stirred it several times, fist-sized clumps had formed. I bravely sniffed a chunk. The dry, chalky mixture smelled like clay that had sat too long on the potter's bench. I couldn't summon the courage to taste it.

The ground shook. The bowls bounced and silverware clattered. I gripped the edge of the heavy table. Was it an earthquake?

Giant men lumbered past the window.

The earth was shaking, not quaking.

One by one, the unsightly hulks filled the doorway. Their clothing was torn. Their hair was too long. Their faces were horribly dirty. Helmer, who appeared to be the squattiest, was the fourth to enter.

I glowered at him. I'd made the mush, exactly how he'd said: two cups to one.

"Get to the stage. Gid wants the cooks to sing," Helmer pointed to the middle of the room. "You don't want to make him mad."

"I can't sing. And, look . . ." I waved a hand to the porridge. "I did exactly what you said. Look at it!"

"You did not do what I said."

"I did exactly what you'd said. Two to one, times ten and quadrupled," I said, holding my little patch of ground.

"Two cups of water to one cup of oats?" The lines deepened in his forehead.

"Yes, two cups of . . .Oh-hhh!" I moaned as the truth hit me.

"Sing before Gid gets mad." He pointed to the giant rock sculpture in the center of the room.

Was the rock named Gid?

"Get on stage and sing!" Helmer pointed to the grand piano sized boulder.

Oh, it was a stage. The rocks that dribbled down one side of it were steps. I saw it now. I clambered up to stand on its flat top.

The bowls bounced on the tables as a second round of giants strode past the window. Like the giant men before them, they did not stop at the sink to wash their hands and faces. They lumbered straight to the tables and crouched down on the benches. None were as massive as Remford outside. I was glad he was not one of my diners.

"Me, mie, moe, mush," said the youngest looking giant, staring into his bowl.

"Mush! Urrgh!" The others groaned, staring at the clumps.

"Sing!" They glared at me.

Helmer had told the truth.

I rocked back and forth on the giant boulder—heel, toe, heel, toe—and although I tried to think of a song, any song, my brain was void of the words to every tune I'd ever heard.

"Sing!"

Neither my voice nor my cooking would win their hearts. I needed my viola, and I'd left it on the table at Crauley's.

"Sing!" The last of the giant men shifted his shoulders through the doorway, which were far too wide for him to get in otherwise. I knew his name was Gid. His disheveled dark hair hung in his eyes, and his stature made Herbert look like a scrawny school boy.

"Sing!" Gid's gravelly voice bellowed.

The only lyrics that came to mind were from *The Ballad of Blue Sky*—our country's national anthem. Were we even in my father's kingdom? I didn't know.

"When skies are blue, when skies are gray . . ." My pitch was off. The ballad that I'd probably learned in my mother's womb might send me to an early grave.

Only Helmer placed a hand over his heart. His other hand was supposed to be there, too, but he used it to cover his eyes. No one else appeared to recognize the tune enough to stand, place both hands over their hearts and sing their allegiance. Wherever Blaird's Giant Farm was, we were not in Blue Sky Kingdom.

"I shall defend thee with my heart. I shall serve thee with my life." To see if anyone was listening, I was tempted to sing my own rendition: *I will become Prince Vincent's wife.* I paused for a moment, and closed my eyes, trying to remember the correct lyrics.

"What 'appened to me mush?" Gid bellowed. Now was not the time to correct his English.

"I . . ." I stared at the giants. "I made a mistake."

"Me mush looks like rocks in me bowl."

Maid Kimberlee's murmurings, so sweet and kind, teased me at this inopportune time: *We are never to grumble or complain about anything. To whine is to complain to God.* I chose not to repeat her counsel at this moment; as I had so often done with her wisdom, I simply tucked it away in the corner of my soul for a later time.

Gid slammed a fist on the table. "Sing!" the giant bellowed.

I'd brought this upon myself. Running away. Disobeying. Justifying.

"When skies are blue, when skies are gray, I will defend my beloved Blue Sky." Both my voice and my legs were wobbly.

Chin lifted and eyes narrowed, Gid turned an ear toward the stage. He set his meaty hands on top of the table and rose to his feet.

The others followed his lead, pushing back the benches to stand hands over their hearts. Swaying back and forth in the cavernous room, their tone-deaf voices sang, "I shall defend thee with my 'eart. I shall serve thee with my life." Had I not been weaned on the lyrics, I never would have understood their partial pronunciation.

We were indeed in my beloved Blue Sky.

Please don't leave me, Lord. I don't want to through another dark tunnel alone.

"That was the worst singing I 'ave ever 'eard and the worst me mush 'as ever tasted," Gid bellowed and downed a glass of milk. "Dinner better be better or…"

Cook's Cemetery came to mind and my five-word epithet:
Ennie. Fired after two meals.

ΦΦΦ

As the giants returned to their labor, Remford stood near and repeated his earlier mantra, "You are too dumb; you cannot flee—"

"Helmer . . ." I chased after him as he lumbered toward the door. "What do I make for dinner?"

"There are recipes in the drawer. Make me mum's Gruel Cakes. It's been a long time since we've had Gruel Cakes."

I'd never heard of them.

"What else do I make?"

"Always begin your meals with meat. Use the salt beef in the pantry."

Back home, the first course was often soup or a fancy appetizer, but here in Gruel Kitchen, dinner began with meat.

"Is it already cooked?" I asked.

"Yes."

I'd begin the meal with the salt beef and end with the Gruel Cakes. What would I serve in between?

"When you sing, we want to hear of home, not of war," Helmer said as if he were certain of ten giants' hearts.

The Ballad of Blue Sky was of home. Perhaps Helmer was a romanticist. Could I trust his opinion? War was the only thing my father talked about, breathed—his passion. So unlike Crauley, whose passion had been music and me.

I swallowed.

The door closed behind Helmer.

Remford dropped the wooden slat into place with a thud. I turned to face the mess—the kettles in the sink, the messy tables—and sighed. Apparently, I was not only the cook but the dishwasher as well.

I rustled through recipes in the top kitchen drawer. Grease and coffee dribbles stained the yellowed pages. In the middle of the pile, I found Beulah's Gruel Cakes.

I rounded up all of the ingredients, except for the baking powder from the pantry. One jar was labeled "Ovich's powder" and its contents were white. Was Ovich a brand of baking powder? I'd ask Helmer. I carried the jar to the counter and set it among the other ingredients.

While I cleaned the dining area, I watched the window for Helmer. Giants lumbered past carrying wood, but there was no sign of the squatty giant. I couldn't wait any longer for his answer, so I added what I prayed was baking powder to the mixture. Sadly, I lost count of how many tablespoons I'd measured, so I added a few more. I mixed the batter thoroughly and slid the pans inside the hot oven.

When the evening sky faded to dusk, the pewter plates on the tables bounced as horsemen with whips escorted the giants' return. The gruel cakes were in the oven and just beginning to turn a golden brown. They would still be warm when it came time for dessert.

While the dirty hulks seated themselves, I suppressed a nervous sigh and hurried about the room, sliding a plate with a mound of salt beef in front of each of them. I would try and learn at least two more of the giant's names. Anky had a speech impediment and a limp; and Rhino had smooth, dark gray hair. If I could remember their names, perhaps I'd be less apt to end up in Cook's Cemetery. I slid a plate in front of a giant who had the neck of an ostrich and peach fuzz on top for hair.

"This is the most boringest meal EVER," he groaned, looking down at the mound of beef. His breath smelled like garlic and dirt. Even Daisy's smelled better.

"Ovich, stop your complaining," Helmer's voice carried from the other table.

Heat crawled up my neck. *Ovich's powder*.

"'Elmer, I say when 'ee can stop," Gid thundered.

"Here you go, Helmer." I slid the mound of beef in front of him.

"Where's the vege?" His round eyes widened.

"You said to begin with the meat." I stared at him.

"I did not." He glared back. "I, I... I meant... you plan the meal around the meat." He rolled his beefy-sized wrist. "You plan what else you're going to fix around the meat."

I stared at the salt beef alone on the pewter plate. The gelatinous mound reminded me of what Cook served in a terrine back home. Except he added a few more ingredients to it: onion, vegetables...

"Where's the vege?" Helmer asked. Like the other giants, his pores were unusually large. They needed a good exfoliant, maybe a honey mask.

"The carrots are boiling." I glanced toward the large pot on the stove.

"Test them. Drain them. Add butter, salt and pepper. What else did you make?"

"The gruel cakes for dessert."

"Gruel cakes are side rolls, not dessert!" He rocked his head forward to cover his eyes with one hand.

"They are still in the oven." Things were not looking good for me.

"Grab a big bowl and follow me."

He was trying to save my life. I grabbed a large earthenware bowl and hurried after him.

He knelt to the slab floor and removed the lids from three, enormous crocks. The brines were bubbly and fermented like a pond in late summer. Using his bare hands, he plundered his way into the swamp-filled crocks and plunked fistfuls of pickled green beans and sauerkraut inside the bowl. His concoction was only going to add to the torture of my death.

I needed a Goliath-sized miracle

"How long have you lived here, Helmer?"

"Eight summers. We were on our way home from the Twelve Year War when Blaird and his men captured us."

"Eight years," I murmured.

"Ennn-nnie!" The jars' metal lids clamored together in the pantry as Gid's voice thundered. "This can't be all!"

My existence might very well end before the second course.

"After you serve, get on stage and sing. I'll take care of the rest," Helmer said.

"Thank you."

I spooned the second course—Swamp Salad—onto the giants' plates. They didn't appear to mind the odd mixture.

"Finally, something besides meat," said Ovich, the complainer.

While the giants ate, they belched and set their elbows on the tables. Their manners were even worse than Hughie's. I climbed the steps of the Grand Boulder. *Lord, let me live at least until dessert.* My hope rested heavily on Beulah's Gruel Cakes.

"Home," Helmer bellowed behind me.

"Home . . ." I held the note like an empty-pocketed and very poor opera singer. For twenty years, the giants had been away from their home and their families. That could make anyone cranky. "Home…"

Wearing his mother's apron tied about his middle, Helmer delivered the cakes and condiments of butter and honey. I'd made ten cakes, one for each giant. The beautiful golden brown cakes, not my singing would help me win the giants' hearts.

"Sing!" Gid bellowed.

He must not like my one-word song. "Home . . ." I held the note and closing my eyes, pictured Alia. "You were my dearest friend." The room quieted to hear my five-word song. Perhaps my voice was not that bad. "My only confidante." No, my ears told me the truth: my cracking voice was terrible. I dare not look at their faces. From Alia, I remembered sweet Pearl yelling from the upstairs of the farmhouse. *No, I'm not.*

Take your hands off me! As it often did, my memory got in the way of my music.

"That was the worst dinner and the worst singing I 'ave ever 'eard," Gid bellowed.

Ovich, who looked like an ostrich, carried a cello by its neck and climbed the steps to join me on the stage. Instead of resting the base of the cello on the ground like a normal cellist, he lifted it like a viola and tucked the giant instrument under the left side of his chin. Then he drew the bow for one very long screechy note.

Helmer, tired of trying to save me, returned to his seat; and covered his eyes with one hand.

In spite of my gruel cakes, Ovich's music sounded like a funeral march. I'd lasted only two meals in Gruel Kitchen. Was it a new record?

"That was the worst song I 'ave ever 'eard," Gid bellowed. "And what did you do to me cake?" He smacked the golden brown delicacy against the side of the table. It didn't crumble. Instead, it sounded like a rock.

"Ennie, you didn't use the jar that's on the counter, did you?" Helmer pointed to the jar labeled *Ovich's powder*.

I bit my lip and nodded.

Would he put a flower on my grave when he visited his Mother's?

"Don't eat the cakes! She used Ovich's tooth cement!" Helmer yelled.

Ovich drew the bow across the strings for another dreary, screechy note, and ten giant pairs of eyeballs stared at me with somber clarity—like a jury who'd reached their final decision.

In the face of battle, my father was brilliant. I had to think like him.

I scanned the battlefield: I was locked in a rock room with ten, unhappy giants. The only giant who remotely liked me was Helmer, and he now covered his eyes with both hands.

There was no outlet. Otherwise, I would've run.

"Father in Heaven," I mumbled beneath my breath. "Save me somehow. I'll be a good girl. I'll go home. I'll apologize. I'll do anything You say. Just let me live."

In the face of my giant battle, I wanted to live.

Chapter Thirteen

War wasn't only survival of the fittest, but also, of the brightest.

I needed to get the cello away from Ovich. A cello was basically a giant viola with a deeper pitch. My gift might not be singing, but I could fiddle among the best.

"May I?" I asked Ovich, glancing to the cello.

"No!" Curbing his left shoulder to me, he played a series of dreary notes that I'd heard once before when everyone had been dressed in black.

"Please, I, um . . ." I faltered for words.

"Sing!" Gid thundered. Swinging both of his arms off to one side, he flung the disc of gruel cake toward me. I barely ducked in time as it whizzed over my head. My gruel cakes might very well prove my demise.

I ducked again as another disc spun in the air like an out-of-control comet. Instead of me, it struck Ovich in the temple. Staggering back a step, he dropped the bow before tumbling off the stage. I was near enough to grab the neck of the cello before its base hit the floor. Amidst the flying rounds of cakes, I retrieved the bow.

I had never played the cello before. Held upright beside me, the large instrument was at least a foot taller than me. With my left hand on the fingerboard, I ducked as another gruel cake whizzed past. Then, I nestled the bow against the strings and prayed the cello would deem me a dear friend, instead of the stranger that I was.

For one, long beautiful note it did just that.

My third draw of the bow stilled the anarchy in the cavernous room.

I stuck with *The Ballad of Blue Sky*. I would let the giants sort through their own memories.

After I completed the fourth verse of the poignant tune, I lowered the bow to my side.

"Play." Murmurs echoed in the stone room. Perhaps they were like Crauley. Perhaps, in its own way, music was more important to the giants than words.

ΦΦΦ

After my long day in Gruel Kitchen, I thought I'd sleep like a baby. Instead, I lay awake listening to the giants. Their wispy little snores sounded like they were trying to keep a feather afloat in the air above them. Even Maid Kimberlee snored louder. Although I tried to picture black, my mind was awake with convictions: I had to learn the giants' names. I had to learn to run a kitchen. I had to learn to cook.

Not all of the giants were asleep. I heard sniffles about the room. Anky, whose bunk was below my own, mumbled, "Me, mie, mo, mum. Me, mie, mo, mum." I didn't understand his gibberish, but I heard one word distinctly. "Mum."

I could not think of my mother right now, or I would be like Anky and need a giant-sized hanky.

I swallowed my tears instead.

ΦΦΦ

As a child, I'd been fascinated by what appeared to be synchronized activity in the kitchen, but Mother had always made sure that our visits were brief. *We are to serve our people, but not in that way,* she often said. *We are royalty. We are looked up to. We are not to take our God given position lightly.*

What Mother had truly meant was: everything I would learn was merely for other's entertainment—not my own self-preservation. Someone else buttoned my dress, brushed my hair, boiled water for my tea… I was taught French in an English-speaking country, the waltz and the complicated krassant, yet I could not dance at a ball until I turned sixteen. My upbringing made me dependent on the people who were my subjects; and now that my life depended on preparing simple meals, I lacked the training. My education was a paradox for which I was not grateful.

Yet… lucky for me, Helmer befriended me and taught me everything he knew.

"How many of the cooks are buried in Cook's Cemetery?" I asked, flipping the bacon.

"Only my mother." His dark brows gathered.

I didn't understand. "Then why is it called Cook's Cemetery?"

"After the Cooke's—Blaird Cooke," he said, matter of fact. "Three generations of the Cooke family have been buried there."

"Oh, but . . . where are the other cooks buried?" I had to know.

"What other cooks?" His thick brows furrowed.

"Every week, Blaird buys a new cook at auction." I repeated what I'd overheard in Stockford.

"They don't all die. They're fired and become housekeepers, wash women or…."

"Oh . . ." I sighed, relieved. I hoped I wasn't fired. I'd much rather cook than clean all day.

"Today is Friday. We don't like Fridays."

"Why is that?"

"Blaird makes the giants race."

"Oh." Maybe he didn't like losing.

"Whoever loses is whipped."

"Is it Anky?" I tried to prepare myself. If it was a running race, his limp would prove a huge setback.

"No, you'll see."

From the somber note in Helmer's voice, I didn't think I wanted to watch.

After supper, Blaird and his men entered the arena and sat on the top seats on the other side of the stadium. Guards stood on every post; even Remford had left his usual station.

I sat on the counter beneath the window.

All of the giants were gathered in the center of the arena. It was an odd sight. Ten strong giants, fit and muscular, ruled by skinny men with whips, a few rifles, and Remford. I already knew this about the giants: they weren't planners. They couldn't think past the next meal. Helmer said planning hurt his brain, *made it feel all knotted up, like when he did basic arithmetic.*

The clap of two boards together marked the start of the race. Two horsemen accompanied the giants as Helmer led the way out of the stadium. Swift of foot, he drove his knees high and raced off to my left toward the woods at the bottom of the gully. He was so far ahead of everyone that I felt certain he would not be the loser. Sadly, I watched Anky limp and run, limp and run. He was as far behind the giants as Helmer was ahead of them.

Ten minutes passed before I realized that it wasn't only a running race. Near the grove of trees, Helmer rolled a huge cylinder-shaped bale of hay that was as tall as he was. But his progress slowed. He took far too long on the hill. It was as if he'd stopped and had a four-course dinner. Everyone passed him. Even Anky.

"What are you doing, Helmer?" I shook my fists. But, I was afraid I knew. He was losing on purpose.

I could no longer watch. I knelt down in front of the counter and prayed that God would see what was going on and send help.

I waited in anguish. Then covered my ears to the crack of the whip and Helmer's cries.

ΦΦΦ

That night when I cleaned the stripes on Helmer's back, I wept. Blaird's cruel show of entertainment had gone on every Friday for the last eight years. The giants took turns losing so that their wounds could heal, and they made sure that Anky never lost.

That night at the cello, they expected me to play happy music of home. My heart was filled with vengeance, and in my grieving, I stilled the bow.

"I am going to get you out of here," I told the giants. Perhaps it had been the regal note in my voice, but the room stilled to a deadly silence.

Years spent eavesdropping on my father, and I'd made this basic mistake: *Never let your soldiers know your plans until it is time to enforce them.*

The giants stared at me.

"How?" Gid asked.

"We've tried before, and everyone gets whipped. Even Anky," Helmer said.

My gaze drifted to the kitchen. One butcher knife and a paring knife would not win this war.

"I don't know." But I knew this: Blaird's cruelty ravaged my soul.

The next morning while I stood at the sink, the giants passed Remford on their way out the door.

"Ennie is going to get us out of here," Ovich said.

I closed my eyes and felt around in the sudsy water for the paring knife. *Lord, please help me. Please help me.*

"How?" Remford bellowed.

Helmer grimaced as he and the other giants walked past my window.

The fact that they couldn't keep a secret was a hard lesson for me.

There was no thud of the bolt dropping into place. Remford stood in the doorway instead.

"How?" His mouth bunched as he shook his head.

"How what?" I swallowed, pretending I hadn't heard.

"You going to get the giants out of 'ere?" he bellowed.

"I don't know." My hand finally found the knife's wooden handle. "I'll let you know when I do."

He slammed the door shut, and the bolt dropped into place.

I slumped over the sink and with short, shallow breaths, tried to collect myself.

ΦΦΦ

A month slowly passed. Now that I'd cooked over eighty-four meals in Gruel Kitchen, Helmer no longer needed to help me decipher his mother's handwriting, or explain what a term meant or that a *giant* pinch of salt really amounted to a full teaspoon. I was now deemed the boss of Gruel Kitchen; with that title came the privilege of making rules.

I made the giants wash their hands and faces before they sat down at the table. Rhino would bless the food, and belching was no longer allowed in a woman's presence. With a somewhat dull pair of scissors, I cut their hair, so it didn't hang in their eyes when they ate—or in their food for that matter. As a sailor might say, I ran a tight ship.

Now that I was no longer studying recipes each night, and learning to cook for pure survival, my mind turned to other things, and how we might escape.

I feared that like the giants, I might very well watch the years fly by and no longer know or care what day it was. So, I drew a calendar on the blank side of Beulah's least favorite recipes. I hung it on a nail next to the only picture in the room, a cross-stitch of a thatched roofed cottage bearing three words: Home Sweet Home. Beulah had probably stitched it here in Gruel Kitchen.

When we were settled in our bunks that night, I cleared my throat. "Today is Saturday, August 5th, 1876," I said to the darkness. Trying to rise above my circumstances, I pictured my future. In less than two months, I would marry Prince Vincent and be in line to be the Queen of Davenport—the wealthiest, most affluent country in Northend. Compared to my present existence, my future sounded like a fairy tale.

"I don't care what day it is!" Ovich moaned.

For once, I understood his complaining. They'd worked hard seven days a week, for the last eight years. When they'd left for war, Ovich and seven of the others had left brides behind. Anky and Helmer had only been twelve at the time. Not even teenagers.

"Do you think your wives will search for you?" I asked.

"No, I told the women not to leave Shepherd's Field," Gid said. "They are to wait for us there."

"Do you think Myrtle is still waiting for me?" Ovich's voice cracked.

"Yes," Gid said.

"Of course, she is, Ovich," Helmer said into the darkness.

I stared overhead at the rock ceiling. Despite their loss, the days still mattered to me. In less than three weeks, I'd turn sixteen. I wanted to know when August twenty-third arrived. I'd make myself a cake; and, in keeping with my country's coming-of-age tradition, I would choose the recipient of my first kiss.

Heaven forbid that I should still be here. I did not want to kiss any of the giants!

Father in Heaven, we need to get out of here. Help me to come up with a plan.

That night I dreamed of gruel cakes whizzing through the air and Ovich falling off of the stage. I sat bolt up in bed and knew it was the start of my plan.

ΦΦΦ

The next day, Helmer carried in a large crate. "Blaird got these from a man in Stockford. He said that turnips are good for giants—help us to stay strong and healthy." He set the long wooden box of what must be turnips on the table. They were round and white with purple tops and long green stalks still attached. I'd never knowingly eaten a turnip before.

"Sounds like he sold Blaird a load of hoopla," I said.

"No, they are turnips." Helmer was obviously not familiar with the term. "Chop them about this big," he held his fingers a half-inch apart, "and roast them in the oven for a half hour."

After I put away the dry goods, I carried the round root vegetables to the sink. I would bake five per giant. Below the second layer of turnips, I glimpsed what looked like black leather similar to a... I dared not finish my thought as I pulled a viola case out of the box.

My heart pounded in my ears while I unclasped the locks. My viola and bow lay nestled inside on the green velvet. I hugged the precious instrument against me, and sank to the floor, sobbing.

Gruel Kitchen was not forever. Someone knew I was here.

It was just a matter of time before Father, and his cavalry arrived. I heaved a heavy sigh and rose to my feet. A folded piece of paper lay where the back of the viola had settled in the velvet.

I unfolded what was indeed a message. The choppy print read: *I tried to get word to your father, but the raven returned to Stockford injured. I have tried twice, but Blaird will not hire me. Fear not, we have God on our side. Burn this. A-F-K.*

A-F-K. What did it stand for? What did it mean?

"All for King," I whispered Brody Hew's favorite sentiments.

I had to read the note three times before I fully gleaned what he had written. He was in Stockford, perhaps alone. Father didn't know. But, surely Brody would get word to him, somehow. It was just a matter of time.

I popped the paper into the hot oven and watched it burn to ash.

All for King.

Brody Hew was more faithful to my father than I had ever been.

ΦΦΦ

The following Tuesday, after breakfast dishes, I returned to my other chores and lifted the heavy wooden bolt of the pig pen door. As was routine, several of the pigs followed me to the trough where I emptied the bucket of scraps. At the far end of the room, sunlight streamed through the open paddock doorway, and Helmer lifted a large pig over his shoulders. As he turned, I caught a glimpse of Daisy's straw hat.

"Where are you going with her?" My heart knotted in my chest.

"To slaughter."

"No! You can't!"

He pulled the door closed and dropped the bolt into place behind him. Gone was the large swath of sunlight.

"Helmer, no!" Hurrying along the edge of the pig berries, I closed the pig pen door behind me and raced to the kitchen window in time to see him amble past with Daisy over his shoulders.

"Not that one, Helmer! Not her." I scrambled up on the sink and gripped the bars.

He swiveled around to glare at me.

"Not Daisy. Not her."

"You're not supposed to name the pigs. Mum said never to name the animals that go upon our table." He turned and strode away.

"Helmer!" I cried. "You're my favorite." I could think of no other bargaining chip.

He turned to smirk at me this time.

"You're my favorite giant, and Daisy is my favorite pig." I gripped the bars, pleading. "Please, I'll help you catch another."

One of Blaird's new guards walked around the corner of the building and into view. With his auburn hair longer than I remembered, and dressed in gray, not blue and white, I recognized him all the same. Even though I was dressed in an old rag of a dress and hadn't had a bath since I'd left home, I stared at Brody Hew like a moonstruck school girl.

"Hello," I breathed.

He merely nodded in passing. Had he sent word to Father? Did anyone else know that he was here? Where was his white horse? I scanned the open farmland and the gully as far as I could see from my limited viewpoint. There were no signs of Dilly, which meant that—like our usual recruits—he'd arrived in Blaird's wagon.

Over his shoulder, Brody glanced back at me. From his somber gaze, I knew he was here to protect me. Should I ever call out, he would risk his life for mine. He would die in my place.

ΦΦΦ

That afternoon while I peeled turnips, I watched through the window for Brody but saw no sign of him. I returned to the stove and shed some tears for Daisy while I basted the pork ribs with clover honey. I paused with my basting spoon mid-stroke and pictured her frolicking in the flower beds of Heaven.

Something bounced across the stone floor, almost hitting me in the leg. It was a twine-wrapped rock, the size of a piano key, with a note tucked inside.

I ran to the window. Guards were stationed at their usual posts, overlooking the nearby stadium and the farm beyond. Someone must have tossed it in passing.

Helmer wheeled a load of potatoes beneath the window. "Make mashed turnips. They're always good with pork."

I scowled at him.

"I put your pig back." He grinned. "I wanted to stay your favorite giant."

"Helmer!" I almost choked with joy.

"Don't name any of the others. We like pork."

"I won't," I promised, smiling.

"The ribs smell good." He strolled away, humming *The Ballad of Blue Sky*.

I turned my back to the window. Untying the twine from around the rock, I felt certain that Brody was the sender. The note was the same off-white paper as the one he'd left in my viola case. It read: There's a note for you in the corner of the sill. Look there from now on. Leave one for me under this rock. Burn this. A-F-K.

I held Brody's second note to the flame on the stove and then went to search the sill area. A small, folded piece of paper lay on my side of the window. Because of the bars, he'd simply reached in to deliver it.

Although no one was in the kitchen, I closed the pantry door behind me before unfolding the note. It read: We are not alone. We have God on our side. A-F-K.

What? He'd already said that! Didn't he have a plan for our escape, everything figured out to a T? His note was more dismal than I'd expected; it was simply a reminder to pray.

I stared at the stone floor.

I'd write him a nasty letter and vent.

I found Beulah's old quill pen and a bottle of ink and returned to the pantry. On the back of his note, I wrote: *Thank you for your reminder to pray.* He'd risked his life to be here; I should at least be amicable. *We are in this together.* I penned Pearl's sentiments. Even though I wanted to tell him off for not having a plan, I chose to be diplomatic. *Thank you, you have exceeded all expectation of service. I hope you do not regret your decision in coming here. Burn this.* I set my note under the rock in the left corner of the outer window sill and prayed that Brody would be the one to find it.

ΦΦΦ

After the giants left for work the following morning, I stole away to the windowsill, moved the rock and found a slip of paper. On the counter lay a buttercup—a little yellow flower that was really more of a weed. Had Brody left it when he'd delivered the note?

I again closed the pantry door behind me before I unfolded it. His print was much smaller than his prior messages; but to my delight, he'd written more.

No, I do not regret my decision. I must say, your music is as dreary as ever, but I understand why. Y-H-S.

I knew only too well what those initials meant. *Your humble servant.* I was glad that he did not end this note with *burn this*, for I wanted to keep this one. It was my favorite so far of the three he'd given me.

I tucked the note deep behind the velvet in my viola case for safekeeping.

Throughout the morning, I laughed about his comment *your music is as dreary as ever,* and I found myself glad that he was close enough to hear me play.

After I served lunch and the giants returned to work, I stole away to the pantry to write Brody his second note. Already, paper was becoming an issue. Below one of Beulah's recipes, I snipped off the lower inch of blank page.

Thank you for my viola. In case you don't already know, I'm glad that you're here. The paper looked too empty. **Fridays are hard for the giants.** I penned, wanting Brody to be aware of the difficult day ahead of us.

Chapter Fourteen

I spent the afternoon baking gruel cakes, but this time, I'd purposefully used Ovich's tooth cement instead of baking powder. I hid the cakes in my bed lest the giants find them. To appease their strong sense of smell, I baked gruel cakes for dinner, this time with real baking powder.

"Fee, fie, foe, fum, I smell the cakes of an English woman," Gid and Ovich bellowed as they entered at dinnertime.

I was glad I'd gone to the extra effort. Alongside sliced ham and steamed carrots, I served the cakes with honey butter.

Before the war, Gid had been an elite discus thrower and boasted about it to no end. Though we needed the stadium to practice in, I had to be content with the cavernous room.

"Gid," I said, carrying a roasting pan full of gruel cakes up the rock steps of the stage. "I have a game I would like to play tonight, if it's all right with you."

"What? No music?" he groaned.

"Please, just tonight. Can you show everyone how to throw a discus?" I knew there was a specific technique to the way it spiraled out of the hand.

"What game?" He stuffed a piece of ham into his mouth.

"Whoever gets closest to the target with the gruel cakes, wins." I pointed to the round silver pan that I'd hung on a nail high on the far wall. Before I planned our escape any further, I wanted to be certain the discs could fly with precision.

"Wins what?" Gid asked.

"A giant cookie." Fortunately, there was still one left from yesterday's baking.

Gid pursed his thick lips, thoughtfully. "Ovich, go first," he said.

Skinny-armed Ovich was the most uncoordinated of the giants. Why had Gid chosen him?

Ovich joined me on stage.

"How should he hold it?" I asked, wishing Gid had been the one to demonstrate.

"'Old it at the bend in the fingers." Gid curled his fingers above the table like he was studying his fingernails. "And release it off of this one." He bobbed the pointer finger of his right hand.

"Try and hit the tin." I handed Ovich the gruel cake and pointed to the round silver pan on the far wall.

Standing stiff-legged, Ovich swung his arm back and forth, and then with a wild early release, flung the gruel cake toward Gid's table.

"Are you trying to kill me?" Palms, up, Gid waved his arms.

Without being prodded, Helmer climbed the steps. Gruel cake in hand, he pumped his arm several times behind his back, transferring his weight to his front foot, he released the disc. The cake struck the far wall, several feet to the right of the pie tin.

I inhaled deeply, suppressing elation. The cakes might indeed prove to be effective weapons.

With each participant that took the stage, the banter in the room increased. And, as I'd foreseen, Ovich's attempt had been the worst. Anky's aim was surprisingly close—a foot beneath the tin. Finally, Gid took the stage.

The cake appeared small in his massive grip. He bent his sturdy legs, eyed the tin a few times over his shoulder, rocked back, and uncoiled with a swish of his hips. The disc whizzed through the room, denting the tin and knocking it to the floor.

"I won." Gid puffed out his chest and strutted down the steps. "Where's my cookie?"

My plan for escape had officially begun.

ΦΦΦ

I began to watch through the barred window of the kitchen, taking notes of the guards, their habits, their routines, who carried a whip and who carried a gun. I needed to know the strengths and weaknesses of Blaird's men and the strengths and weaknesses of mine.

I pieced together this much of our plan: our escape would take place on a Friday when Blaird and his men were in the arena; the gruel cakes would be our weapons, and the giants would have to hide them until the time was right.

How to hide the gruel cakes was the piece of the puzzle, I couldn't figure out.

I'd awaken in the middle of the night hearing my father's voice, snippets from my childhood. *Attack in the evening. Attack with swiftness.* I'd sit up trying to repeat what I'd remembered so I wouldn't forget come morning. Never let your soldiers know your plans *or they will tell someone else.* I'd already learned that one the hard way.

One night, I awoke to Pearl's voice saying: *We don't want to make an ugly pocket on the outside for everyone to see. It should be one that doesn't show—a hidden pocket.*

I bolted straight up in bed. That was it!

I needed to sew a pocket in each of the giant's shirts for their gruel cakes. The pockets were the missing link.

By candlelight, I spent several nights sewing two gruel cake-sized pockets near the inside hem of each of the giants' shirts. Hidden pockets. They were so hidden that the giants wouldn't even notice they were there. In Gid's shirt, I sewed four pockets. He was the best aim, by far.

In my notes to Brody, all I dared to tell him was *Next Friday, be ready.*

Chapter Fifteen

One by one, I planned to take the giants into the pantry, Gid being the first.

I stared into the giant's dark eyes. He was no more endearing than my first impression of him.

"Why can't I eat me supper?" he groaned.

"I've made a plan, to take down Blaird's men. Today is the day." I had to get straight to the point as we didn't have much time.

"What?" His nostrils flared.

"I've made a plan."

"Why now?"

"Because they'll all be in the stadium. If you strike before the race, when you are all together, you'll have more energy." He stared at me. "I've made gruel cakes into hard discuses for you to hide in your pocket and use as a weapon."

"I don't have a pocket."

"You do. I've sewn four pockets in the bottom of your shirt. Everyone else has two."

Gid fumbled with the bottom of his shirt and his eyes widened and then narrowed.

"Go on."

"Each of the giants will have a guard they are to take down." I inhaled deeply and forced myself to continue. "You are to target Blaird and his two men."

He nodded. "Only I can throw that far."

I'd taken that into account in my planning. "Anky will take out Remford," I said, adding a prayer.

Gid nodded.

I called in Helmer next.

Gid would not leave the pantry. It was so crowded that we could barely shut the door.

I told Helmer my plans and then added, "You are the fastest. Run like you do every Friday. After you round the bend, hide in the trees. With your disk, you are to take out the lead horsemen. Then head back through the woods, and release the rest of their horses. This way Blaird's men cannot follow us."

Gid appeared confused, so I repeated my earlier instructions to him. "At first, all of you must run out of the stadium like every Friday. You must do this, so Blaird and his men will turn their backs to the arena to watch the race. You and the other giants will return and take out as many men as possible at one time with the discs. I will tell each giant who they are to target." Then I reminded myself to tell them about Brody near the end when we were all together.

"I run to the bend, and then I go through the woods and release the horses?" Helmer asked.

"Yes. And, after you release the horses, you're to open the door for me."

"We can't remember this much." Gid clamped his hands on his head.

"Helmer, send Ovich in. I have to tell everyone before lunch is over," I said. Maybe if I repeated it ten times in front of Gid, he would remember.

"What did boss say before battle?" he asked Helmer.

"'To follow orders; and to never talk about *home* because he needed men, not babies.'"

It sounded like something my own father would say.

"Do not talk of home," Helmer repeated to me. "Before battle, King Francis said never talk about home."

All of these weeks together and we could have been sharing war stories. "What else would King Wells say?" I asked. Never had I needed my earthly father as much as I did right now.

"Courage, men." Helmer breathed a smile. "He always called us men."

ΦΦΦ

There was mumbling amongst the giants. Ovich and Gid were unsettled.

"Stop it! We're going to do this for Ennie," Helmer said.

They didn't believe in my plan. It wasn't a good start.

One by one, I handed the giants the gruel cake discuses and remembered to tell them, "No one is to hit the new guard. He is on our side."

This irritated Gid further. "You only think."

"You have to trust me. He is." I held my ground.

We knelt in a large huddle and I said the prayer. "Dear Heavenly Father, help these men to defeat Blaird's. Guide them, give them wisdom and protection. Give these men courage and help us to win. Amen."

Then trying not to draw Remford's attention in any way, I simply washed dishes and prayed while my giants exited Gruel Kitchen.

Not one looked back, for which I was glad. I might have cried, otherwise.

Anky was his usual self, mumbling gibberish; but this time, the other giants were good about sandwiching him between them as they stepped past the giant guard.

"You are too dumb," Remford said.

"Me, mi, mo, mum." I heard it distinctly. Anky was already thinking about his mum.

"You cannot flee. Your work is Blaird's for eternity." Remford dropped the bolt into place and followed my giants to the stadium.

There was so much that could go wrong; yet, I could not let fear strike me. For my giants' sake, I also had to have courage.

Chapter Sixteen

Through the barred windows of Gruel Kitchen, I watched my plan unfold.

Swift of foot, Helmer ran ahead.

One guard on horseback followed him.

The rest of the giants ran out of the stadium together. They paused in a semi-circle and took the gruel cakes out of their pockets.

Gid mumbled their orders and then they ran back inside the arena, many out of my vision.

Discs took flight.

Boom. Ba ba boom. My heart pounded against the walls of my chest as I gripped the bars.

Blaird and another one of his men fell.

Even Remford tumbled from the nearby post as Anky's aim hit its mark.

Too nervous to watch further, I knelt below the window, clenching my hands together tightly. "Father, God, please watch over them. Help them to work in unison."

Outside, the yelling and the murderous sounds of war raged on while I petitioned Heaven in prayer.

The fighting continued for what felt like hours. Horses ran free, and the ground shook as giants, held captive for years, sprinted east toward freedom. In the settling dust that followed, I sensed the abysmal silence of victory. I was afraid to look, but I had to know.

Through the bars, the bodies of Blaird and his men littered the ground.

To my grief, Brody Hew lay crumpled beside his post.

ΦΦΦ

The Hews were Father's favorites. Edwin's baby brother had been more loyal to Blue Sky than I'd been able to be. Brody was dead. I grieved for the young man and his little slips of paper. If I had not run away, he'd still be alive. I could never go home. I could never face Father. Not now.

To make matters worse, Helmer had not unlocked the door to Gruel Kitchen. I tried the heavy door a second time, shaking it. The bolt was as firm as ever. Was he hurt or…? No, I couldn't let my mind go there. In the thrill and adrenaline of freedom, he had simply forgotten me.

Below the window, I clasped my trembling hands. On my knees, I prayed and prayed. "Father, God, watch over my giants and me. Send someone back for me."

While I prayed, the earth shook. At least one giant had survived and approached with thundering footsteps. I stifled my exuberance.

"En-nnnie! You are to blame!" A voice which sounded more like Remford's than Helmer's bellowed through the bars. "En-nnnnnie!"

If I had not been kneeling, he would have seen me.

My biggest nightmare was not over.

There was only one place for me to hide. Hurrying, I pulled the door to the pig pen closed behind me and stepped shin-deep into the pig berries. Six pigs fattened for slaughter roamed the dimly lit pen.

I moved to a dry, patch of darkness in the far left corner of the room. The light from the tiny upper windows did not reach this area. There I huddled into a tight bundle, wrapping my arms around my legs.

I heard the muffled sounds of Remford in the kitchen, yelling and slamming things about.

The pig pen door flung open.

"En-nnnie! En-nnnnnie!" His voice echoed in the stone room.

He slammed the door closed, dropping the wooden latch on my casket.

I was afraid to move or breathe, lest he hear me, but my limbs betrayed me and shook violently.

Were any of Blaird's men, outside of Remford, alive? If they were, would they stay here or run?

Night fell, and so did the temperature. The pigs grunted and lay down for the night. A large one sniffed at my uncovered toes. I shifted my legs toward the wall behind me, in case the pig thought my toes were something to eat. The large creature bent at the knees and lay down beside me and heaved a muffled breath.

I patted at the animal; near its ears, I felt a crumpled hat.

Hugging Daisy's wide neck, I curved my body around her's and sniffled.

"You should never have gotten into Mother's garden, and I should never have run away. Brody Hew is dead, and I'm still here." I cried softly, pouring my heart out to the pig. In my brokenness, I could not let myself focus on one glaring truth: My giants had forgotten about me. Even Helmer, my favorite, had forgotten me.

ΦΦΦ

The crow of a rooster woke me, and I opened one eye. It was still dark out. The bird's timing was off. The pig stirred a bit and then we both drifted back to sleep.

The next time I awoke, the sky was an early morning gray. Someone unbolted the door to the kitchen. I dared not move an inch.

"Ennie, you're dead." Remford bellowed into the dark cell.

While my heart fluttered like a wild bird inside a cage, I made no sound. I barely breathed.

Daisy rose partially to her feet and then flopped down in front of me.

"Where are you?" Remford breathed.

The pig now blocked my view of him.

Father, God. I closed my eyes and felt my lids tremble. *You know. You know.*

The door slammed shut, and the bolt dropped into place with a thud.

Did Remford think I was still here because of my viola and bow? I'd left them on the table, hoping to grab them when I left.

He knew I was in Gruel Kitchen; he just didn't know where.

ΦΦΦ

I didn't know if it was due to lack of food or water, or both, but I found myself unstrung and continually weepy. In the giants' absence, the pigs were not being fed or watered. I would have eaten their food if there'd been any to fight them for.

For the second night in a row, Daisy lay curled up beside me and grunted softly in her sleep. The moon peeked through the upper windows, and I began to face the truth. This might very well be how my life would end: I'd be alone with my thoughts—the mistakes I'd made, the wrongs I would never be able to right, the goodbyes I would never be able to say—only I was to blame. Not my father this time.

The rooster crowed.

I opened my eyes to darkness. The impatient bird was again too early. I returned to sleep.

In the gray of morning, I tried to wet my mouth, but it was difficult.

On day three—or was it four? I'd already lost track—I tried the outer paddock door again. It was still securely locked. I crept along the wall toward the trough. The pigs roused themselves, following my lead. The half-inch of water in the trough was muddy and fermented looking; I couldn't bring myself to sample it.

Empty and exhausted, I returned to my corner and slept. I sailed in and out of various dreams, the last one being the most real. Even though I was full grown and too big to hold, Crauley was holding me in his arms. We were in his cabin and the light from the fire flickered in his gaze.

"Do you hear that bird, Wren?" His eyes sparkled as he listened above the crackle in the hearth. "Such a happy, little bird. Not plain at all. It's time, dear girl, for you to be happy. To fly."

With a gasp, I awoke.

I was still in the pigpen, not in Jesus' arms or Crauley's.

Was my body close enough to dying for my soul to fly to Heaven? Is that what Crauley had meant?

"I can't go home to Heaven before I've seen Alia," I whimpered. "I just can't."

I flitted in and out of dreams. This time, Maid Kimberlee sat by my bedside as I said my prayers. "Remember to listen for His voice." She patted my hand.

I woke myself up with a sad laugh. I'd been such a naughty girl. God wouldn't talk to me. I'd broken my family's heart. Now, I wouldn't even be able to tell them how sorry I was.

I sailed in and out of another dream. Amy, the old woman, held the lantern handle high as she peered into my face. "Repeat it again."

"To knock and keep on—" I woke myself up with my gibberish.

I stared into the darkness. If I announced myself, there was a chance Remford wouldn't kill me. But if he did kill me with one of his powerful blows, death would come quicker, and the pain of it all would soon be over. I may not have been thinking clearly, but I was still thinking.

The old lady's verse kept me awake. My pulse quickened and pounded in my chest. If I knocked on the door, I might very well awaken a sleeping giant.

Was there a chance that God would change Remford's heart? He'd changed Saul's, the man who'd once been a slayer of Christians, and renamed him Paul. I crouched in the sludge beside the door and rapped against the hard, coarse wood with one hand.

No one answered.

I continued knocking until my knuckles hurt. Then I knocked with the soft pad near my pinky finger.

Remford's laugh reached me. He was back. Or perhaps he'd never left. His deep belly laugh made the emptiness inside my stomach curl upon itself.

The sun's fingerlings of light slipped through the tiny windows. Daisy and I watched side-by-side what might very well be our last sunset, and then she lay down beside me near the door.

Over and over, I flung my hand against the hard wood *Knock and keep on knocking.*

Crashing sounds from inside the kitchen startled me awake. Remford cursed and bellowed. Listening soon took too much energy, so I just lay there, waiting.

ΦΦΦ

The rooster's crow woke me to the first rays of light. The bird was finally correct. The crashing sounds were still going on inside Gruel Kitchen, but not as loud as before, and Remford was no longer yelling.

I raised my arm away from the pig's side and flung it against the door. It didn't even make a thump. I flung my wrist again, and my knuckles tapped the solidness of the wood. Tired, I rested. A short time later, I summoned the energy to knock once more.

Remford lifted the heavy wooden bolt. He was finally checking on me.

Daisy and I lay beside the door and didn't move when it swung open.

Light streamed into the dark space.

The pig didn't move to cover me this time. We were both tired of this life.

"Wren . . ." A man too short to be Remford stood in the doorway. Silhouetted by the light behind him, I recognized Brody Hew.

He was alive, and he was my angel of mercy in my darkest hour of need.

"Here," was all I could rouse my voice to say.

Brody's gaze lowered to the pig and me and then he bent to one knee for a closer look. "Praise God," he whispered. "Praise God."

Chapter Seventeen

Although I was covered from head to toe in muck, Brody carried me over his shoulder through Gruel Kitchen. Remford's limbs were tied in four directions to bedposts and stove legs. He looked like a fly trapped in a giant spider web. Mouth gagged, he feebly flailed and twisted.

I merely blinked at the unfathomable sight.

Near the kitchen island, Brody bent to pick something up off the floor. Attached to the scroll piece of my viola was a smashed object of some kind. It took me several blinks to comprehend that it was my beloved viola.

A teetered gasp escaped me.

Brody swiped a blanket off of one of the beds, and then continued to the door. Daisy followed us halfway across the room before becoming sidetracked by spilled grain on the floor.

"Dais . . . Daisy," I managed. As we crossed the threshold outside, the gray light of morning stung my eyes.

With long and hurried strides, Brody carried me past the kitchen window. At the edge of the long building, he set me to my feet beside a dark horse. He stuffed my smashed viola in his saddle bag, along with my bow and case. Then he shook the blanket out, lowering it to the ground. He picked me up and laid me down in one corner of it like a muddy baby. With my arms at my sides, he quickly swaddled me, and I didn't have the sense to protest.

My viola was smashed, and the giants had forgotten me.

Brody lifted me up and set me sidesaddle. Just before he swung a leg behind me, I saw Daisy round the side of Gruel Kitchen, to stand in the open.

"Pig," I said, trying to moisten my mouth. "Pig… gy."

Brody prodded the horse to a gallop. I bounced against him, my chin pressing into his shoulder.

Daisy sat on her hind legs, watching us ride away. As the distance increased between my beloved companion and me, I began to weep.

Brody rode hard toward the west horizon, like a madman racing the sun's climb into the sky. If my hands had been free, I would have pounded them against his chest.

Many hours later when he finally stopped, we were in the middle of nowhere with only the moon. He dribbled water into my mouth and made me swish it around, and then continued riding. We rode through the morning to mid-day before he finally slowed the dark horse to a halt beneath the shade of an oak tree. Again, he dribbled water into my mouth from a flask and fed me crumbled crackers and snippets of jerky.

"My pig . . . we need to go back for my pig."

"We can't, Princess Wren." His dark brows gathered.

If my hands had been free, I would have hit him.

"You're to obey me. You must do what I say. Everything. Go back for my pig." I began to weep. "She is my most valued possession." Though he didn't say anything, I argued with him in such a manner for an indiscernible length of time.

He gathered the reins, continuing his race with the sun. "Go back for Daisy," I commanded. "I love her. She is my only… confidante."

The endless ride rocked me like a baby to sleep. I slept for hours with my cheek pressed against his solid chest. I nuzzled my nose unashamedly into his warm neck and heard myself make contented sounds like Daisy often made in her sleep.

Several hours later, I awoke from a veiled dream. I tried to lift my hand and knock, but I found I couldn't because my arms were pinned at my side.

"You're delirious," Brody whispered.

"I am not!" I rocked back my head. "I'm a terrible cook."

He made me swallow more water and take bites of crackers and jerky.

With one hand on the reins and one arm wrapped around me, Brody rode through another night. When darkness turned into day, he finally found shelter for us beneath a Camperdown elm—a tree that looked like a giant umbrella that touched the ground. We remained on horseback and slept, completely hidden by its foliage-laden arms.

Early the next morning, I awoke to dappled light. In the drowsiness of sleep, I thought the tree's gnarled limbs had grown around me and had grown skin.

I blinked.

Beneath the canopy of the elm, a magical little world of sunlight sparkled and Brody's arms encased me like a fortress. With my left cheek pressed against his chest, his chin rested on top of my head. I bit the inside of my cheeks, embarrassed by our coziness.

A disagreeable earthy smell greeted me. I tried not to breathe too deeply. I no longer smelled like lilac and French powder.

I moved my head only slightly, and Brody's eyes flashed wide. Peering around, he blinked himself fully awake.

"Do you have soap?" I peered up at his strong, unshaven jaw line.

He nodded and yawned, rolling a kink out of his neck.

"I will do my best to find ya soap *and* water, Princess Wren." A faint smile teased his lips.

ΦΦΦ

Later that morning I sat drying my hair while Brody cooked a brook trout over the fire. Though I'd scrubbed, Pearl's old dress would never be white again.

"I thought you were dead," I told him. "I saw you had been hit." My stomach knotted at the awful memory.

"I don't know how long I was out fer." He laid wild asparagus over warmed rocks in a corner of the fire. "But, my mum's always said that I have a very thick skull."

I laughed softly. "What happened to your horse, Dilly?"

He shrugged at first and then cleared his throat. "I had to sell her in Stockford with the agreement that I can buy her back when I'm able to."

"Why did you have to sell her?" He loved his horse.

"The guards I was with didn't agree with me about staying in Stockford, even though I was certain I'd found yer boots."

"They were mine." I nodded.

"A waif of a girl was wearing them." Brody shook his head. "With the money from Dilly, I paid for a messenger to deliver a letter to your father about where I was and why. But, now I wonder if I was conned." He rubbed the back of his neck.

"I'm sorry about Dilly. I hope you get her back." It was only a matter of time before Father and his men caught up with us. My bath in the stream had taken all of my energy, and I was too tired to get angry.

"Princess Wren . . . why'd ya run away?"

I lowered my gaze to the fire between us. He'd saved my life. I was too weak, too broken to continue on my own. "I wanted to see my sister, Alia—the future queen of Yonder." As I said it, a deep sadness filled me. "She was taken from me when I was seven. I wanted to see her one last time before I marry. But, it doesn't appear to be God's plan for me."

He nodded and his mouth drew into a straight line. "We're to always honor our parents, even when we don't agree. But, I am sorry."

The smell of the fish had earlier inspired appetite, but I no longer felt like eating. I lay down on a nearby blanket and only wanted to sleep.

Brody sat beside me and without asking, squished slivers of the white fish meat into my mouth.

I chewed and swallowed, grateful for his insistence.

"When we obey our parents, there is blessing." He stuffed another bite of fish into my mouth.

I wondered if his father was a minister or someone of the cloth. He made me sit up so he could hold the flask to my mouth for small sips of water. I was too tired to be embarrassed that he treated me like a baby bird that had stepped too early out of the nest.

ΦΦΦ

Brody didn't appear to be worried about time. While we rested by the fire, he picked a buttercup that was nearby and twirled it between his fingers. "These were blooming beneath yer window. I kept thinking it would be nice if ya could see them." He twirled the weed-like flower between his thumb and forefinger. Then, he eyed my ear a couple of times before he inched his hand close and tucked the flower in my hair.

"It's a buttercup." I shifted my gaze to the sun-dappled tree tops.

"The day I arrived, when ya were yelling at Helmer about the pig, I never would have recognized ya, if it hadn't been for yer polished voice."

"And why is that?" I smiled at his description.

"Ya were so skinny. Dirty. Wearing rags and yer hair was so much darker than right now when it's clean."

"I worked hard." I pulled my lower lip between my teeth and shook my head.

"Yeah, I know. If only yer father could have seen ya. Ya would have made him proud."

"No more." His words made my throat burn hot with emotion.

"Ya know there are wild pigs in this part of the country. I'm glad ya no longer smell like one of them."

Though he'd meant to be funny, his sentiments reminded me of Daisy sitting on her haunches as she'd watched us ride away. In my darkest hours, the pig had shown me that I had a Heavenly Father who cared deeply for me.

"What is it?" he asked.

My encounter with God confirmed that He did indeed have a plan for me. Despite Father's and God's plans, I felt a tad breathless as I met the young guard's gaze.

"Thank you." My thank you was expansive and included a great many things. "For your little slips of paper and for saving my life."

"All for King." The corner of his mouth twitched. "All for King."

ΦΦΦ

Our third night while we sat across from each other at the campfire, I asked Brody to tell me more about the ocean. I loved his introspection, the way his voice changed when he spoke of home and his beloved Corra.

"No, you tell me more about Alia, first."

"Hmm . . ." I studied the midnight blue sky. "She's very fond of shoes or at least she used to be. And, she was my best friend." I peered over at him. "Now, tell me about the sea."

"Well . . . it's vast." His voice held a faraway note in it like when my mother spoke about Alia. "There's a sense of freedom because it's so open. There's the sound of the waves crashing, and, when ya look out, it just keeps going. There's no end to it. We used to watch the ships head out until we couldn't see them anymore."

"We . . . ?" Was he married? Or betrothed?

"My siblings and me, all seven of us." He looked up from poking a stick at the fire. "Edwin's the oldest and then me. We always thought it strange how ya could hear one wave crash, and then another off to the side like an accordion. And then there's the smell of the salty, cool air. The sea's always moving, just like my mother." He smiled and stole a glance at me. "She's a hard worker, too."

I nodded.

"Yer eyes are sometimes blue-green and sometimes just green," he said. "Just like the sea, they change color."

Was Father right? Did I have my great-grandmother's blood?

"Yer father placed you in the right kingdom. Davenport's on the sea," Brody said as if the color of a woman's eyes should determine her fate.

"Back to the sea," I reminded him.

"Let me see . . ." Brody scanned the night sky. "When you're looking out over it, salt is in the air and on the breeze. You can taste it. In the morning when there's no wind, the waves are perfect and smooth. Then later in the day, everything gets choppy, and all messed up. The wind makes a mess of things."

The soft staccato in his voice tugged at my heart. He was homesick.

"You've sold me the sea, Brody Hew." I smiled across the firelight at him. "Now, I want to see it, and then we'll visit my sister." I waited, hoping he'd take the bait.

His gaze held none of its usual mirth. "You're going home, Princess Wren."

Heat pricked the corners of my eyes. Though negated, my attempt had still been worth the try.

ΦΦΦ

The next day while we rode, the air began to feel heavy and damp. Brody halted his horse in a meadow of tall, purple lupine. Over my shoulder, he pointed toward the horizon. "See there," he said. "Way off in the distance… it's the ocean."

"You're not taking me home?" I gazed at the vastly different scenery. He'd known all along.

"No, not yet."

I stared at the thick line of blue. Could it possibly be that he intended to take me to Alia? No. Everything Brody Hew did was for my father—all for King.

"What day is it?" I asked. I was to marry on September tenth.

"August twenty-second."

"Oh . . ." There had been no hesitation in his voice. Tomorrow, I would turn sixteen. I would miss my coming of age party—the cakes, the dancing, the dress. In the beginning of my travels, I'd hoped to be back home by this time, but that was before Gruel Kitchen had skewed my plans.

I sighed. Brody was the younger brother of Edwin—my father's favorite soldier. "You're taking me to Davenport."

"No." We were seated closely, and I saw his Adam's apple bob in his thick neck.

"Then why have you taken me to the sea, when I am to marry in less than three weeks?"

"I want to fix yer viola." His chest expanded. "I'm taking ya home to Corra. My father is a cabinet maker. Between the two of us, I believe we'll be able to fix it."

"And then after you fix it?" I questioned.

"I'll take ya home."

He was lying to me.

"You won't have time."

"After my father fixes yer viola, I'll take ya home."

"Do you mean Blue Sky or Davenport?"

Brody pulled on the reins, turning his horse west. Without answering me, we continued riding.

ΦΦΦ

I stood on a green velvet bluff gazing out over the ocean, and the view was so beautiful it was hard to stay mad at Brody Hew.

He tethered his horse to a twisted, wind-bent tree and stopped behind me. "I will stand here to protect ya from the wild pigs that roam the hills. They try to butt newcomers into the sea."

He liked to talk about wild pigs. "You make your pigs sound half billy goat."

"Aye, they are." He laughed softly. Now that we were at the sea, his Corra brogue was more pronounced.

The ocean was as vast as he'd described. Along the cliffs, the windblown trees resembled a woman's hair, rippling behind her in the wind. As we stood overlooking the sea, I felt the closest I ever had to comprehending the imagination of our Creator.

I wanted Brody to take my hand, somehow join us in this memory—the new buffet of sights and sounds—of the surf crashing upon itself, the caw of the gulls, and the salt-nipped breeze. But he didn't. I was to be the future Queen of Davenport; I reminded myself. I had to be content with simply his nearness as we took in the awe-inspiring sight together.

"With yer rust-colored hair, ya belong near the sea." He gave me words instead.

"It's more of a coppery red." I eyed him over my shoulder.

He chuckled. "With yer coppery-red, rust-colored hair, ya could easily belong to the people of Corra. Our roots are Scottish like yer father's."

"Aye." I mimicked his accent.

"See the town?" He pointed up the coastline to a wooded peninsula.

I cupped a hand over my eyes, following his gaze. Before the point, and nestled against a verdant green hillside overlooking the sea, sat stark white cottages. Several dozen townspeople were gathered in the streets.

"What's going on?" I asked.

"Mr. Sutharlan must have his binoculars out again. He's spotted us and informed everyone that I'm home and . . ." His voice trailed off.

"We're in Corra?" I couldn't hide my delight.

"My father will try his best to fix yer viola." His chest inflated.

I smiled at the thought of taking a real bath and sleeping in a real bed and having a real dinner.

"While we're here, you'll have to be Ennie again." Brody's whisper sounded almost hesitant.

"I'm used to being Ennie."

"If anyone found out who ya are, it'd be too hard for me to guard ya all by myself."

"I understand." And I did, completely.

"And . . . the only thing that'll make sense to my mum and dad is that you're my girl," he said so quickly that it took me a while to catch up with his thoughts. "I'm sorry." He breathed. "It'll only be for a little while, while we're here. Soon as yer viola's fixed, we'll leave."

"You don't have to fix it. You broke it to save my life."

"I want to fix it, make it right for ya. A birthday present of sorts from me." A corner of his mouth twitched. "It'll take a couple of days, and then we'll leave."

He meant *leave for Davenport*, but he knew me well enough not to mention my future.

ΦΦΦ

"It's so quaint," I breathed. From the top of the last hill, the white-painted homes of Corra with their thatched roofs and red doors were a bright contrast against the Cashmere Hills that rolled to the sea.

"Brody," I said over my shoulder, "You didn't tell me your homeland is so picturesque." His arms rested against my sides, his hands holding the reins.

"We're simple people, we Hews. Not like yer people." His voice was unusually soft. "My dad's a cabinet maker, and he says that a tree is for shade and for making cabinets. And my mother, she's full of her own wisdom, too. She'll tell ya that God gave us arms for holding babies and each other."

I wanted my life to be so simple. I wanted Brody's arms to… I stopped my mind from rambling.

"I'm sorry, Ennie. I'm a tad nervous." He sighed. "They're going to think yer my sweetheart, maybe even my bride."

"Oh-hh." I laughed softly. That was a problem. I already knew that I liked him a little too much.

Up ahead, an elderly man reached the top of a grassy path, a fishing rod in one hand, and a silvery fish in the other. "Have ya brought home yer bride, young Brody?" he asked.

"I brought home me girl, Mr. Pittendrigh."

Had I ever heard Brody's voice so happy?

"The wedding will be here in Corra, then?"

"If me mum has anything to say about it." Brody laughed and softly flicked the reins.

"My mum," I corrected him.

"You're in Corra now. Things are different here. But, I'll watch me mums for ya."

I couldn't tell if he was being cheeky or not. He probably was his voice was so soft.

As we rode down the hillside toward the edge of the town, I could see the differences. A crowd had gathered in the wide cobblestone street—men in woolen blazers and caps with cigars poking out of their pockets and women wearing shawls and bonnets. Many a face wore a pair of windblown wood glasses like Crauley's.

"My grandparents founded Corra, and Hew means heart," he said.

Hearts were everywhere, carved into the bric-a-brac of each home and in the eyes of the townspeople who'd gathered for this young man's homecoming. From the rejoicing in the streets, you would think that he'd been gone for twenty years. I thought of my giants going home, and the celebrating that in all likelihood had already taken place.

"Brody, Brody!" Standing near the front of the crowd, a wiry, lean woman with silvery streaked hair and twisted wood glasses gripped her hands beneath her chin.

While he slid off of his horse, the woman stared up at me. Not as a dressmaker—sizing me up—but much, much more. In one long look, she tried to read everything about me. She tried to determine my love for her son.

I smiled back, wondering what she saw.

Brody hugged his father and then his mother before returning to the horse's side. "Ennie." He held his arms up for me.

When I reached down for him, our eyes met as if for the first time and a knot twisted in my gut. He'd saved my life. His strong hands gripped my waist before he slowly lowered me to the ground. In a truce unspoken, I smiled up at him. I wasn't going to run from him anymore. While his father fixed my viola, I'd stay here in Corra with his family and be his girl.

Chapter Eighteen

I sat squished between Brody and his younger brother, Scot, on the couch in the Hews' cozy front room. The walls were painted a sky blue. Above the brick fireplace hung a heavy framed oval painting of Blue Sky Kingdom with its red turrets, sweeping lawns and distant blue hills. On each side of the picture hung oval portraits; one of my father, King Francis II, and one of my mother, Queen Irene. Mother's had been painted before her red hair had turned gray. With her blue-green eyes, the resemblance between us was very strong.

No one appeared to notice.

"Those pictures were given to us after our son Edwin lost the use of both of his legs in the war," Trev, Brody's father, said.

Misery Hill. I knew the battle only too well.

"How is Edwin?" I asked.

"Surprisingly well, considering. 'Win has always been an over-comer. They have three children, ya know. A girl and two boys," Trev said.

If I had heard correctly, he'd called his son *'Win*. Did my own Father know the nickname of one of his most beloved men?

"Tell us about yourself, Ennie," said Margaret, Brody's mother. Her graying chin-length dark hair framed her lean face.

"Well, I . . ." What could I tell them about myself that wouldn't raise suspicion?

Brody took my right hand in his. His strong, calloused hand quickly emptied my brain of any answers I might have been able to conjure.

Perhaps holding hands in Corra was a prenuptial feat, for his siblings stared at our clasped hands with wide-eyed fascination. So did I, for that matter.

Uneasy with the situation, I dug my nails into the palm of his hand.

He patted my hand before returning his to his knee.

Maybe I'd overreacted. I wasn't used to being his girl.

"How did ya and Brody meet?" asked his oldest sister, Lydie, a pretty girl of thirteen.

"Well, we . . ." I peered up at Brody's profile, his strong unshaven jaw, and remembered the first time we'd met when I'd been crawling through the tall grass, trying to escape.

He peered down at me and his lopsided grin cut short my thoughts.

Perhaps he should answer this question.

Instead, he lifted his nearest arm high up in the air and settled it around my shoulders.

I sat up taller, and catching my breath, told myself to blink.

My gaze returned to the pictures of Father and Mother above the mantel, and the oath "All for King" carved into the top of the gilded frame. My disobedience must have deeply disappointed them.

Brody and I were under both of our family's watchful eyes.

I clasped his hand that rested on my shoulder, curved my thumbnail in and pinched him good.

He removed his arm, returning his hand to his knee.

Heat crept up my neck and into the hollows of my cheeks.

"We met one fine afternoon when Ennie was walking to town for candy," Brody said. "We even had a small picnic of milk and cookies." He smiled down at me and pretended adoration.

"Aw, a sweet tooth! Just like yer mum." His father slapped his knees and chuckled.

"Where are you from, Ennie?" Margaret, his mother, asked.

"Blue Sky." I managed to speak two whole words.

"Oh, what does your father do?" Trev asked.

I did not let my gaze drift toward the mantel.

"He's a soldier, and highly regarded," Brody said.

"Do you have siblings?" asked one of the four girls.

"Yes, three sisters and a brother." My cheeks warmed as I realized my slip.

Brody turned his head slightly to regard me.

"I'm so relieved to hear that." Margaret fanned her face with one hand. "I was afraid that Brody had brought home Princess Wren." She looked toward the portrait of my mother. "Her hair is said to be a fiery red like Queen Irene's. But, there are only four children in the royal family, ya know."

"Yes, I know." I nodded.

"Ennie is princess enough for me." Brody's arm snaked behind my lower back and then his hand settled above my hip.

What was he thinking? My heart tied into what I hoped was a knot that I might undo later.

Perhaps it was due to the warmth of the room or the squishiness on the couch, but I felt myself relax against his side.

"When's the wedding?" Margaret beamed.

"Ennie wants me to meet her sister first before we speak of marriage." He smiled. "And, Father, I'd like to rebuild her violin while we're here."

I elbowed him. He knew very well that I played the viola.

He dug his thumb into my side.

"Owh!" I said under my breath.

"You play the violin!" Lydie clapped her hands together. "Princess Wren plays the vi-ola. You are so like her!"

"Vee-ola," I corrected her, adding a smile.

"Ennie's sixteenth birthday is tomorrow, Mum," Brody said.

He'd remembered. I glanced at him. Was it wrong to feel touched?

"Sixteenth?" Lydie beamed. "We know who *you'll* be kissing."

I stiffened and felt my mouth go dry.

The giggling children had obviously heard of Blue Sky's oldest coming-of-age tradition: On her sixteenth birthday, a young maiden chooses the recipient of her first kiss.

"Yes, but will it be yer *first* kiss?" Margaret asked.

"It will. We have waited," Brody said.

His mother rolled her eyes and waved a hand like she didn't believe him. Then, she eyed me.

"We've waited," I confirmed.

The children giggled amongst themselves.

Would they be disappointed when they learned the truth? That it was all an act? That Brody was simply guarding me with his life? *All for King.*

"Tomorrow night!" Lydie clapped her hands together as if the kiss were something to be celebrated, perhaps viewed.

Why had Brody informed every one of my birthday? The same soft look as when he'd tucked the buttercup in my hair resurfaced. Did he want to kiss me?

"How long have ya two been in love?" Margaret asked.

"I think since they sat on our couch." Trev slapped his knee and chuckled.

"What are they doing?" asked the youngest boy. "They just keep looking at each other."

Heat climbed my face.

"Shhhh! They're in love," whispered Jewelee, the youngest.

"That's what happens when ya fall in love," Lydie said. "Ya can't think. Yer in a world all by yerself."

I didn't correct her or any of them. I didn't want to look away from Brody's velvety soft gaze.

Chapter Nineteen

The morning of my sixteenth birthday gifted me with common sense. I could not kiss Brody Hew. I would soon be married. I would fulfill my duty to my country and marry Prince Vincent. My marriage would make our enemy an ally and Father could have his railroad.

In the meantime, it was wrong to think about Brody, much less kiss him! Glad that I'd come to my senses, I joined Margaret in the kitchen.

"Can ya cook, Ennie?" she asked.

"Yes, a little." I tried not to think of the Gruel Cakes and how my baking had served as implements of war.

With my hands clasped behind my back, I noted that a heart had been meticulously carved into the top of each door of the bright yellow cabinetry. It was that way throughout her sparkling clean kitchen.

"The Heart of the Home cabinetry design is my husband's bestseller." Margaret must have followed my gaze. "Here in Corra, we like to think that the kitchen is the heart of the home."

She sifted dark brown and white ingredients into a long glass pan. Next, she made three holes in the dry mixture and added oil, vanilla, and vinegar, which I thought quite odd. She dumped two cups of water over the top and began to stir her mystery mess with a fork.

"Brody went to the forest to find a violin piece for ya." Margaret looked up briefly from her stirring.

"Oh, I wish he'd asked me to go, too."

"Well, he wanted it to be a surprise."

"Ohh . . ." Then why had she told me? Now, I would have to pretend that I was surprised.

"What are you making?" I asked as she continued stirring the concoction.

"Yer cake." She attacked every remnant of white with her fork until the mixture in the pan was a dusty rose color.

"Doesn't it require eggs?"

"No, it's a Wacky Cake."

She could say that again.

The cake couldn't be all that special. Margaret hadn't even cracked an egg or dirtied a bowl.

"Does yer family go to church, Ennie?"

"Yes." Our cathedral back home was larger than her town.

"Do ya believe in God?" While Margaret waited for my response, she appeared to have stopped breathing. "That He sent his Son to pay the debt we could not pay. To die in our place."

"Yes, without a doubt."

"I'm so glad." She blinked and continued stirring. "What do ya love about my son?"

I knew she'd always remember my answer, so I had to word it wisely, with care. "His arms," I said, and warmth crept up into my cheeks.

"Aye, God gave us arms for holding babies and each other." She nodded. "And, what do ya love about…" she rolled her wrist, "his spirit?"

My answer had not been insightful enough for her. I had to dig deeper.

"Brody's always been sensitive like his father. He won't take kindly to anyone breaking his heart," Margaret said.

"I've always been honest with Brody." I wouldn't break his heart.

"About what?" From behind her windblown glasses, her dark eyes narrowed. "Are ya saying ya don't love my boy?"

I had stirred the ire in Margaret Hew.

"No." For a moment, my rib cage felt knit together too tightly.

"What are ya saying then?"

The woman I was conversing with deemed herself, my future mother-in-law. She was not a woman to take lightly.

"Do ya love my son?" Margaret pulled open the heavy oven door and slid the Wacky Cake inside. After she closed it, her face was red, and it wasn't from the heat of the stove. She set her hands on her narrow hips that had somehow born seven children and stared at me.

Did I love her son? I gulped and looked to the cabinets where carved hearts adorned each of the upper doors. During our travels and our time alone together, is that what had happened? Had the mysterious softness in Brody's eyes when he'd twirled the buttercup possibly been love?

For several days, far removed from the rest of the world, I'd simply been a girl and he a boy. No titles between us. Is that what had happened? Had I fallen in love with Brody Hew?

"I can see that yer still coming to grips with yer feelings for him." Margaret sighed. "Well, ya'll know after tonight, won't ya? I can say that about yer country's odd custom. Ya'll know after tonight."

She meant after the kiss. My heart stretched in a wild panic. If a kiss helped determine one's true feelings, then I should not kiss her son!

ΦΦΦ

I enjoyed a warm bath that the girls prepared for me. The room was filled with steam when someone knocked on the door.

"Mum wants me to burn yer dress and give ya something of mine to wear. I'll leave it here for ya," Lydie said.

"Thank you. It's near the sink." I was relieved that Pearl's old dress would no longer be mine.

After I finished bathing, I found my birthday dress—an unfitted checkered sage green jumper with an attached white shirt with half sleeves. A dark green tie was sewn into the pointed collar. I believe it was the only thing in Lydie's wardrobe that she was willing to part with, as it was very ugly and reminded me of a school uniform.

Hopefully, the dress would be so ugly that Brody would not want to kiss me.

When I strolled into the kitchen, Margaret's eyes widened. "Really, Lydie, is that the best ya could do?" she asked, loudly.

"It's the only thing I don't wear anymore, Mum," Lydie said from the front room.

Margaret eyed me and then like she was giving the hideous outfit her permission to stay, she sighed and lowered her shoulders.

"Isn't that Lydie's old school uniform?" Brody asked, entering the kitchen.

"It is. I thought she got rid of it three years ago when they retired the style," Margaret said but did not call Lydie into the kitchen for a lecture.

"Ya look like a schoolgirl, Ennie." Brody's voice was so soft that it made me feel like bread pudding.

I promptly returned to the bathroom and braided my clean, dry hair into two long pigtails. I hoped to make myself so unattractive and school girlish that Brody wouldn't want to remember the Blue Sky tradition.

After dinner, Margaret lit all the candles on the Wacky cake and then carried it to the table. The candles were arranged in the four far corners of the pan. It would be nearly impossible for me to blow them out in one breath. Obviously, Margaret did not want my birthday wish to be granted.

I inhaled, eyeing the cake.

"Make a wish!" little Jewelee reminded me.

"Thank you, Jewelee." The day had so befuddled me that I'd almost forgotten the order. I paused, taking my time. I couldn't waste my birthday wish on not kissing Brody. I had to use it on something more important. I recalled my vow to self. *I wish to see Alia one more time before I am married.* And because all wishes should be shared with God, I prayed the same.

I inhaled deeply, and traveling to all four corners of the cake, managed to blow out all sixteen candles.

"She should have played the bagpipes," Trev said.

Margaret watched as I sunk my fork into the Wacky Cake.

The texture was as pleasant as any of the cakes our cook baked back home; and although I was not fond of chocolate, I was able to force it down. I wished I'd had this recipe when I'd been in Gruel Kitchen. The Wacky Cake would have made winning the giants' hearts easier for me.

"Thank you, Margaret. Thank you, everyone," I said, looking around the table. Throughout the day, I'd been showered with birthday wishes and little candies that the children had bought with coins they'd shaken out of their piggy banks.

As soon as I'd finished my piece of cake, Brody rose abruptly from the table. "The sun's getting close to setting. We best make haste."

Something important was going on. I tagged along with the rest of the family as we made our way out the door and up the front walkway.

"These are my rugosa roses." Taking her time ahead of me, Margaret pointed toward chest-high shrubs bearing deep pink blossoms. The roses and their bright green foliage flanked both sides of the picket gate. She leaned down to smell an open flower and waved a hand for me to do the same.

I already knew from walking by that their fragrance was heavenly, but for her sake, I leaned very close to one and inhaled its sweet perfume.

"It's lovely, Mrs. Hew."

"Hurry, Ennie," Brody called from the street.

I slipped out the gate and caught up with him. Over my shoulder, I saw Margaret fall in step with her husband and take his arm.

While the sun slipped to half-mast in the sky, we climbed the gentle slope of the Cashmere Hills.

"Where are we going?" I asked.

Brody's strong hand took mine, and he nodded ahead of us toward the knoll. "We're going to walk up to the top to watch the sunset."

"Everyone?" I asked, glancing behind us to his family, who carried blankets.

"Just ya and me," he sounded matter of fact.

He'd gone ahead and planned the evening with his family, without conversing with me. Somewhere along the way, his clan was going to stop and set up an observation point.

"Why?" I dared to ask.

"Because it's not their sixteenth birthday, it's only yers." I saw a dimple in his profile.

I let go of his hand and stopped in my tracks.

A step later, he did the same and turned to face me.

Even though I'd worn the old school garb and my hair in pigtails, he was going to follow the Blue Sky tradition, and he had the fellow picked out for me.

"Brody . . ." My mouth pursed as I inhaled deeply.

"Am I to be the recipient of yer first kiss, Ennie?" he whispered.

Simply holding his hand made my stomach crash over upon itself like the surf below. And, I couldn't think with his gaze on me. I turned to face the sea and tucked a strand of loose hair behind one ear.

He stopped beside me, his shoulder touching mine.

"It appears I have no choice in the matter," I said. "And your mother does not approve of me." Over my shoulder, I eyed Margaret's front row seat.

Down below us, his parents and all of the children—were camped on blankets. In Corra, kissing appeared to be a spectator sport.

"Mum does not know what to make of ya." He chuckled and then his voice dimmed. "Is it me ya want to kiss, Ennie?" he asked, softly.

The question was like the long rifle he used to carry. Loaded.

In less than three weeks, I was to be Vincent's bride, yet... here I was in Corra on the night of my sixteenth birthday. I reached for his hand.

My actions were my words unsaid. My silent "yes."

A heavy sigh escaped him.

"If it's not me ya want to kiss, we'll march back to town right now, and ya can have yer pick of any fellow in Corra."

Brody wanted words.

Because of our audience, everyone in Corra would know about tonight. After I left this magical little place, what was to become of him?

"I'm scared," I admitted.

"You?" He chuckled. "Yer not scared of anything." He grabbed my hand again and led me the rest of the way up the hill.

He was so wrong. I was scared. I was scared of leaving my heart here in Corra. I was scared I'd never forget him or these days we'd spent together.

We reached the ridge and, knowing what was next, I grew awkwardly shy. Ever so slyly, I tugged at the bands securing my hair and tucked them into my pocket. Brody Hew planned to kiss me. I may as well look my best.

ΦΦΦ

While I stared at the horizon, Brody wrapped his arms around my waist, and he stood so close behind me that his breath was warm on my neck. His chin pressed gently into my shoulder as we watched the sun like a ball of fire set into the mirror of the sea.

Eyes wide, I stared out over the fuchsia-orange rippled waters. *You'll know after tonight, won't ya? I can say that about yer country's odd custom. You'll know after tonight.* Margaret's sentiments worried my heart.

I was Brody's girl in Corra. Our lives had become entangled and what could never be was happening here.

He nuzzled his chin softly into the curve of my shoulder.

"What are we going to do?" I whispered. In less than three weeks, I would be married, and Brody would return to Blue Sky. What were we to do with our memories of Corra?

"Well . . ." He cleared his throat. "To make the kiss believable, you should turn around."

He'd misunderstood me. But it was for the best.

I closed my eyes and listened to the waves crashing against the cliffs in the darkness below. If kissing Brody was as pleasant as his arms about me, I would never want to leave this place, and Father had his plans for me. God had His plan for me as well.

But, I reasoned . . . Tonight was mine. Years from now, I would look back on my sixteenth birthday and remember what it was like to have been in love.

Slowly, I bid my feet to turn and meet Brody's softly misted gaze.

"I should not kiss you, Brody, for I am to be Prince Vincent's wife." It hurt to tell him what he already knew. "I'm sorry." Feeling bumbly and shy, I tucked a wisp of hair behind one ear.

His fingers knit about the small of my back and he nodded. "Then a lollyberry kiss would be all right."

"What is that?" I didn't have the heart to giggle. The evening felt like a vow that we were secretly sharing in front of everyone.

"Ya hold yer left hand to my cheek, and then ya move closer, until our foreheads touch, and then the sides of our noses will touch. From the distance, my family will not be able to tell that we have not truly kissed."

I pulled my lower lip between my teeth then felt it uncurl. "The lollyberry sounds like a lot of hoopla." Though I did not fully trust the calm in his eyes, I lifted my left hand to his cheek and proceeded to lose myself in his sparkling gaze. Already, the lollyberry had swept my breath away. I liked his strong arms about me. I loved his home, his family, and yes, even his mother.

For the lollyberry kiss, I leaned toward him until our foreheads touched, and the sides of our noses touched, too. His mouth actually brushed against mine. Instead of pushing him away, I returned his kiss.

I did not want to think about my future. For my first kiss, I only wanted to think about Brody. The sea was our melody, and its spray a reminder of our audience. Then our foreheads touched once more.

"Happy birthday, Ennie," he whispered.

We simply smiled at one another for a moment before we remembered our audience.

We turned toward them and bowed. Warm cheeked, I lifted my gaze to his family. Hands clutched beneath their chins, Margaret and the girls looked like they were at a play and had just seen the best part. A deep smile was chiseled in Trev's ruddy face.

Even though I belonged at the sea, my home was not Corra. My father had already given me away, and the truth ripped at my heart. When I was the Queen of Davenport, I would look back on my days with Brody Hew and regard them as some of the finest and most heartbreaking of my life.

Chapter Twenty

Over the next few days, Brody never mentioned the kiss. He avoided being alone with me. He never told me of the feelings he might hold. Instead, he ventured endlessly into the windblown forests of Corra. One afternoon, he returned with a figure-eight shaped piece of wood, perfect for my fiddle. He showed it to his father and together the two began to work on it in the cabinet shop behind their home.

Though I wanted to be with them, I stayed behind in the kitchen and folded clothes fresh off the line with the girls.

"It was the most beautiful kiss," Jewelee, Brody's youngest sister, sighed as she gazed across the table at me. The girls often mentioned the kiss, but it was the first time I'd been alone with them since the night of my birthday.

I   didn't   know   what   to say.

"Mother says it's not Corra's custom for a sixteen-year-old girl to kiss a boy, but I will," Lydie, the oldest, whispered. "When I turn sixteen, I'm going to grab the boy I like, and we're going to walk to the top of the hills and look out over the sea. I'm going to wear my hair down, just like you did." A fire shone in her pale green eyes.

"Only if it's all right with your mother." I lowered my gaze to the pile of tea towels and felt the burden of my guilt.

"I'd die an old maid before Mum would allow me to kiss a boy," Lydie said, rolling her eyes.

"She may surprise you." I recalled how their parents had sat on blankets.

"It was the most beautiful kiss." Moira, the ten-year-old, gazed dreamily at me.

What had Brody and I started in these girls? I hoped it was not a rebellion of Corra custom.

"Mother says that the wedding should be soon," Lydie whispered.

"Father agreed." Moira nodded. "He said the knot is already tied in Brody's eyes."

"Mother said as soon as she saw him crest the hill, she knew he'd brought home his bride," Lydie said, adding a heavy sigh.

I remembered our arrival to Corra. I was still in awe about seeing the ocean for the first time, and then the whole village had gathered—the sweet homecoming, the reunion, the love. And even though I was a stranger to them, I too had been caught up in the emotion of the day.

"Ya look so sad, so far away." Moira leaned her head to one side, gazing at me.

"Things are different here than in Blue Sky." I shrugged. "That's all."

"When I turn sixteen, I'm going to Blue Sky," Lydie said, energy in her eyes.

I shook my head. "Things are better here."

"How can they be better? The streets of Blue Sky are brick, the turrets red and there're dress shops on every block."

Who had Lydie been listening to?

"You cannot see the ocean or smell the salt breeze and… you'll miss your family." Then I repeated something I'd once overheard. "But, sometimes you need to go away to miss the ways of home."

I glanced toward the back shop, anxious for Brody's return and for him to rescue me from this difficult conversation.

"Ennie, Mr. Jiggins has a violin. I'll go ask if he'll let ya borrow it." Without waiting for my response, Lydie rose from the table and strode into the front room where Margaret was ironing. "Mother, may I take some of yer bread to Mr. Jiggins? We want to see if he'll let Ennie borrow his violin."

"Yes, that would be nice," she said.

I knew enough about the violin to play it, but it would be a first for me. My heart and fingers warmed at the thought of playing for Brody's siblings.

A short while later in the Hews' front room, I placed Mr. Jiggins' violin on my collarbone and rested the left side of my jaw on the chin rest. One would think that one inch is not so much, but when you are holding a violin instead of a viola, one inch feels as awkward as a tippy canoe. I drew the bow and reminded myself that the violin does not have a middle C.

My memory drifted to Brody, beginning with the time we'd met, how I'd been the one to drink the chalky milk, and his strong arms had caught me. I remembered his arms about me in the saddle for days on end until we'd reached Corra; and lastly, his arms around me as we overlooked the sea. His arms were an extension of his heart, pulling me close. His sparkling eyes were a reflection of his soul. While I played, I didn't think about what could never be; I thought about Brody and his gentle ways and the buttercups. While I played pure happiness, his siblings gathered cross-legged in front of me on the floor, and Margaret continued her ironing.

The backdoor clicked open and closed, and then Brody leaned in the doorway to the front room. Shoulders low, he gazed at me. Had I ever seen such a soft look in his eyes?

I stilled the bow, gazing back.

"I've never heard ya play so happy, Ennie." He swallowed, then cleared his throat. "Never. Not in all the... times, I've heard ya play."

Didn't he know why?

My most beautiful music should also have been my saddest, for outside of my sixteenth birthday, Brody and I could never be. I could see in his sparkling gaze that the truth had not hit him yet. When it did, it would feel like another of my Gruel Cakes to the side of his head.

He returned to the cabinet shop out back, and I continued playing.

Someone knocked at the front door. Lydie flung her thick auburn hair over one shoulder and rose to answer it. Through the picture window, I saw that a crowd—three people wide— had gathered on the walkway all the way to the front gate, the entire neighborhood from the looks of it.

"We heard the most beautiful music," a middle-aged woman said.

"It's Brody's girlfriend, *Ennie*, playing Mr. Jiggins' violin," Lydie said my name with sweet inflection.

Brodie's girlfriend, Ennie. What could never be was—for a little while.

"May we come in?" the woman asked.

"Yes, please come in," Margaret said and folded up her ironing board.

While the neighbors gathered in the front room, Mrs. Hew pulled brightly colored tins from a lower cupboard and set bickies upon plates. She set two large kettles on the stove and made several pots of hot tea, serving it with a pitcher of steamed milk.

"Brody's brought home Ennie, his future bride, to meet us all." Margaret beamed as she waved more and more people inside. *Future bride*. If only my future were so simple.

Did Margaret approve of me now?

She continued waving more visitors inside their small, little home; soon, there was standing-room-only in the kitchen and front room.

"Play something, Ennie," Margaret said.

I drew the bow. *Future bride?* Is that what a kiss on the Cashmere Hills meant? My worries turned to music as I played my way up Misery Hill. *Future bride.* Now, the entire town believed we were betrothed. When I became Mrs. Vincent von Drake of Davenport, would Brody's reputation be forever scarred?

For some reason, the children's glee had turned to sadness, and they stared at me with mournful eyes.

The back door in the kitchen clicked open and closed, and Brody made his way through the crowd of people. "Ennie, play *happy* music fer our guests. Play something like..." his chest expanded, and a smile lit his lips, "buttercups."

Buttercups.

Outside of Brody, every memory that came to mind was sad: Father, losing Alia, my future... The only happy times I could remember at the moment were of him.

"Happy ones." His smile reminded me of his words.

Instead of misery, my heart drifted to the window with its view of the Cashmere Hills. How could I ever leave here on my own? How could I leave Brody's family, the unity, the love? He'd have to poison me with the chalky milk plant and cart me off in the middle of the night. He'd have to remind me that I still wanted to see Alia one more time. Falling in love with him had almost made me forget my vow to self.

At dusk, the neighbors finally made their way home. Margaret's tins were empty and it was time to prepare dinner. I took the trash outside to the bin and heard the men's voices. I paused to listen near the corner of the building where Brody and his father worked on my viola by lantern light.

"I've never seen a woman sit up so straight," Trev's voice carried through the open window. "Did her parents make her walk around with a board tied to her back and books on top of her head?"

"I don't know. Do you think the scroll area matches her old one, exactly?"

"Yes. And, her voice sounds like it's been sanded and polished," Trev said.

"Yes, Ennie has a polished voice."

"But, son . . ." Trev's voice held concern. "Does she know how to cook, clean and take care of a home?"

"She's had some training, and I'll teach her what she doesn't know."

Brody. If only it were true. His father would remember this conversation and the lies.

"Sometimes men go to their graves teaching a woman who has not had the proper training." Perhaps, Trev did not approve of me.

Even though the conversation was difficult, I didn't want to miss one word.

"I would gladly go to my grave teaching her."

"I don't think you'll go to yer grave teaching her, only loving her."

I tucked Trev's words deep into the cabinets of my heart.

"I was so proud of ya, son, one of Blue Sky's top guards. But, now that you've brought Ennie home," Trev sighed, "we can't help but hope that yer future will be here in Corra; and for the rest of our days, we'll get to share in yer lives."

How in the world would Brody respond? The tears that knotted in my throat told me to leave, but my feet would not budge.

"Father, I may not know tomorrow, but I know this . . ." Brody paused for two full heart beats, "I will go to my grave loving her."

Brody's words slipped deep into my soul. Did he really feel that way? Or were his beautiful sentiments merely for my protection, to make his father believe that we were truly in love?

ΦΦΦ

The next day, I couldn't handle Brody's aloofness any longer. When his father was in the house for midmorning tea, I went and found him in the cabinet shop where he was working on my viola.

"Brody . . ." I took a step toward him and folded my arms in front of me.

"Yes." His head remained bowed while he sanded.

"I'll do what you've always told me was right. I'll obey my father, and there will be a blessing." I inhaled deeply and nodded. "I promise." I came to grips with my decision.

"Aye," he said, but he didn't look happy, not like I thought he would. "You are a daughter of the King, Ennie." His chest expanded as he gazed sadly at me. His lips pressed together tightly, and he swallowed. "I shouldn't have…"

A corner of my mouth twitched downward. He was sorry that he'd kissed me.

The truth was more painful than I'd expected.

I backed away from him.

"I should not have." He inhaled deeply, pulling back his shoulders. Was it the soldier in him that spoke or the man?

"You should not have what?" I waited near the door for him to break my heart completely.

"But it was your sixteenth birthday." He smiled like his alibi was believable.

Had he thought he'd been serving the King in kissing me? I had not had to follow tradition; I'd chosen to.

I wanted to take the beautiful slab of wood that he was working on and smash it over his head.

"Ennie . . . every day . . ." He shook his head as his tender gaze softened me. "I wish every day were yer sixteenth birthday."

"Aye . . ." I stuffed my fist into my mouth and fled the shop. His words were not what I'd expected. Hurrying around the side of the house past Margaret's rugosa roses, I flung open the front gate and took the sandy path beside Mrs. Campbell's home down to the sea.

I ran through thick, loose sand and tall grass over the rippling hills to the ocean that I loved. Ankle-high in the surf, I told God my problems even though He already knew.

"I love this man. I love Brody Hew. You know my future, but, here I am in Corra," I inhaled a shaky breath, "and just like the wind with the morning calm, I am making a mess of my life... and my heart." Tears coursed down my cheeks as I said more gibberish. "You have a plan for Pearl..." I inhaled deeply. "And I know that You have a plan for me, too." I tried to believe the best: that Vincent was decent, that he would not be too great of a disappointment, that someday, I would be able to look in his eyes and not remember Brody's.

I quieted and stared at the distant horizon—God's plumb line that divided the sea from the sky. The foam crested at my feet. The waves continued to ebb in and out with the tide. I waited for Brody to follow me, as he always had, and for him to tell me that everything was going to be okay.

But, this time, he didn't.

He left me alone with God.

Chapter Twenty-one

Early the next morning when the sun was uncurling its fingers over the hills, Brody tiptoed into his sisters' room and woke me. I met him near the front gate and from there we ran barefoot on the path along Mrs. Campbell's home down to the sea. He took my hand while we ran near the water's edge, our footprints erased by the surf. My soul felt weightless as he chased me up a winding path, halfway up the hills.

Instead of reaching the summit like the night of my birthday, we stopped on a lower knoll to catch our breath. Brody's strong arms wrapped around my waist, his chin rested in the curve of my shoulder, and we watched the sun's belly inch over the distant hills.

"Turn around, Ennie."

The tender note in his voice made me shake my head. Within a month, I would be married to Prince Vincent. We shouldn't be here, tempting fate. What were we thinking?

"Brody, it's not my birthday anymore," I tried to face the cold hard truth.

"I'd still like ya to turn around."

His voice held no humor, but I questioned if he'd come up with another lollyberry tale. More hoopla. I inhaled deeply and then turned to meet his velvety gaze.

Opening his hand between us, he unveiled fragile yellow buttercups that he must have picked when he'd been lagging behind me up the hill. He slid a few of the wispy stems into the side of my hair above my ear and gazed softly at me.

The flowers were fragile, wispy, too delicate for a bouquet.

As we looked out over the calm waters of the sea, Brody nuzzled his cheek against my hair. "The family story is that we're from Scotland," he said, and although his arms were wrapped around my middle, his voice sounded faraway. "Our great grandfather was very wealthy, of nobility. It was a sorry time in the old country—a time of killing—and grandfather's beliefs and his family's worship of God made them fear for their lives. So, he hired a captain to bring his family here to Northend. They packed all of their belongings and trunks of gold and jewelry into the hold of a cargo ship and set sail."

"Go on." I took one of his hands in mine.

He shook his head. "For weeks they only ate hard tack. My grandfather trapped rats on the ship and tossed them into the sea. My grandmother and their five children cried a lot for their loved ones and the comforts of home they'd left behind. Then one evening after night had fallen and they only had the light of the stars, the captain spotted land." I followed Brody's gaze miles up the craggy coastline. "Back in those days, there wasn't a lighthouse, and only the locals knew of the rocky point and the lives that had perished there. The captain barely spotted the danger in time to save their lives. Shifting the sails, he was able to change their course. Instead of wrecking his ship on the rocks, the wind pushed them further down the coastline."

Though I wanted their misery to be over, Brody's voice still held a note of unease.

"At the edge of the turbulent waters, a ship sat all alone. Though the captain tried to readjust the sails, the wind continued to push them toward the dark ship. As they drew even closer, they saw a woman with a shawl over her head, standing on the gangplank, holding out a wee bundle in her arms and wailing. 'Take my baby. Help my baby.'" Brody inhaled deeply. "While their gaze was mesmerized by this woman, men dropped from out of the sky, swinging on ropes onto their boat. Dirty men with dark curly hair, and one with a wooden leg, threw my grandfather and his family overboard, into the sea. The captain threw vests out, trying to save them. But the pirates threw him over the side, too. They were all swept out to sea, miles down the coast before they finally washed to shore. Of my grandfather's family—his five children and his wife—they lost one soul to Heaven that day, baby Corra."

"Oh-hhh . . ." I let out a broken breath. He hadn't prepared me. Tears that had burned my throat now streamed down my cheeks.

"Aye, 'tis a sad story. Though my great-grandmother walked the shoreline every day for years searching, her wee body was never found."

"How old was she?" I stared sadly at the swirling waters of the sea.

"She'd just turned two. A beautiful baby with auburn curls like her mother's."

I pictured my sweet Odessa as a babe with her auburn ringlets.

"Grandfather had to start over. He became a fisherman, founded our little village, and named it Corra—after his little girl."

I inhaled the salty air deep into my lungs, tipping my head back against his shoulder. Davenport was also on the sea. In my future, I might very well become like Brody's great-grandmother, walking the shoreline searching for these memories.

"You wonder, lass, about our allegiance to Blue Sky and yer father." His cheek pressed gently into mine as he shook his head. "Because of yer father's pledge to stand by us in times of trouble, we won't lose our Corra ever again."

"Do you think Father's heard the story?"

"I know he has. After Edwin told him our family's story, yer father made his pledge to stand by Corra."

"Oh-hh." I breathed a painful sigh. *Father, if only he'd explained himself more, I might have understood him.* My marriage would protect Corra. Understanding this gave purpose to my present happiness. My marriage would protect Brody's homeland.

ΦΦΦ

After dinner that evening, the family gathered in the front room. I was seated in the stuffed chair that Brody's siblings often fought over and piled into. The fire blazed in the hearth, and the room felt heavy with anticipation. Mouths pursed and eyes wide with stardust, it appeared that I was the only one who wasn't in on some very special secret.

"Ennie . . ." Brody bent to one knee in front of my chair.

"Yes." I gazed happily at him, trying to dismiss the otherwise serious aura. The fire crackled in the hearth, and his siblings were unusually quiet.

While he remained on one knee, a knot formed in my gut. He knew my future. Even though his eyes were softly lit with love, I remained confident that he was not going to propose. He was a sensible man. Except for my sixteenth birthday, we could never be. I breathed in a shallow breath. Still, the moment felt very much like a proposal.

I sat stiffly. While I tried not to let my love reach my eyes, my left hand betrayed me. In front of everyone, my hand lifted to cradle the curve of his cheek. Eyes dancing with moonlight, he leaned into my touch.

Like a rock skipping across the water, sighs surfaced about the room.

"Your violin is like new." Brody pulled the viola out from beneath the ruffled skirt of the nearby ottoman, and handed it to me, smiling.

The wood, like the frames of Crauley's glasses, was windblown and finely polished in burgundy and cream tones. Never had I seen such an exquisite viola. Two small hearts were carved close to each other on the same side of the bridge.

"It's beaut-iful." My voice broke as I ran my fingertips over the engraved hearts, the signature of Corra.

"I don't know how it will sound, but..." Brody's voice trailed off.

The viola's completion meant that we'd be leaving soon, perhaps in the morning. The gift was bittersweet.

"Play something happy, Ennie." Perhaps he doubted that I could, for the corner of his mouth twitched.

I rose and crossed the room to stand in front of the window for a better view of the hills.

"Play something happy, Ennie," Jewelee's sweet voice echoed her older brother's.

Happiness was not my childhood or my future. Still, I forced my memory to return to the evening I'd turned sixteen and turned from my endless view of the ocean to see the look of forever in Brody's eyes.

My first draw of the bow was the saddest and longest note that I had ever played.

"Happy," Brody reminded me.

How could I leave here tomorrow on my own accord? How could I willingly leave this little hamlet that had captured my heart? Instead of Misery, I forced my memory up the

Cashmere Hills and knew that my stay in Corra would be the most beautiful music of my days.

Chapter Twenty-two

Brody and I did not take off the next morning as we'd earlier discussed because his mother had changed his mind. Margaret wanted to make us a special going-away meal of fish and chips. So instead of leaving Corra, Brody and the men were going shark fishing.

Margaret poured pancake batter onto the hot greased griddle. "The cakes will help settle the men's tummies for when they cross the bar into the deep sea," she informed me.

"Deep sea?" I murmured, picturing Brody at the helm through giant swells.

"Yes, for shark."

"Shark?"

When bubbles formed on the surface of the cakes, I slid the spatula underneath and flipped them.

"Yes, shark meat is best for my fish and chips."

"What are ya girls doing today, Mum?" Brody asked, setting his burly arms on top of the table.

"Women's work, nothing special." Margaret set a bowl of fresh raspberries on the table.

"Mum's taking Ennie down to the swamp to pick berries," Jewelee said. She stood on a chair beside me near the stove.

Perhaps, it would be more exciting to go fishing with the men. Would they invite me?

"Why the swamp, Mum?" Brody asked.

"No special reason."

"What kind of berries?" Brody's gaze remained fixed on his mother.

Margaret opened the oven and set a spatula full of pancakes on a pan inside to keep them warm.

"Mum! What kind of berries?" His tone was unusually firm.

"Tis the season for nangoonberry jelly."

"Not this year. It's not a good idea."

"The nangoonberries are ripe for the picking." She laughed lightheartedly and carried a pitcher of warmed honey to the table.

Head bowed, Brody rubbed the back of his neck.

Perhaps, there were snakes amidst the bushes. Or perhaps, the bushes were prickly. As always he appeared concerned for my safety.

Trev puffed out his chest. "There's an old nangoonberry ledg—"

Margaret rocked the point of her boot down on her husband's toe before she stepped away from the table.

Maybe there was a steep ledge.

"Is nangoonberry picking dangerous?" I asked.

"No, not necessarily," Trev said.

"Are they poisonous?" I knew some berries were.

"No, Ennie. Nangoonberries are just a lot of hard work." Brody's chest rose. "I don't want ya picking them with my mum."

I smiled back at him. I knew shark fishing was a lot of work, too, but I didn't argue with him.

We saw the men off at the docks, and I waved until their boat was just a dot on the sea. I wondered if it would be the last time I'd ever see Brody. I worried about him now, and it wasn't only because of the kiss. Or was it? I sighed, measuring the ache inside me. No, I worried about him with my heart and soul.

ΦΦΦ

"Now, Ennie . . ." Margaret whispered over her shoulder as we trekked through thick, scratchy brush into a gully-like area. "This is where I usually find nangoonberries. It will take at least a half-gallon of the berries to make the jelly. So it will take time, love. But the jelly will be ever so special. Not only will Brody love it, he will love ya for it."

"I've never had nangoonberry jelly." Today was also the first time I'd heard about it.

In the bottom of the basin, Margaret set her bucket down and hunching over, scanned the ground for something. I followed her lead and searched on my knees. But unlike her, I didn't know what I was looking for.

"There's a little jewel," she whispered. Pointing, she bid me closer to her vantage point on the ground. She behaved as if the berry were alive and might slip away upon hearing us.

"See." She plucked one, the size of a small raspberry, off a single-stemmed plant that stood no more than a foot off the ground. Shoulders touching, we marveled at the wine red berry in the center of her palm. "Don't eat any, love. It will take thousands of these to make Brody's jelly."

"May I try one?" I eyed the pretty little berry.

She shook her head. "They're just sweet enough that it's best if ya don't even try a one. Remember, it takes thousands of them. Nangoonberry jelly is a labor of love, it is."

I knelt down. Six feet away from me, I spied my first berry. On my hands and knees, I plucked it free of the plant. When Margaret wasn't looking, I popped it into my mouth. The berry was packed with a tarty-sweet juice. I believed Odessa and Edwin would enjoy nangoonberry picking; it was like going on a treasure hunt.

I spotted my next prize and popped it into my mouth, instead of my bucket.

"Remember, my bucket is for my family and your bucket is for Brody's jelly," Margaret said. "Tonight, I will make scones for dessert, and Brody will have his with fresh whipped cream and *yer* nangoonberry jelly. He will love ya for it."

The next berry that I picked, I forced myself to pop it inside my pail instead of my mouth. The berry bounced, making a delightful sound on the bottom of the bucket and I caught a hint of a smile in Margaret's profile. I would at least pop every other berry into the pail.

By the time I could no longer see the bottom of my bucket, the sun had climbed high in the sky and beat warmly upon our backs. Fortunately, I'd worn one of Margaret's wide-brimmed hats.

"Nangoonberry picking is like waiting for yer first child to be born, a labor of love it is," Margaret said.

What was she talking about? I glanced over at her.

"Work on filling your bucket, Ennie, or we'll be out here until dark."

My picking became more focused. For the next hour, I did not pop one berry into my mouth; all of the berries went straight into the bucket. Nangoonberry jelly must be very special for all the work we were putting into it. I hoped Brody would love it.

I soon lost track of Margaret. While I searched the area for her, I spotted a wide-girth man standing near the top of the gully. Although he whittled a large stick in his hand, I felt certain he was watching us.

"Margaret." I spotted her on the other side of a nearby thicket. When she looked over at me, I nodded toward the man on the hill. "Who is he?"

She turned to look. "No one to be afraid of. That's just Niles, Brody's school chum. Brody asked him to watch over us today while we're picking. My son can't even go fishing without worrying about ya." She smiled.

"How is your picking coming along, love?" With a lift of her chin, she eyed my bucket.

Only half an inch of berries covered the bottom of the pail.

"Why couldn't God have made nangoonberries bigger?" I asked.

"God made precious things tiny like nangoonberries, diamonds and... babies."

From diamonds to babies had been quite the leap. How disappointed would she be when she found out who I really was?

"Nangoonberry picking is a labor of love, it is," Margaret said again, her voice wistful.

Though my knees and back ached, I brainwashed myself with her sentiments: *Brody will love it. Brody will love me for it.* For the next couple of hours, while I picked, my heart remembered the night of my birthday and Brody's later sentiments—*I will go to my grave loving her.* I hoped he wouldn't go to his grave while shark fishing. I paused from berry picking to peer out over the vast gray sea and whisper a prayer on his behalf.

ΦΦΦ

We spent the rest of the afternoon in the warm kitchen. Then Margaret, the younger children, and I walked down to the wharf to wait for the return of the men's fishing vessel. The sun was setting as their boat drew near, and sea gulls flew behind them. Cupping a hand over my eyes, I spotted Brody onboard, and my heart leaped. With his windswept hair and sturdy build, he belonged here at the sea, with his family and the people that he loved.

Shark meat made the best fish and chips. After the delicious dinner, the time came for dessert and the unveiling of my day's work. Strangely, I was nervous as I'd felt my first time on stage singing for the giants.

Margaret set a plate of homemade scones and freshly whipped cream on the table. Following her nod, I set before Brody the small glass bowl of the nangoonberry jelly. After many hours of simmering on the stove, the berries I'd picked had amounted to less than a quarter cup of preserves. All the same, Margaret was pleased with my day's work.

I sat down, kitty corner from Brody, and folded my arms on top of the table. My stomach was a knot of nervous energy.

"Get the chair! Mrs. Campbell has it," Margaret murmured to Lydie.

"I told ya, Mum, I don't think this a good idea." Brody glanced at me before taking a golden brown scone from the top of the pile. "You didn't really make the jelly for me?"

"You are not to touch another thing until Lydie returns with the chair." Margaret waved a bossy finger.

"Mum." Brody sighed heavily, glancing at me.

I was greatly puzzled by the events of the day and the way he was acting.

Margaret paused in the doorway, watching the front room window. "Don't touch a thing; Lydie's almost here."

The door clicked open and closed. Flush cheeked and smiling, Lydie carried in a short stool that looked like it belonged in a torture chamber. Thousands of pins, maybe needles, had been driven vertically through the wood with the prickly side up to sit on.

"I'm sorry, Ennie. It's an odd West Coast tradition continued by the matriarchs," Brody said, casting his mother a glum look.

"What is that for?" I swallowed, staring at the infinite points of the stool.

"You have to sit on it." Lydie motioned for me to get up, so she could set it in my chair. "So yer sitting on pins and needles while Brody eats yer jelly. Here, I'll show ya." She slowly sat down on it and swallowed, wide-eyed. "Ya won't want to move around much," she said.

"What's the tradition for? What does it prove?" I asked, and because everyone was waiting, I slowly sat down on the stool of pins. It was prickly and, like Lydie had said, I didn't want to move around much.

"The tradition proves whether ya love my son," Margaret said with a lift of her chin.

"I know how she feels about me, Mum." Brody sighed and shook his head. "She doesn't need to go through this. It isn't right."

Did he truly know my feelings for him? Did he? I stared at Brody.

"Well . . ." Trev finally interrupted, "anyone can tell ya that the test is more for yer future mother-in-law than the groom." He chuckled. Under Margaret's stern gaze, he cleared his throat.

"I don't understand." Uncomfortable in the chair, I leaned slightly to my left. Already the stool of pins had got its points into me, and I wanted whatever was at hand to get going.

Brody took my discomfort as his cue to slather the precious thimbleful of jelly on his biscuit and top it with the billowy whipped cream. The table quieted, and we all watched as the scone bearing the translucent red jelly neared his lips.

Margaret clutched her hands in front of her.

Brody swallowed and swished his mouth around as the scone neared his lips. Then he lowered his arm to the table, looking at me. "Are ya sure ya made it for me?"

"Who am I staring at, Brody Hew?" I heaved a befuddled smile. "I made it for you and you alone." I sighed, recalling all the work I'd poured into this small decadence of which even I was deprived a taste.

"Did Mum tell ya that now ya just have to sit and watch me eat it all, all yer hard work?" His gaze was as soft as my mother's velvet robe that I used to wrap round about myself. "Did my mum tell ya that?" His eyes were the richest hazel hue.

"Aye, she did." While I'd stirred the jelly on the stovetop, she'd softly warned me that I could not even dab a drop on my tongue.

I smiled across the table at Margaret. "You didn't tell me the waiting would be so painful."

"Like yer first child waiting to be born, a labor of love it is."

"Did Mum tell ya that nangoonberry jelly is an old wives' tale?" Brody asked. "A tradition along the West Coast to see what kind of—"

"I'm sitting here on pins and needles waiting for you to taste my jelly." I stared at him. "Tell me it's good, Brody. Tell me it's the best jelly you've ever tasted."

"Awh . . ." Lydie crossed her hands above her heart. "It's my first time witnessing the nangoonberry . . ." Her voice faded under her mother's stern gaze.

Brody's chest expanded beneath his cambric shirt. With a heavy sigh, he finally took his first bite. He chewed, and taking his own sweet time, swallowed. With one eye open, he smiled at me—a soft, lazy smile. He took another bite, chewed and twisted his mouth around for every last bit of the morsel.

"It is the best, most heavenly jelly that I will ever have the privilege of tasting." A mist filled his eyes as he softly gazed into mine.

"You must finish it all," Margaret said, firmly.

We watched as he slowly completed the task. After Brody had captured and devoured the last crumb, his family turned to stare at me. Narrowing their gaze, they stared intently at me, like George when he'd painted my portrait.

"What? What are you looking at?" I felt like the sun must with all the planets orbiting around it. And then under their gaze, I felt a tingling sensation inch its way up my neck and over my jaw to settle warmly beneath the curve of my left cheekbone. Whatever was happening, its prick was similar to that of a smallpox inoculation. My left eye fluttered open and closed while I waited for the sting to end.

"There it is." Margaret lifted a hand to her mouth. "There it is. Do ya see it?"

"I see it, Mummy . . . I see it!" Mouth agape, Jewelee stared.

"See what? What is it?" I asked. My face felt altogether too warm.

"Aye, there it is." Trev leaned toward me in his chair, studying my cheek. "As clear as day."

Brody stared at me, pale and unblinking.

Whatever was on my face, was it something bad?

"Follow me." Margaret rose, took my arm, and walked me into the front room. She stopped in front of the oval mirror above her mother's bureau. I turned slightly to survey my left cheek, where the warmth had taken up residence. A bright reddish-hue, the color of a nangoonberry, stained a wide swath of my cheek. The crescent moon shape followed the curve of the bone clear to the side of my nose.

"It's the nangoonberry mark of a bride-to-be," Margaret gushed. "The sign of unforgettable love. And, it will stay there until the day ya are wed." With her hands clasped against her heart, Margaret gazed lovingly at me.

"Till the day I'm wed?" My voice wavered.

"Yes, love, till the day Brody and you are wed."

Chapter Twenty-three

I returned to the kitchen. Thankfully, the pins-and-needles stool had been removed from my chair. I sat down and stared at Brody.

What did it all mean?

"I tried to . . ." He set his chin on top of his fist, returning my gaze. "Not in a million years did I think that ya'd…"

"She worked hard all day, and not once did she complain, all so ya could have a biscuit-worth of jelly," Margaret said. "The sign of a very good bride."

"Ya love me." He took a sharp intake of air. "Ya really love me."

"Brody, it's been etched on her face since ya first arrived. But that's right, love is blind," Trev said.

"Love is blind to faults, not to love itself," Margaret said.

"Ya love me." Eyes wide and unblinking, Brody gripped my hand.

"Yes. Yes, I do." I nodded, giving into the moment and what could never be.

"Ya love me, Ennie." Tears filled his eyes, and then I watched as his mind marched up Misery Hill. I knew where his thoughts were going, and I was already ahead of him, waiting at the top.

If we ran away together, we'd be forever on the run. Fugitives from both our families. Although I knew that I would lose both Corra and Blue Sky when I married into Davenport, I could not let that happen to Brody.

We stared at one another.

We could never be. Yet, the irony was, we already were.

And, no one could take that away from us.

The soldier in him blinked, and a somber clarity entered his gaze. "What are we going to do, Ennie?"

"Ya ask her to marry ya, son." His father beamed. "It's easy. Ya get down on one knee. Go ahead, right now."

"Ask her, Brody; we're all waiting." His mother gripped her hands above the pockets of her apron.

"Not now, Mum." His Adam's apple bobbed.

"Diamonds before babies," Margaret said.

"For once, son, yer mother is right. You've had the look of knot-tying ever since the two of ya arrived."

Brody watched me and shook his head.

"We're leaving in the morning, Mum. I need to meet her sis and family."

"No, the two of ya can't be traveling alone together. Not now. Not with the Nangoonberry stain and that look of diamonds in your eyes." His mother fanned a hand in front of her face.

Tears were close. All this happiness and heartbreak.

A knock sounded on the front door. We had not heard anyone approach. Like everyone else at the table, our focus had been on Brody.

"I'll get it. Wait till I'm back to say another word." Trev rose to his feet and left the kitchen.

In his absence, I sighed and wiped at my eyes.

"What in the world?" Trev uttered in the front room.

"What is it, Dad?" Pinning his legs beneath the table, Brody leaned back in his chair. Then eyes wide, he rocked his chair down.

"Is this the home of Brody Hew?" I heard the soft lilt of the Blue Sky accent.

Rising from my chair, I stopped beside Brody in the middle of the doorway.

In uniform, my father and two of his men stood in the Hews' front room. Lean and haggard, my father looked worse than when he'd returned from war.

His gaze locked on me.

"Wren," he whispered.

Chapter Twenty-four

A legion of Blue Sky soldiers on horseback surrounded the Hews' little, love-filled home. Through the front and back windows, our guards in their blue-and-white uniforms were a sharp contrast against Margaret's pink roses.

I began to shake. Just like Crauley had said, I had caused my parents pain.

"What's going on here?" Father asked.

Margaret squeezed past us through the doorway into the front room.

Trev asked before she could, "Now, this is my home. I'm the one to ask what's going on here." He turned to regard Brody. "What's going on here? Are ya in some kind of trouble, son?"

"Wren," Father said my name again, louder this time.

I stepped away from Brody toward my father and inhaled deeply. I'd faced the giants. I'd faced Margaret, a woman who would do anything to protect her son; and now, it was time to face my father.

I paused halfway across the room. "I'm ready to go home now." I summoned the speech I had practiced a thousand times. "And, I'm very sorry for any pain I've caused you." I didn't want my future to be a Davenport. "But, I cannot fulfill the marriage you've aligned for our country." I inhaled deeply. "I'm sorry, Father, but—"

"That's enough, Wren. The arrangement has been made." He exhaled a rumpled breath. "Now, say goodbye to these good people."

I gulped.

"Too bad you didn't just tie her up and haul her home," Father said, staring at Brody. "Instead, the two of you appear to have run away together."

"Margaret, and, Trev," I held out my hand, "meet my father, King Francis II of Blue Sky," I added, spoiling our little party.

Their countenance paled further before they bowed.

A child's whimper interrupted the silence. "Brody was going to ask Ennie something very important," Jewelee said. Tugging on Trev's shirt tail, she gazed up at him.

"Then I got here at the right time," my father said. His gaze settled on the stain upon my cheek. "Wren, it's time to leave."

While I stepped further and further away from the man that I loved, I began to worry for his life. "I have one wish, Father, one request." I dropped in front of him, hugging the his leather boots.

"Stand up, Wren," he mumbled under his breath.

"I owe Brody my life. Please spare his." I sobbed.

My father lifted me up by my armpits until I was standing. I could see in the dark depths of his hazel eyes that he wanted to shake me; instead, he gripped me firmly.

"In keeping you safe, he has served the crown. Because of him, we were able to find you." He turned his gaze to Brody. "The blue strips were clever; but, you are still dismissed from service for one year. If you are seen anywhere in Davenport or Blue Sky, you will die a traitor's death."

Trev sucked in a deep breath.

"Oh, dear, dear, dear . . ." Margaret clasped a hand to her mouth.

I stared. *Blue strips. Did he mean strips of cloth?*

"You are to report back to service, September of next year," Father added.

"Yes, King Francis. Thank you," Brody said his gaze downcast. "Lydie, get Ennie's things. Jewelee, find her viola," he said.

Though they were in shock, the girls hurried about the house.

Still clutching my arm, Father started for the door.

"Goodbye, Trev." I had to blink aside tears to see him clearly.

"Goodbye." He didn't blink as he patted my arm.

"Goodbye, Margaret . . ." I managed a sorry smile.

Even Margaret, with all her clever sayings, was at a loss for words. Her thin lips formed a straight line while she shook her head.

"Goodbye, Scott. Goodbye, Moira, be a good girl," I whispered each child's name as I numbed myself to leave.

"Goodbye, Brody," I inhaled deeply, meeting his solemn gaze.

Father escorted me out of the house.

Brody hadn't even say *goodbye*. After everything we'd been through, that couldn't be how we ended.

Near the sparkling white gate, where Margaret's rugosa roses spilled their perfume, I saw a strip of blue cloth tied to the picket fence. Strips of a soldier's uniform, a Blue Sky blue. How many times had I walked by and not noticed? Had he left strips at all of our stops between here and Gruel Kitchen?

I'd fallen in love with a soldier fiercely loyal to his king. What could easily feel like betrayal only confirmed to me his heart. *All for King.*

Only twenty minutes before, he'd gazed across the table at me. *Ya love me*, he'd whispered. *Ya really love me.*

The girls caught up to us with my things.

"Thank you, Lydie." I gazed into her thirteen-year-old eyes and prayed that I had not been too large of an influence on her adventurous soul.

"Thank you, Jewelee." I patted her head of curls, and tried to rally other sentiments; but, like everyone else, I was in shock.

Father slid my viola case into his saddle bags, and then he boosted me up onto his horse to sit like a man, stationing himself behind me. It was useless to argue with him. Besides, I didn't want to sit sidesaddle, for it would have meant seeing his face. I tucked the old school uniform beneath the sides of my legs and tried to appear as proper as possible.

I blinked aside the tears that stung my eyes. I wanted to see everything one last time: the Hew family standing behind their gate; the tidy homes that lined the streets of the town; and the cliffs that through the centuries had been carved by the crashing tide. I filled my lungs with the salty air. This little village that I had fallen in love with at first sight would be the haven of my heart, and was even now as my world came crashing down.

While our army crested the Cashmere Hills, I knew the green velvet would be the material of my life's fondest memories. Tears dripped down my cheeks and splashed onto Father's forearms, but I did not weep.

Over my shoulder, I saw Brody on foot, scrambling up the hillside behind us. I held my hair away from my face, hoping for another glimpse of him.

"Father, may I please say goodbye?"

He shook his head. "I forgot how much you look like your mother." He sighed heavily behind me. "The spitting image of her."

Had he ever said that to me before?

"You loved Mother before marriage. I will not be so fortunate."

"Wren . . ." The break in his voice was in sync with the lull of the crashing waves. "You haven't even met Vincent yet."

"I have met the man that I love, and I owe him my life." A sob escaped me. "Please, let me say goodbye."

He inhaled deeply, his chest pressing into my back before he slowly brought his thoroughbred to a halt. "Promise me you will not throw yourselves off the cliff."

"No-oo! To do so would be wrong with God."

He inhaled and nodded. "Then you may say goodbye."

I slid off.

Father remained on horseback and followed me while I walked through our legion of men toward Brody.

It was love's coincidence that Brody and I should stand in the same spot as the night of my sixteenth birthday. Father halted twenty strides back, too far for him to hear, even if the wind should carry our words.

I walked toward Brody, my gaze locked on his. I knew him. I knew the contents of his heart and had found myself there.

"I forgive you," was my greeting.

He wiped his left eye with one hand. Lowering his chin, he looked at me. "After the nangoonberry jelly, I was granted one wish," he shook his head, "and I have used it up to say goodbye. But, I don't think I could have gone on if we hadn't."

My left hand, which seemed to have a will of its own, lifted to his cheek. Even though my father was watching, Brody leaned softly into my touch. The wind ruffled the top of his hair as I tried to memorize everything about him.

His wide, high cheekbones, his hazel eyes, the little nick of a scar in his dark brows...

"Ennie."

The way his voice ached when he said my name.

"You have shown me the sea, the love of family, and… *happiness*." I managed to say the word without breaking. For so long I had held back my words, afraid of my feelings. Now words were all I had to give him.

"Please don't only play sad." He rested his cheek against my hand. "I can't bear to think of ya only playing sad. In yer future, remember Corra."

"Our memories will only cause me pain." I knew it already.

"That's where yer wrong. Ya hang onto the good for the hard times ahead." He cleared his throat. "I wanted it with all my heart, Ennie . . ." he shook his head, and I dropped my hand, "but, we could never be." Our goodbye had officially begun, and the soldier in him stood taller now.

"You're wrong. We were." With this insight, I smiled up at him. "No one can take that away from us."

One last time, I lifted my hand to his cheek. "I will never forget you, Brody Hew." I meant it with all of my heart. With that, I returned to Father.

Chapter Twenty-five

If I ever see my sister Odessa again, my advice to her would be: when you turn sixteen, don't kiss your father's guard.

I kept waiting for Father to say, *no more tears, no more tears*.

But he didn't.

In view of the sea, we stopped for the night and camped. Following a dinner of biscuits and beans, we sat by the fire. In its light, Father gripped my chin and studied the stain.

Afraid to meet his gaze, I focused on the gray stubble on his cheek. The firelight lit half his face as bright as daylight, and I know it did the same for mine. He called over Larkin, the army doctor.

"What is the remedy for the nangoonberry stain?" Father asked.

The wiry, middle-aged man studied me, clucked his tongue against the roof of his mouth and sighed. "I haven't seen a lot of cases. It's mainly a West Coast malady here, where the berry grows. But, the only remedy I've heard of that works is… marriage."

"Marriage?" Father said.

"Yes, to the man she made the jelly for. From the looks of it, King Wells, your daughter has a most difficult case." Dr. Larkin touched his forefinger softly to my cheek. "You see, the deeper the shade of red, the deeper the stain. The deeper the stain, the deeper the love."

"We could camouflage it somehow with skin tone paint," Father said.

"It's worth a try. But, in the end, I've always heard that honesty is best."

"This marriage is in lieu of war, Doctor. I don't think showing up in Davenport with a nangoonberry stain on my daughter's face is a good political move. Do you?"

Dr. Larkin scratched his neck. "Teens often surprise their parents." He lapsed into a crooked smile. "Look at the bright side," he patted Father's shoulder, "your next daughter will be easier, for she's seen the pain that this one's put you through."

I had not put Father through any pain, only inconvenience.

"Raising daughters is the same as going to war, except you have even less control over the outcome," Father said. It hadn't helped that he'd been away at war while I'd been growing up.

With a seafoam sponge, the doctor dabbed some army paint on my cheek and then stepped back, waiting for it to dry.

Father grimaced. "The stain's even darker in an ugly sort of way."

"I think so, too." Dr. Larkin wet the other side of the sponge and gently washed it off.

ΦΦΦ

The next morning, Father sat across from me in the royal carriage and stared glumly at my stain.

"How is Odessa?" I asked, hoping to break his pensive silence.

"She's hurting. Your actions have caused great pain for her, your mother... Maid Kimberlee. Everyone who knows you cares about your well-being." He shifted his gaze to look out the window.

"And the twin?" I asked, knowing I should have clarified.

"Edwin misses you, also."

"And Odessa's true twin—my other sister." My heartbreak had left me tactless and unafraid of Father.

He inhaled deeply and looked out over the craggy cliffs that lined the coastline. "How long have you known?"

"I witnessed her birth. I saw the exchange. I saw it all." I swallowed hot, bitter tears.

"There's been a price to all of your eavesdropping."

"Yes, there has." I agreed. "I waited, Father, for what felt like hours, and then I heard a baby's cry. Little did I know that it was someone else's baby." Hot tears burned my throat while I waited for Father to explain the unforgivable.

"Edwin is Edwin Senior's boy. I talked with him about the possibility beforehand."

"Edwin Hew?"

"Yes, I thought having his son on the throne might help ease his spirits in the loss of his legs. And, the doctor had already informed me that your mother should have no more children. That I might lose her if we tried again for a son."

Brody's nephew would be the future king of Blue Sky, and I might not ever be able to tell him.

"Edwin and his wife have taken very good care of Elaina, your sister," Father said her name with loving inflection.

I bit my knuckles, stifling a sob. Father voicing my sister's name with such tenderness, shredded my insides. I gazed out the window and dwelled on her beautiful name. *Elaina.*

"Are the girls identical?" I asked.

"No." He laughed softly. "Out of you four girls, Laynie, as they've nicknamed her, looks the most like my side of the family. She is a lovely combination of her three sisters, and she has the gift. Perhaps, it is a blessing that she and Odessa have not grown up together."

Odessa was beautiful, but I knew what Father meant. She already found it difficult being the first of the girls not to have the gift, much less growing up with a twin sister who did.

"And in Edwin junior's absence from their lives, Edwin Senior and his wife, Jessie, have been blessed with two more boys."

"They will always long for the one they don't have." I knew from my own longing that it was human nature. They would always long for Edwin, their son—a prince and future king.

"Yes." Father nodded. "We love most what we cannot have."

Had he said it for himself or me?

"Elaina is a very determined one like her father... and you, Wren." His gaze locked on mine. "Why did you run away?"

Crauley had not told him because he was no longer among the living. I swallowed a knot of emotion.

"I wanted to see Alia one more time before I'm married." My admonition spurred tears.

"It's too late for that now, isn't it?" Father's lips pursed into a thin, straight line. "You should have told us. We would have given you the world if you'd only asked."

"I did ask."

"Not enough for me to know how desperately important it was to you."

I couldn't believe him; I had seen too much betrayal. What he said couldn't possibly be true. They were only words.

Chapter Twenty-six

Three days later, we stopped in an obscure little town called Cliffton. With the hood of my cloak over my head, Father escorted me inside a hostel. After a warm bath had been drawn for me, I was left alone. Today, I would meet my future husband. I undressed from the school girl attire, bathed, and changed into a long, soft blue gown, new for the occasion. The sleeves fit snug to the elbow and from there, frilled out like petals of a flower in bloom. Without my consent, my mother had given into her splash for fashion.

Iridescent pearl buttons lined the high neck and bodice. Had she been given the chance, Pearl might have made her own wedding pillow from this dress. Even though I still questioned my friend's motives, my mood lightened as I recalled our time together.

I dried my hair in front of the fire in the hearth and then rolled it into a high bun as mother would have deemed appropriate for the occasion.

In an aged mirror, I gazed sadly at my reflection. Following the curve of my cheekbone, I traced my fingers over the nangoonberry stain. The stain exposed my heart.

In my absence, our soldiers—all two hundred of our men—had changed from their soiled uniforms into bright white-and-blue. Their procession on horseback would prove a strong contrast against the mossy green, craggy hillsides of Davenport.

"Wear your hair down," Father said, sitting across from me in the carriage. "Up like that, it only draws attention to the stain." The corner of his mouth twitched.

My heart's scar was more visible than most.

While we rode through the downtown streets of Davenport, Father moved across the aisle to sit beside me. "Do not let any of your future countrymen see the stain," he said.

I pulled the hooded cloak over the left side of my face.

From the same window, we viewed the expansive port city that stretched for several kilometers along the coast and bustled with commerce. Factories and mills lined the waterfront; massive sailing ships the harbor, and pedestrians the boardwalks. The people stopped and stared at the arrival of our entourage. No welcome was in their eyes.

With the cloak half hiding my face, I stared back.

There were two sides to Davenport. On the factory side of the street, the townspeople wore as somber of clothing as when I'd worked in Gruel Kitchen. Quaint shops lined the opposite side, and the pedestrians' clothing was expensive and finely tailored. I noticed the women's most—hoop skirts, layers of petticoats, complete with reticule and parasol.

"There is no middle class," I whispered.

"No, I'm afraid not. You are marrying into wealth—the richest city in Northend. Before the war, Blue Sky used to be the wealthiest. Now, Davenport with its steel industry and exports is years ahead of us. The new railway will help   us all."

I was indeed a valuable commodity in my Father's eyes.

I gazed sadly out the window. My view eventually changed from tightly packed buildings and busy streets to farmland and hills off in the distance.

We rode in silence for several miles.

"Stockford needs your attention, Father," I said.

Our carriage began to climb. The road was narrow and rocky, with switchbacks up the craggy green hills.

"I know, it's been brought to my attention," he said and pointed out the window on my side of the carriage. "There," off in the distance, a gray stone castle was built into the side of cliffs lining the deep blue waters of the bay, "the von Drake's." Three turrets with pointed roofs reached for the sky. Sailing vessels dotted the harbor, and a modern looking bridge crossed the ravine to the fortress's doorstep.

My future inched closer, and there was nothing I could do about it, but feel sick.

God has a plan for you.

Pearl's verse had been so much more comforting than mine. Could it possibly be that the elderly woman had intended the same verse for me?

Father and I bumped shoulders as the carriage jostled over the rutted road.

"Milton spent a sizeable fortune on his steel suspension bridge," he said.

"It doesn't look like a very good military design to me," I peered over the edge of the steep hillside to the castle up the coastline.

"You're observant. The bridge is an open invitation for trouble."

"I meant the castle, itself," I admitted.

"It's more strategic in design than meets the eye. There are hidden passageways. Some go all the way down to the sea, where their navy is stationed."

"How do you know?" I asked.

"I have my spies."

Of course, he did, I was marrying the enemy.

I hoped Father would align Odessa's marriage with an ally, for her sake.

"The nangoonberry stain will prove a problem for us." He frowned.

Father's admittance knocked boulders loose from the rock wall inside my belly. My love for Brody, so visible on my face, would not be a great start for my marriage. I had to think about Vincent now, as I was only a few minutes away from meeting the man.

"Most likely, the von Drakes are aware of the folklore that runs up and down this coast. We can pray that they are understanding people and will overlook the stain."

Oddly enough, I found myself in agreement with Father.

ΦΦΦ

Father and I, accompanied by ten of our guards, walked across an immense, steel footbridge over a very deep ravine to Davenport Castle. It was a good thing I was not afraid of heights, for the von Drakes' home, situated on a cliff, had towering views of land and sea.

"Most of their wealth has come from shipping and steel," Father said as he pointed overhead to the cables. "Articles have been written all over the world about its design. But tell me, Wren, why build a bridge with a road like that?"

I agreed; the road traveled was not very welcoming.

A tall, elderly doorman greeted us and pulled a cord that must have rung a bell inside the castle, for it made no noise in the immediate vicinity.

While we waited for the royal family, I peered around. My future in-laws were very fond of gold—both the element and the color. The chandeliers were gold. The furniture was inlaid with gold. The seams of their furniture, the fringe on the pillows, lampshades and drapes were gold.

In the white marble corridor off to our right, Queen Mary approached. Even from a distance, I knew that the threads of her royal clothing and the locket about her neck were gold. Pure gold.

Her gown was fitted at her expansive waist, and she wore a round crinoline cage. In my mother's opinion, the hoop skirt had been out of fashion for over six years and replaced by the smaller crinolette, which I presently wore. Mary's silvery-gray hair was cropped short at the neck in a boyish cut. She nodded briefly in our direction and then dismissed the doorman. Without a word, she led us straight ahead through the wide corridor. On our left was the ballroom, with arched windows overlooking the sea.

"That's an elevator," Father whispered, nodding to a wide steel door on our right.

I'd never been on an elevator and held no desire to change that.

On the next span of wall was a floor-to-ceiling painting of Queen Mary, younger and less portly.

"The library is more intimate and less drafty," she said, while we followed her up a winding marble stairwell.

"Irene, my wife, sends her regards." Father cleared his unusually raspy voice. "I have not been home for a spell; otherwise, I would have brought her letter and gifts."

"I look forward to them on your next visit." Her voice was pleasant, if not sweet. At the top of the stairs, she took a left in the wide corridor.

My stomach knotted tighter with each step. I had disappointed my parents, made things more difficult than they should have been. But in the end, I wouldn't trade my memories of Brody for the world. I breathed deeply and rested in this epiphany.

Mary's hand rested on the knob of a dark, six-paneled door.

Despite my convictions, my stomach was in knots.

"Milton will be pleased that you are *finally* here," Mary said, opening the door. The room was wide and only a few strides deep. The shelves lining the far wall were filled with books and a varied collection of sitting ducks.

"King Francis and his daughter have arrived," Queen Mary said.

Upon her announcement, two men rose from wing backed chairs situated to the right of the doorway.

"Are you a day late, or were my speculations a day early?" King Milton, a wiry built man with silvering curly hair and a noticeable stoop, addressed Father.

"I'm afraid we are a day late." Father set a hand on my lower back, ushering me deeper into the room.

My gaze narrowed to Vincent. He was simply a younger version of his Father. His hair was curly and dark, almost black, and his eyes were a slate gray.

"Vincent, meet King Francis II, and your betrothed, Princess Wren." King Milton's deep voice reminded me of a foghorn in the gray of morning.

Vincent lifted his chin and with his arms folded in front of him, studied me. "I'd hoped your hair would be golden in color, not red," were his first words to me.

"We've raised our sons to be honest and forthright," said his mother. While she fanned her face, I waited for Vincent to survey mine.

"Sons? I was aware of only one," my father said.

"We have three boys. Our younger two are away at boarding school in France," Milton interjected with a roll of his eyes.

I glanced at the ducks sitting on the nearby shelves. They were either well trained or dead. On closer inspection, their posture was unnaturally stiff, and their plumage needed to be dusted. Instead of pictures, dusty ducks—with their wings spread—adorned the walls.

The art form of taxidermy was new to me. I'd heard stories about it, but this was my first time seeing mounted specimens. I found them more interesting than my future husband.

A square grand piano with lavishly carved legs and case sat on the far right side of the room beneath tall arched windows.

"I'd hoped your skin would be flawless." Vincent's gaze had locked on my stain.

"I understand your disappointment," I said, politely.

"I hope that's not what I think it is." Queen Mary took a closer look at me. "The nangoonberry stain. Not a good start. Not a good start, at all."

"What are you talking about, Mary?" King Milton studied me with a wide, toothy grin before his gaze narrowed to the stain. "Looks like you've spent a little too long on the West Coast before you got here."

"Ten days." Father nodded and rocked heel to toe in his fine leather boots.

"The West Coasters are fond of their berries," Milton said, holding his mouth pursed as he nodded.

Father managed a light chuckle, and then he sat down on a paisley upholstered couch with gold stitching. I followed his lead and sat a few feet away from him.

A servant poured dark coffee for us and handed each of us a cup without asking our preferences.

"I'd hoped your eyes would be pure blue." Vincent regarded me from where he sat in the high back chair, six feet away, one knee crossed over the other.

"They are blue-green." Chin lifted, I swallowed.

"I'd hoped they'd be more of a *blue-sky* color."

I disliked my future husband.

"And I wished you played the piano, instead of the violin." Vincent's honest wishes continued.

"Viola," I corrected him.

"Oh, how unfortunate. We already have one of the best violists in the world residing here in Davenport." Mary said, fanning herself.

I wondered if his name was Lambert.

"Father, there's something I'd like to speak with you about," Vincent said.

"Now is not the time," Milton said, turning to me. "The Queen of Nearton said that you were a concert piano-ist. That she saw you play when you were a young child. You couldn't even reach your feet to the pedals, but you played like you were Beethoven."

"I no longer play piano," I said and inhaled deeply.

"Wha-aat?" Vincent laughed, glancing at his mother.

Mary's jaw hung so slack it appeared to touch the extravagant gold locket that she wore. "We bought the rosewood Chickering from America, just for you." She glanced toward the square grand piano.

"I'm sorry. I no longer play." Hoping to change the subject, I focused on Vincent. Like Beethoven, he had a cleft chin and broody eyes. He was nice enough looking, but he was not my Brody.

"I'd hoped your hair would be auburn and your eyes hazel, not gray," I said, inspired by his honesty.

"Wrrr-een!" Father groaned, and like Helmer had so often done, he covered his eyes with one hand.

"I'd hoped you'd be taller and have a mole right here, not a..." Vincent's voice trailed off as he swished a finger near his left cheekbone. I noted a dagger-like gleam in his eyes. I had to be careful. He was trying to get me to describe Brody to a T so he might threaten him, maybe even kill him.

"I'd hoped you'd be nine feet tall," I said. Vincent was six feet at most.

"I've heard about your escapades, how your father spent months searching for you, and how you're fond of giants." His dark eyes flashed. "I was hoping you'd have a voice as soft as silk and a dash of freckles right here." He swished a finger over his nose.

His wishes were concise, if not particular. "I do have a dash of freckles." If this was his style of diplomacy, Davenport did not have a bright future.

"I wish you had only nine fingers, and that your hair was a mop of tight, kinky curls." I'd, of course, described Remford. I could think of no one finer to pay the punishment for my stain.

"Go!" Vincent pointed toward the double doors. With his gaze locked on one of their guards, he bellowed, "Take ten of our strongest men and bring me back a nine-foot giant with a mop of kinky, tight auburn curls and only nine fingers. Dead or alive."

I dropped to my knees on the Turkish carpet in front of him and feigned great agony. "No! What will you do with him?" I sobbed. "What will you do?"

"We shall see." He breathed. "We shall see."

"Get up, Wren," Father said, sternly.

My future husband was a fool. I rose to my feet and returned to the sofa to sit within arm's reach of Father. If Davenport ever went to war, I would have to assist with strategy. Perhaps, I'd have Vincent killed in battle and make this a very short marriage.

"Something has to be done about the stain." Vincent cast me another look of disapproval.

"Let her be," Milton said good-naturedly. "She'll come 'round to love you soon enough. Takes time, is all."

Takes time, I pondered the expression. It would take more than a lifetime.

ΦΦΦ

"A dress appropriate for you to wear to dinner is in your *boudoir*," Queen Mary said with poor French inflection, pronouncing the "r" at the end. "It is more the Davenport-style than what you are wearing." Wrinkling her petite nose, she eyed my petal-sleeved gown.

Too bad she hadn't seen me in Lydie's old school uniform.

In my room, four doors down the corridor from the library, my dinner dress hung alone in the open, and otherwise empty, armoire. The gown was a dusty pink with layers of satin and lace and required the dreaded, steel-hooped crinoline.

With the help of Flora, a servant girl, I stepped inside the cage's inner circle, which lay flat upon the floor. From there, I lifted it to my waist and fastened the front hook-and-eye closure. Two petticoats were layered over the top so the ribbing would not show through the top garment. I shrugged the heavy gown over my head, and Flora gently tugged it into place. I viewed my reflection in the armoire mirror.

I looked like a bird wearing its cage.

In less than eleven days, Vincent and I would be married; our countries would become allies of blood. I would be under Queen Mary's controlling thumb and trapped in a loveless marriage, all so Father could have a railroad. Yet, I'd forgotten one reassuring side to the equation: my marriage would help protect Corra. As Davenport's future queen, I would do everything in my power to protect her.

Chapter Twenty-seven

The first course of the evening meal was a cream-based seafood chowder. The entrée was wild duck in a puddle of raspberry sauce teamed with sweet potatoes, asparagus, and herb-flecked rolls. Dessert was cheesecake—Mary's favorite.

Vincent wore a copper-colored ditto suit with only the top button of his knee-length coat fastened. His shirt was ruffled at the collar. If I didn't know any better, I would guess that his mother had also chosen his apparel.

"Wren, do you speak French?" Mary asked, taking an inch-sized bite of cheesecake.

"Oui."

"Pardon me?" She half-smiled, turning one ear.

"Oui."

"What was that, dear?"

I clamped down on my cheeks to trap the laugh.

"Yes, she does, Mary. My wife hired a French tutor for the children," Father said, with his most endearing diplomatic smile.

"Did you attend the same French school as your younger brothers?" Father addressed Vincent.

"No, I wasn't keen on the subject," Vincent said.

I sensed there was more to it. Most likely, his mother could not bear to be away from him for that great distance and time. Or perhaps it was the other way around.

"Father, there's something I'd like to speak with you about," Vincent said.

Milton shook his head. "Now is not the time."

The decadent meal, the company, and my heavy, warm dress all inspired a nap. We adjourned upstairs to the library, many of us yawning. Vincent and I sat on the large couch, with his mother in the middle.

"How long have you been in the export business?" Father asked. He was seated in a high-backed chair next to Milton's.

Milton crossed one knee over the other. "The Drakes have always been in international trade."

"Have a chocolate, Wren." Mary held a gilded plate toward me. Even their candy dishes were trimmed with gold. "This one is exceptionally lovely." She pointed to the center, square-shaped piece, in which a rose had been masterfully painted in the cream-colored fondant. Though each chocolate was pretty, great artistry had gone into the one she'd suggested.

"It *is* very lovely," I said.

"It is yours." She nudged her shoulder softly into mine.

"No, thank you. I'm not fond of chocolate."

"Not fond of chocolate!" Mary patted a hand over her heart.

"I know, it's unexpected for my gender." After the decadent dinner, I was fit to be stuffed like one of the nearby mallard drakes.

"Oh, dear, dear . . . Did you hear that, Vincent?" Mary patted above his knee. "Your future bride is not fond of chocolate."

"How unfortunate," he said, dryly. "What sweets are you fond of?" The corner of his mouth curled down.

Why was he asking if he didn't care?

"Chewy candies—licorice pinwheels. . ." I shrugged.

"Milton, don't take that one!" Mary's voice rose.

Despite his wife's plea, Milton popped into his mouth the beautiful chocolate that she'd wanted me to take.

"It's unfortunate that you don't like chocolate." Vincent leaned past his mother to stare at my stain.

Perhaps he, like many others, regarded chocolate as a cure for unforgettable love.

"What did you say, son?" Milton asked.

"I said something should be done about *the stain.*"

"Let her be. This sort of thing takes time; that's all." Milton chuckled. "Now, Francis, tell me about my future daughter-*of*-law."

"Wren's a good listener," Father said thoughtfully. "She takes it all in, and then she surprises you with what she pieces together."

I didn't appreciate his sharing this about me with my future in-laws. But, as Margaret would say, *what's done is done.*

In the silence that followed, King Milton's pipe-holding hand dropped suddenly to his side, and he began to snore. I glanced at Mary. Were smoking and snoring his typical evening behavior?

An acrid smell permeated the room.

Mary sniffed the air several times.

Our eyes locked and I nodded to where Milton's pipe lay wedged between his leg and the side of his chair's dark upholstery.

"Vincent, your father's smoking!" she wailed.

He slowly rose to his feet and, without bending, tipped his crystal goblet. A thin stream of apple cider coursed onto his father's pipe and chair. Vincent returned to sit down beside his mother, and his father's snoring resumed.

"Wren plays the viola as well, if not better than she does the piano," Father said as if music would pardon my nangoonberry stain.

"Better than Beethoven?" Vincent said, dryly.

"Beethoven played the violin, not the viola," I corrected him.

He rolled his eyes.

"I would like to hear your piano, but I will listen to your viola," Mary said, adding a sigh. She held up one finger for a guard's attention near the door and then pointed to my case that had earlier been deposited on a side table.

A middle-aged guard carried it over and handed it to me with a bow.

"Thank you." Remaining seated, I flipped back the lid and gazed at the highly polished burgundy and cream-colored wood. Brody had found the perfect piece. I ran my fingertips over the two hearts. Even when I am an old woman, I will remember my days in Corra. Is that why he'd taken such great care? When he'd etched the hearts into the wood, did he know—perhaps hope—that this piece would always remind me of him?

"Your daughter is a decisively slow creature," Vincent said.

To survive, there are dreams we must tuck away from self.

In my birdcage dress, I forced myself to stand and stroll to the corner of the heavily furnished room, where an arched window overlooked the rocky cliffs, the ocean, and its horizon. With my back to everyone, I closed my eyes, and the sun warmed my cheeks through the leaded glass. I could almost smell the salty air, feel the wind in my hair, and see Brody climb the Cashmere Hills for our goodbye.

Four days already divided us.

Warm tears lapped against my lids. *Happy, Ennie, play something happy like Buttercups.*

As the years passed, would I forget the sweet sound of his voice? Or would my dreams remind me? I set the bow to the strings. Instead of playing misery, I focused on Brody and the day he'd picked the buttercup and slid it into my hair. With the next draw of my bow, verdant greens and golden hues infused the air. Even though Brody had gilded his way about my heart, I was to marry Vincent, someone I cared very little for, someone I might never even like.

Oh, how the wings of my heart wanted to fly along the coastline and over the hills to Corra, but Father had caged me here.

You love me. Really love me. Would I ever forget the ache in his voice when he'd said it?

I'd known my fate since I was a child: I would turn sixteen, leave home, and marry… just like Alia. I'd known that my life would be rife with heartbreak. Yet, never had I imagined it to this extent.

"Wren . . ." Father's hands settled on my shoulders. "It's been a long day. With all of our travels, sleep will do you good."

I had stopped playing. The bow hung motionless by my side as I gazed north.

"Follow me, Wren." Queen Mary's kind voice reminded me of a peppermint—small and soothing. As portly as a ship in all her royal threads, she escorted me into the corridor, pulling the door closed behind us.

I had the sense to pause for a moment and get my bearings.

"Follow me." Mary strolled ahead down the wide corridor.

Six feet from the closed library door, I bent and set my case on the dark wool carpeting, to nestle my viola amidst the velvet.

"No one can see her, not until the stain is gone. No one," Vincent said with emphasis.

"To remove the stain is very, very difficult. It isn't even worth discussing," said his father. Milton was awake again, and I was glad.

"Wren!" From the far end of the hallway, Mary had just discovered that I hadn't followed her.

"Love is patient," my father said.

"I will not be known as the king with the nangoonberry bride," Vincent said.

"Come, Wren." Mary strode all the way back to me and extended her hand.

I remained in my crouched position. Slowly and with great care, I nestled the bow into its proper place in the velvet-lined case.

"This union will create an alliance of blood, not to mention the future railway that will connect both of our countries." Milton's voice was low and firm. "Did you hear me?"

"Did you see her face?" Vincent asked.

Heat crept up my neck. I closed the lid and quietly snapped the locks into place.

"Love is patient." Perhaps it was the strategist in Father that sounded like an idealist.

"You are a deliberately slow young woman." Mary motioned for me to rise.

"I agree." Her husband's voice reached my ears, but not her own. "It may take years, Vincent, but you'll know when you've won *this* woman's heart."

Amongst the men's laughter, I heard Father's.

I saw his strategy: *Laugh with the enemy and they will think you an ally.*

At last, I followed Mary down the corridor. *Love is patient.* I'd never heard Father speak of love, or give advice to anyone of that nature before. He'd always been so militaristic, so stern.

"Did you see her face?" My betrothed's sentiments hardened my heart even more.

I would be known by my future kingdom—the people of Davenport—as the nangoonberry bride, and my husband might never be an ally of love for me.

Chapter Twenty-eight

In my boudoir of gray-blue wallpaper and heavy furnishings, a nightgown was laid out for me on top of the bed. No lady-in-waiting attended me, and I was too tired to change on my own. I remained in the heavy garment with its crinoline cage, climbed beneath the covers, and sank into a deep sleep. So deep was my sleep that when someone shook me, it paralleled my dream of being on a ship. While the shaking increased, the waves grew taller and taller.

"Wren, it's time to get up."

It was Margaret's face and willowy form that reached out to me in the fog, bidding my return. She wanted me to come back for her son. Was it on account of my nangoonberry stain that she finally approved of me? Or my royal birth?

Queen Mary, not Margaret, stood beside my bed, along with another gray-haired woman with massive shoulders. I blinked hard, staring up at her. Was it Helmer wearing a gray wig? Although the woman was tall, she was too short to be him; besides, Helmer would never wear a fluffy pink robe.

"Wren, it's time to wake up," Mary said.

"For breakfast?" Slowly, I flipped back the covers, and yawning, touched my stocking feet to the floor. I'd been caught sleeping in my gown by the royal mother. I ran a hand through my loose hair, mildly embarrassed by my disarray.

"Yes, a snack. Wren . . . in Davenport, a woman is not to sleep in her crinoline. It'll lose its shape, and you'll look like a…" Mary paused, searching for the right word.

"Squash?" offered the broad-shouldered woman.

"Yes, you'll look like a crookneck squash. You need a bite to eat, a midnight snack," Mary said.

Up ahead, the henchwoman held open the door for us.

Shaking off sleep, I paused in the doorway. They'd awakened me for a snack? How odd. Perhaps midnight snacks were a nightly tradition in Davenport.

"Where is my father's room?" I peered across the dimly lit hall, hoping one of the doors was his.

"He's camping in the North Forty with his men," Mary said.

Back home, our royal guests did not camp. Unless we were at war with them, they were always welcome to stay in one of our resplendent rooms.

The Queen pressed a hand to my mid-back and gently pushed me into the corridor. She was not a patient woman.

Dimly lit gas lamps flickered on the walls, casting our shadows on the gold wallpaper. The design appeared to be of sailing vessels. Half-asleep, I peered closer. No, it was simply toile.

Ahead of us, another old woman, this one short and heavy-set, stepped out of her room. Her curly white hair was loose about her shoulders. Large, sea-blue eyes were lost in her pudgy face. "What took you so long? We haven't got all night." She had a twangy accent like she was from the New World. She ambled ahead of us, a wooden cane in her left hand.

We were staged like a train—Old Blue Eyes out front, the Queen one stride behind me, and lastly the henchwoman as the caboose.

"We just passed the stairs," I said, glancing over my shoulder at the balustrade.

"We have a sitting room on this floor for the... uh... servants," Mary said.

"We do?" asked the henchwoman from the rear.

"Did we have to bring her?" Old Blue Eyes asked, over her shoulder.

"You know we did," Mary said.

"That's right; she's the brawns, and we're the brains."

"That's enough, Edith."

Midnight snacks appeared to be a tradition in Davenport. Or were they lying? A shiver ran down my spine. Could I make it to the North Forty on my own? If I found Father, what would he think about the three old ladies wanting me to join them for a late night snack?

He'd think I was sleepwalking.

Up ahead, the corridor changed from dark Turkish carpet to slate. Through the arched windows, the last turret on the west end of the castle came into view. I knew enough about war to know that turrets were for torture.

Lord, help me. With a lift of my skirts, I dashed ahead, out of the Queen's long reach.

Something solid tripped up my feet. I flew through the air, landing chest-first with a thud! Air knotted in my ribcage for a painful moment before finally reaching my lungs.

I tried to get up, but the end of Old Blue Eyes' cane pinned me mid-vertebrae to the cold hard slate. In my birdcage dress, my future mother-in-law undoubtedly had a view of my undergarments.

"Don't worry, girl, it won't hurt," Old Blue Eyes said.

It already hurt.

The others caught up to help me stand and hold me hostage.

"What are you doing? What's going on?"

Old Blue Eyes grabbed one of my ears.

The henchwoman grabbed a handful of my hair.

Without explaining anything to me, the old biddies manhandled me into a stone room with only an old desk and chairs. Mary guided me to a wooden, captain-style chair; without a word, she pushed on my shoulders for me to sit down.

"What's happening?" I grimaced while the henchwoman retained her grip on my hair.

"Be quiet!" Mary's voice was no longer peppermint sweet.

She and Old Blue Eyes tied my wrists and ankles to the chair with strips of old royal stockings. Gold threads frizzed out the sides.

Cobwebs straddled the walls in the dusty, old room. Grit coated the floor, and dust bunnies congregated in the corners.

"Please, tell me what's going on."

"You'll know soon enough," Mary said.

The midnight snacks they planned to feed me were probably spiders.

"Why are we here?"

Instead of answering me, they sat down in chairs to the left of the door, entwined their hands in front of them, and twiddled their thumbs.

"I knew she'd be late," Old Blue Eyes said, leaning toward Mary.

"She's always late." Mary's voice had returned to its angelic sweetness, but I knew now that my future mother-in-law was not a saint.

I missed Margaret. A large lump formed in my throat.

"If this is simply a future daughter-in-law talk *without* midnight snacks… do we need all the knots?" I asked, looking at Mary.

"We're here to see what you're made of."

The heavy door creaked open and a mildly plump woman with short, silvery curls waddled inside. Her feet, squished into black, high heels, appeared swollen and uncomfortable.

She rounded the side of the crude wooden desk, set a squatty doctor's bag on top of it, and clicked it open.

"You're late," Mary said.

"I'm here."

"The Sweeper Woman is here." Old Blue Eyes leaned forward, smiling at me.

She had a lot of sweeping to do. I looked about the room. Instead of a broom, the elderly woman had brought a bag.

"My name is Ma-dame Sweeper."

At her ill pronunciation, I clamped down on the insides of my cheeks. French was my second language. The Sweeper Woman's accent was not French, but Davenport. She was no Madame.

Behind wire spectacles, the woman's half-opened eyes studied the stain.

The old biddies elbowed each other, yet no whispers were exchanged.

The Sweeper Woman rummaged inside her case. "Where is it?" she mumbled.

"Where is what?" Old Blue Eyes asked.

"My pocket watch. It's missing." She shuffled through untidy stacks of papers. "What a shame, and I *so* wanted to begin tonight."

"How can a hypnotist forget her pocket watch?" Mary asked.

The truth lodged in my throat like a chicken bone.

"Does anyone have anything shiny?" the Sweeper Woman asked, looking at no one in particular.

"I don't usually wear my shiny things to bed," Old Blue Eyes said.

With a high lift of her brows, the Queen sighed. "I better get this back." She lifted a delicate chain from around her neck, revealing an oval-shaped pendant of solid gold.

My future in-laws must have a gold mine at their disposal.

"I'll be in charge of the chain. Edith, you keep notes." The Sweeper Woman rose from her chair and handed a quill to Old Blue Eyes.

The Sweeper Woman was not going to sweep the room.

"When is the wedding?" she asked.

"September tenth, less than one week. Vincent wants the stain gone by Saturday for the annual Davenport Ball. Ladies, never have two large parties in one week. Very poor planning."

"Yes, indeed," agreed the Sweeper Woman.

The old ladies were Vincent's puppets, not his mother's.

Love is patient, but my betrothed didn't want to walk me down the aisle as I was now—the nangoonberry stain so evident for all to see. Not that I could blame him. But… even though my memories of Brody Hew made my heart ache with misery, I didn't want to forget him.

"We're going to play a game of *Truth*." The Sweeper Woman sat down on a corner of the desk. She was the only one of the women not in her nightwear; most likely she lived outside of the castle.

"I hate this game." The henchwoman let out a long breath.

She'd obviously played it before.

"Be quiet, Ursula," the Sweeper Woman said. Then she began swinging the gold pendant back and forth in front of me. "Honey, what is your favorite memory?" Her voice dripped with grandmother-like love.

"It's not right now." I tried to be amiable, looking at her eyes, instead of the pendant.

"We know that," Old Blue Eyes, also known as Edith, readied her pen.

Perhaps tonight was some type of initiation into this strange family. "How are you ladies related to Vincent?" I felt certain they all were. I regarded Edith first, across the desk from me.

"His grandmother was my sister." My future great Aunt Edith pursed her lips, thoughtfully.

"My brother was his grandfather," said my future great Aunt Ursula.

I regarded the Sweeper Woman.

"I am not related to the sisters. Honey, what is your most treasured memory?" She was obviously in charge of the initiation.

"My sister," I said, not allowing myself to think about Brody. "My memories of my older sister Alia before she was sent to Yonder to marry." Even though I thought myself numb, a sudden spark of tears surprised me.

Vincent would never let me see her. I already knew him well enough to know that.

"Yonder is a dreadful place," Ursula said. "We visited there once before the war. The peasants were very poor and—"

"Peasants are always poor. Remember, Ursula, we're here to listen to Wren's memories, not yours." Edith pointed the quill of the pen back and forth between the two of us for emphasis.

My memories. We were all gathered tonight to sweep away the memories of my first love. My loss far outweighed Vincent's future humiliation. He had the rest of our lives to woo and win me, but allowing this inhumane act proved that patience was not one of his virtues.

I vowed to never love this man, and prayed the memory of my vow would not be stolen from me.

"What is your favorite memory of your *giant* boyfriend?" the Sweeper Woman asked.

A smile betrayed me. She had quickly gotten to the heart of tonight's meeting.

"Get behind her, Ursula, just like when we were kids," she said.

As the shiny pendant swung back and forth, I looked down at the gold threads of my dress instead.

Ursula's mammoth-sized hands clamped my head, pulling it upright.

I closed my eyes tightly to the shimmering gold that mirrored the awful scene.

"Queenie, get her eyes," ordered the Sweeper Woman.

"I hate this part." Mary stood off to the side of me and wove her arms in between Ursula's. The warm pads of her fingertips pulled open my eyes.

Forced as I was by the old biddies, I had no choice but to watch the chain swing back and forth, back and forth. I relaxed under the trance. My jaw slackened.

"What is the giant's name whom you love?" Madame Sweeper asked.

"Helmer?" A giggle escaped me while the two ladies returned to their chairs.

"Giggling already and in front of you, Queenie." Madame Sweeper tsked. "Giggling means the memories are still fresh like manure and will be harder to get off of the shovel. We have our work cut out for us, girls. Now… honey, tell me *all* your memories of Helmer. How did you first meet?"

My mind traveled several months back to Gruel Kitchen and the day of mush. "It all started with my first attempt at porridge," I said. The swinging necklace had seized my attention, and there was no stopping my mouth from dribbling everything. "I met Helmer when I was a cook in Gruel Kitchen. It was more like a prison than anything."

"Awh, you poor, poor thing." The old ladies uttered. Believing themselves on the cusp of a romantic tale, they sighed.

My shoulders began to ache from the weight of holding up my heavy arms. I must have been deep into the trance as

Ursula, and the Queen returned to their chairs and foraged through their pockets for their handkerchiefs.

"How did you end up in Gruel Kitchen?" Madame Sweeper asked.

"Pearl and I were in Stockford when I was grabbed accidentally."

"Pearl?" the Queen asked.

"Yes, she was a friend of mine, or at least I think so." I still didn't know what to make of her.

"Stick with Helmer for now," the old woman said.

I spent the next few hours telling her all my stories of Helmer, about the first day when I'd made the giants the clumpy oatmeal. Helmer showing me how to cook, and always helping me. Then the war and the giants, and how even Helmer had forgotten about me.

The women yawned.

Madame Sweeper held her elbow up with her other hand and continued swinging the pendant. Even though it was still dark, a rooster crowed in the distance.

"That can't be all. There hasn't even been a kiss," Ursula moaned.

"There doesn't have to be a kiss for the nangoonberry stain," Edith said.

"We need to get her back to bed before Milton . . ." Mary's voice trailed off.

"Listen to me, honey," Madame Sweeper said. "You will never remember Helmer or Pearl, ever again. The key to your memory is locked away in these two words . . ." She peered about the room. Except for the cobwebs and the old women, the space was sparsely furnished. "Ugly sisters," she said. "You will remember nothing of your giant boyfriend *Helmer*, ever again. Zip. Zip. May it never slip. You will remember nothing of tonight and this room. You will remain in a trance-like state until Ursula snaps her fingers."

Hunched in her chair, Ursula tried to snap her fingers.

"Not now, later, after you get her back to bed," Madame Sweeper said and then she stopped swinging the necklace to and fro.

Ursula carried the candlestick toward me; and, all four women gathered in front of me to study my cheek.

"It hasn't faded a drop. Not a drop." Mary shook her head.

"Her stain is deep," Edith said.

"Well, it means more work for me tomorrow. Our time has been so lovely today." Madame Sweeper snapped closed her bag. "So lovely, Wren, that you won't remember anything about it. Zip. Zip." Her heels clicked on the slate floor, and she exited the room with a tart laugh.

"What were the two words she called us?" Ursula asked. "Ugly—"

"Be quiet, Ursula!" Old Blue Eyes yelled.

They rolled me back to my room, and I climbed back into bed fully dressed in my crinoline.

I yawned as I tucked my hands beneath my cheek.

Near the door, Mary waited to turn down the lamps. Ursula rubbed the fingers of one hand together, observing them intently.

"Not like that. Your middle finger and thumb." Edith said, snapping two fingers together.

Then, Ursula did the same.

Mary dimmed the lights, and I gave into a yawn.

Our short get-together had been odd. Where were the midnight snacks?

Chapter Twenty-nine

After breakfast, I sat in an armless slipper chair, kitty corner from the grand piano in arm's reach of the Queen. The servants had fashioned my hair into long curls and pinned it up on the sides. Across the room, Vincent didn't appear to approve of my new hairstyle. For one thing, my hair was still the wrong color.

I peered around the lavishly furnished room. When I became a von Drake, I would never have a material worry. At my disposal were all of the silk, velvet, and satin stockings with gold threads that a girl could ever want. But, did my future husband have empathy? If he'd been in Brody's shoes when I'd been in Gruel Kitchen, would he have written me little notes of encouragement? Or left me buttercups? Or would Vincent have been happy that I, a spoiled princess, was finally getting what I deserved?

"Would you play piano for us, Wren?" Queen Mary asked, embroidery hoop in hand.

"I no longer play, Your Highness." She already knew this about me, but I repeated my earlier sentiments. "My older sister plays piano, and I play the viola."

"Let me reword it." Mary smiled smugly. "Please play the piano for us, Wren."

My stomach knotted.

"I prefer not to. Thank you." I left it at that and watched the door for Father.

"We bought this piano for you because we were told you were a concert pianist." Mary lifted her chin high above her ruffled collar. "We already have a wonderful violist. Unfortunately, our pianist leaves much to be desired. When you become a von Drake, you will be expected to play."

My gaze shifted from Mary to the dusty, emerald green-capped ducks mounted on the wall. Wings extended out from their sides, they appeared to be in mid-flight before they'd been shot and stuffed. Had they been in their teenage years as well?

Mary's lips pinched together tightly. "Your parents must have thought you were made of butter."

I would think butter quite moldable, but perhaps she inferred that it melted too easily.

The door clicked open.

Father was finally paying us a visit.

"Good morning, ladies." He smiled at the Queen before his gaze drifted to me.

"Good morning, Francis. Your timing is impeccable. I've just requested that your daughter play the piano for us," Mary said, with a lift of her chin.

"I understand your desire to hear her gift, Mary, but Wren stopped playing the piano years ago." Father was at his diplomatic best. "It reminds her too much of her older sister. They had a special bond, you see."

"Yes, well . . . sentimentality is where the von Drakes and the Wells are quite different."

He nodded. "I am here to speak with my daughter in private, if you will. Wren," he nodded toward me and then stiffened a hand toward the door.

"What is this regarding?" Over the top of her spectacles, Mary peered at him.

"A private matter." His brows furrowed.

"Permission is granted." She pulled a golden thread through the black velvet.

Instead of guiding me into the hallway or the more intimate study, Father led the way down the marble stairwell.

"What's going on?" I asked. My imagination was running wild like a knobby-kneed fawn, and I wanted Father to tame it.

We descended six more steps before he answered. "There is someone here to see you."

"Who?" I breathed. How my heart wanted to believe that Brody was here. But… to be here would cost him his life.

"He said he is a friend of yours, a giant."

Was it Remford, here to kill me? Or could it be Gid, Anky or…?

We continued through the marble corridors, and past two guards who flanked the expansive bridge. When we were halfway across, the wind picked up and due to my crinoline cage, my gait felt much lighter.

"Father!" I yelled, gripping the railing. "I fear I may fly away like a balloon."

He came back for me and to my relief, maintained a grip on my arm while we crossed.

To our left, in the North Forty, our army's camp was pitched in a semi-circle over the rocky terrain. Straight ahead of us, near the end of the bridge, stood a broad-shouldered giant with a horseshoe-shaped rim of dark hair. As we approached, his face brightened to such a degree that you would think I was the dearest person to him in the entire world. His clenched fists shook as he held them in front of his chest.

His lack of decorum made me feel mildly embarrassed.

Father and I halted a short distance away from him.

"That's a pretty dress, Ennie."

"Thank you." The giant knew my nickname, yet he was a complete stranger to me.

"You are to call her Princess Wren," Father said. "Wren, are you familiar with this giant?"

"Should I be?" He was a giant of a man, yet his clothes appeared large on him.

"Ennie!"

"Remember, you are to call her Princess Wren," Father sounded patient enough.

Without taking his eyes off of me, the giant fumbled a bow.

"I'm sorry, have we met?" It wasn't like me to forget a face or a voice for that matter.

"En-nie!" The giant's jaw dropped, and his large eyes widened.

"Helmer claims that he taught you to cook in Gruel Kitchen. I should think you would remember him." Father's dark brows gathered.

My mouth had grown dry. I closed it and forced myself to swallow.

"Why didn't you tell me, Ennie?" the giant asked.

"Tell you what?" I'd never seen Helmer before in my life.

"That you're a princess!" The giant pulled a piece of paper out of his shirt pocket and unrolled it. "I saw this on the side of a fence post when I was running home."

"Give me that." Father reached for the paper.

I knew what the reward poster read.

Father unrolled the paper and read it aloud under his breath.

REWARD for the return of:
 Princess Wren Wells of Blue Sky
15 years old with red hair and blue eyes
Plays the violin.
Ł100 pounds for her safe return.

"Ennie, I thought you played the viola," said the giant.

"I do." Who was he?

"Remember you are to call her *Princess Wren*. And she doesn't appear to know you, Helmer."

"I showed you how to make Gruel Cakes. Remember yours? They were like rocks. Remember what we did with the cakes, Ennie... Princess Wren...nie? Remember?"

"I'm sorry, I don't," I said glad that several of our guards had come to our aid.

"Think hard, Wren," said Father. "Helmer wants to serve as your bodyguard here in Davenport for what he claimed you did for the giants."

I remembered all too well Gruel Kitchen and the Gruel Cakes, but not this squatty giant of a man. What was his ploy?

"Father," I turned toward him and whispered, "I've never met nor seen this particular giant."

"Take him away," Father said to his men.

"Where should we take him?" asked one of our guards.

Father turned to regard the giant. "Helmer, I remember you from the war. You were a fine soldier back then, but who are you working for now?"

"I didn't forget you, Ennie." The giant stared at me. "Gid told me that he'd already opened the door. He didn't tell me the truth until we got home. He felt bad for lying. Your plan worked, Ennie." He smiled. "Gid's never did."

"Take him away for further questioning," Father said.

Several of our guards gripped the giant's arms. "He was jealous, Ennie," Helmer yelled. "Gid felt bad."

I remembered Gid. It was hard to imagine him feeling bad about anything. But I did not remember this particular giant. Who did he represent?

"Why don't you remember me?" Helmer stared. "Why don't you remember your favorite giant? I taught you everything you know. How to baste, peel, bake..." his voice trailed off.

I remembered cauldrons of rice hanging above the fire, and the time I'd scorched my hand. I remembered being all alone in the kitchen and fearing death. How the giants had hated me and then put up with me. Yet, out of all of the giants, I did not remember the one standing before me.

He must have overheard his stories from the others.

"I'm sorry, Helmer, I don't remember you," I said, one last time.

"Take him away." Father heaved a weary sigh.

The giant waved his arms above his head, pulling the men off their feet with his antics. *What are you doing?* He mouthed, grimacing at me.

What was his ploy?

ΦΦΦ

"Who's your spy, here, Father?" I asked when we were halfway across the bridge, and alone at that. Spies were the most important part of war, and whether he wanted to admit it, I was marrying the enemy.

"You'll figure it out soon enough."

"Figure what out?" I glanced up at his profile, stern in the sunlight.

"It's just a matter of time before you see her."

My mind traveled from Ursula to Edith. The Queen couldn't be the spy. Did he mean one of the servants?

"What better spy than a woman whose only claim to fortune is her want for a string of pearls?" A smile ebbed at the corner of his mouth. "We've employed her since Stockford. Try not to act surprised when you see her."

"Ursula?" I asked. But what would she have been doing in Stockford? Other than her, my mind drew a complete blank.

"No-oo. She's quite beautiful," Father said.

Ursula might be considered beautiful in a medieval sort of way.

"Can you give me another clue?" I asked.

Father halted abruptly.

I turned to look back at him. "What is it?"

"Enough of the games." The bright sunlight exposed daggers of gold in his hazel eyes.

I swallowed. It was hard to pin down which one of my offenses he was referring to. So, I simply stared at him, searching for a clue.

"Your mother spent a great deal of time working with Pearl before she was sent here. As I've often said, people with a natural charisma make very good spies."

"Pearl?" I whispered. He acted like I was familiar with a woman named Pearl.

"Enough of the games, Wren!" Then shoulders squared, he strode ahead, leaving me to follow in his wake.

ΦΦΦ

What was happening to me? Pearl. Helmer. Two people that were supposed to be important to me were missing from my memory. Did the old women who watched me oddly throughout the day have anything to do with this? Something was happening to me—something I didn't remember.

Without anyone's permission, I dismissed myself from the library, strode to my bedchamber and locked the door behind me. If I'd forgotten the giant named Helmer and the spy named Pearl, then wasn't there was a chance I'd forget Brody, too?

In the top drawer of the writing desk, I found fine linen paper. I sat down and dipped the quill pen into a bottle of ink. Beginning with the buttercups, I scribed my memories of Brody Hew. My pen flew across the page as I recalled *his family, his burly arms, our walks up the Cashmere Hills, his love for the salty sea air, the sunsets like a fireball on the horizon—*

A knock sounded on the door.

"Wren," Queen Mary said and then rapped again. "Are you in there? I command that you unlock this door at once."

"Coming," I said as I continued writing. *Fish and chips fresh from the sea, Margaret's Wacky Cake,* and *darest I forget nangoonberry jelly. I love this man whom they, whoever they are, might soon take away from me.*

I cannot forget Brody Hew.

While the knocking continued, I filled one page of fine linen paper with everything I felt important to remember about the man I loved. I folded it and slid the page behind the velvet in my viola case for safe keeping. Taking one more precaution, I scribbled a short note to myself and tucked it beneath my pillow.

I tidied the coverlet upon my bed and turned as the door sprang open. Huddled in the doorway stood Ursula, Mary, and—in the middle, Edith, a hairpin askew in her grip.

"You are never to lock yourself away in here. Ever!" Mary spouted. Above her high ruffled collar, her face was flushed. "What have you been up to?" She eyed my bed and then the desk.

If she were to grip the pen, she would ascertain that it was still warm, but she didn't have the mind to.

"I've never been in this room," Ursula said, admiring the four-poster bed and the gold brocade drapes. Lastly, her gaze traveled to the wallpaper. "I like the paper."

"It 'tis lovely," Mary said. "It's called Celestial, from Paris."

Small gold tulips were arranged in a repeated diamond pattern on a cornflower blue background.

"What were you doing in here, Wren?" Mary regarded me.

"I had a knot in my knickers," I said.

"Don't be vulgar." She shot me a look of disapproval.

"How should I have worded it, Your Majesty?"

"In Davenport, we never mention the unmentionables."

"I understand," I said and started after them toward the door.

Mary turned to eye me. "What were you *really* doing in here?"

"I had a knot in my unmentionables."

ΦΦΦ

Queen Mary, Ursula, and Edith yawned off-and-on through the lengthy, five-course dinner; because yawning is contagious, so did I. A headache developed, I was so tired. After the meal, we gathered in the library for dark coffee and sweets.

"Wren, look what I bought for you today in town." Vincent stood in front of me and with a mock bow, held forth a gilded plate. Upon it sat four decadent chocolates and a lone licorice pinwheel.

"Alfred said you bought more than that in town today, Vincent, but we'll save that little secret for another time." Fanning her flushed face, his mother glanced at me. "Still, I wish you would have consulted with me first. I'm quite certain that Wren already has a string in her collection."

"You've said enough, Mother."

Her son didn't even like me, but he'd bought me one piece of candy and possibly a string of... pearls? Not that a man has to like a woman to buy her candy, but pearls? Had Vincent already changed his mind about me? I doubted very much that he had.

"Please reward my efforts by taking it." A corner of his mouth curled up, and he gazed warmly enough into my eyes.

One pinwheel graced the plate. He'd gone to town and purchased one pinwheel for me. Most assuredly, there was poison lurking in the black coil of confectionery. He was very poor at artifice. Very poor.

"Take it, Wren. It was very kind of Vincent," Father said. His low, controlled voice was probably the same tone he'd used on the battlefield. *Now, men, get out of your trenches and take a shot for your country.*

The room was quiet as I bravely popped the pinwheel into my mouth. The candy tasted as delicious as it always had. I smiled at Vincent and then I lowered my gaze to the wool carpet as I recalled Brody and the bag of lollies that he'd bought for me. *Why had he done that?*

A few sentences in conversation passed before I found myself yawning. I yawned so wide that I was embarrassed by my rudeness. I tried to cover my mouth with both hands, but I was unable to squelch the next yawn. Perhaps I should go to bed, but I couldn't hold my eyes open long enough to give it another thought.

"Ursula, help me get Wren to bed," Mary said. "Her manners are lacking, and she's obviously in need of rest."

I couldn't rise or budge myself. I was surprisingly sluggish.

Like they'd been employed in an infirmary, Vincent's mother and two aunts transferred me to a wooden wheelchair. In front of my father, they rolled me out of the library and closed the door. Queen Mary hummed while she pushed my chair down the hallway. Vincent's great aunt Edith hobbled in front, employing her cane, and great Aunt Ursula brought up the rear.

Our procession rolled right past my room. Though I lifted a hand, I couldn't form the words to tell them.

Just past the stairwell and around the first bend, Mary slowed my chair to a halt. Edith hobbled back toward me, a bandana in her grip.

"What, uh . . ." I said.

All three ladies were on me at once, wedging the cloth between my teeth, tying it in back, gagging me. Using strips of dark stockings with real gold threads, they tied my arms and ankles to the chair. Like I'd thought earlier, these elderly women were why I didn't remember Helmer or Pearl. The floor changed from carpeting to slate as they rolled me further down the corridor.

Where were they taking me and what were they doing?

"I can't handle any more late nights," Edith said, over her shoulder. "I need a decent night's sleep."

"You'll get it tonight," Mary said.

"I have a headache," Ursula groaned.

The corners of my mouth ached. They'd gagged me too tight.

The old biddies wheeled me into a cobweb riddled room and faced my chair toward an empty desk. After closing the door, the three sat down in wooden chairs, Mary in the middle.

"She's late," Ursula said.

"*Again.*" Edith shook her head.

"I knew she'd be." Mary frowned.

"Did you bring something shiny?" Ursula asked.

"I'm not letting her touch this one." Mary lifted a lovely gold locket that had lain hidden beneath the V of her bodice and fondled it with her thumb.

Ursula elbowed her. "She'll forget her pocket watch and your gold locket, you watch."

"I'll say it again: it's worth a bauble or two to stay on her good side," Edith said, and slowly shook her head.

"Easy for you to say." Mary sat up taller in her chair.

Who were they talking about?

The door creaked open, and a plump, gray-haired woman carrying a black leather bag entered and closed the door behind her. Swollen feet oozed over the sides of her black high heels. After she'd set her bag on top of the desk, she clicked it open and peered at me.

"The Sweeper Woman is here." Edith leaned forward in her chair to look at me.

"She met her last night," Ursula said.

Did I? I didn't remember.

Tight-lipped, Mary elbowed her.

"Oh, that's right," Ursula breathed.

"My name is Ma-dame Sweeper," the woman said in very poor French. Behind her spectacles, her lids hung heavy over her half-opened eyes. "It's going to be tricky for Wren to tell me her memories of *Brody Hew* when she's gagged. Isn't it?"

My heart lurched in my being.

"The man you're in love with isn't a giant, but a guard from Blue Sky. You thought you could trick us. Didn't you?"

I had been here before. Vincent had given me the pinwheel. The old ladies were his puppets, helping him to steal my memories. I needed to tell Father.

"What else did our informant find out?" Mary asked.

"Seems she fell in love with one of their guards, and he's been banished." The old woman eyed me. "You won't be fooling me again, Princess Wren."

I attempted to swallow around the gag.

"Ursula, take it off of her," Mary ordered.

The large woman fumbled behind me while she untied the bandana.

"Why are you doing this?" I asked, staring up at Mary.

"Where is it?" The Sweeper Woman looked in her case. "Oh, diddly dum, I've forgotten it again."

Mary rose to join her behind the desk. Together they pulled items out of the old leather bag—a blindfold, a tin of Nugget shoe polish, and a heavily boned corset.

"And, I so looked forward to hearing about the man she *really* loves," the Sweeper Woman said, pulling out a forked wishbone that was too large to be from a chicken.

Pursing her lips into a straight line, Mary lifted the gold necklace she was wearing over her head. "You know time is of the essence. I want this returned to me tonight and my Georgian pendant, as well."

"Now, I'll be in charge of this," the Sweeper Woman said, taking the shiny necklace. "Edith, take notes for me. Ursula and Queenie, you know what to do."

My heart hammered in my chest.

Ursula stopped behind my chair and clamped the sides of my face in a strong viselike grip.

"Look here, honey." The Sweeper Woman sat on the edge of the desk.

I stared at her thick ankles instead.

Then, Mary wove her arms between Ursula's and with nimble fingertips held open my eyes.

What was happening? What were they doing? Sadly, I knew. They were going to pry from me all my memories of Brody, using everything in her bag, maybe even the wishbone, if they had to.

"It won't hurt." Across the other side of the desk, Edith readied her pen.

"It's like playing a game of Old Maid," the Sweeper Woman said. "It's so mindless that you won't remember anything about it in the morning. Anything."

But, I wanted to. I wanted to retain everything of Brody. In the chair of despair in this room of doom, I knew that I would rather have the nangoonberry stain for the rest of my days than lose the memories of the man I loved.

ΦΦΦ

"Tell me from the beginning what you remember of Brody Hew," said the plump, elderly woman with half-opened eyes. "The stain will fade as you forget."

I remembered back to the day with Margaret picking berries and how hard I'd worked, wanting to please Brody.

"Give me your memories." The Sweeper Woman swung the pendulum this way and that. Tied in the chair as I was, with Ursula holding my head and Queen Mary my eyes, I could not avoid the old woman's sorcery. "Tell me your memories, and the stain will go away. Then, you and Vincent will live happily ever after."

Though I did not find her sentiments inspiring, my arms grew heavier, and my jaw slackened. I began at the beginning, telling the old woman about the afternoon I'd tried to escape from the Lake House—the first time I'd met Brody Hew, the young, handsome guard.

"I thought she loved Helmer," Ursula said.

"Helmer?" Wasn't he the giant I'd met earlier in the day?

"She tricked us," Edith said. "Brody is the man she loves. Can't you hear it in her voice?"

"Shhhh! You're distracting her. Wren, tell me all your memories of Brody," Madame Sweeper swung the pendulum to and fro.

In the trance-like state, I told her everything—things I'd never told another human being, I told this woman.

"Daisy? Who is Daisy?" she asked.

"My pig. When I was in Gruel Kitchen, she was my pet."

"*You* had a *pig* for a *pet*?" Mary asked from the left side of the room.

Though I wanted to look at her, I couldn't pull my focus away from the pendulum.

"What happened next with Brody?" Madame Sweeper asked.

"After he saved my life, we rode for many days." My mood lightened as I relived my memories. While I told them about the buttercups and Corra, and the first time Brody put his arm around me in front of his family, I giggled.

"He put *his arm* around you?" Madame Sweeper asked.

"Yes, in front of everyone." I lingered unashamedly in my reverie. "Margaret said she knew as soon as we crested the hills that Brody had brought home his bride."

"I hate this," Ursula grumbled.

"Here's my handkerchief," Mary said.

"Continue, Wren," Madame Sweeper said in her honey-dipped way.

"It is a Blue Sky tradition that when a maiden turns sixteen, she selects the recipient of her first kiss." Despite my audience, I felt a moonbeam smile stretch across my face. "My sixteenth birthday fell when we were in Corra. Even though I knew that I would someday be the Queen of Davenport, I wanted the memory of kissing Brody Hew."

"And why did you want this memory?" Madame Sweeper asked.

I swallowed.

"Wren, tell me. Tell me everything."

"Years from now when I am plump and gray, and an old woman like you, I wanted to remember what it was like to be in love." In my trance-like state, I held no sense of tact.

The locket stopped its pendulum-like swing, and behind it, the old woman's pouty mouth gathered. "How dare you speak to me with such disrespect."

Sherri Schoenborn Murray

"You! She's marrying my son," Mary's voice was a gasp. "How dare she say such things in front of me!"

I blinked, and before I could blink again, the pendulum swung to and fro, to and fro.

"Stop it. It's wrong!" Ursula sobbed

"Did we have to bring her?" Edith asked.

"Go on, Wren, tell me everything about Brody, every last drop," Madame Sweeper said.

I told her about picking the berries with Margaret, sitting on the stool of pins and needles while I waited for Brody to taste the nangoonberry jelly and the trial of waiting to see the affirmation in his eyes. Things I wouldn't tell another person or even Daisy, I told her.

Lastly, as the necklace swayed to and fro, I lingered on my final memory of Brody running up the hill to say goodbye.

"How did *you feel*?" I detected a lilt in Madame Sweeper's voice.

"I . . ." I shook my head. "I . . ." Even in my trance-like state, I swallowed tears. "I knew it would be the last time I'd see the man I love."

"Yee-ss, Wren, but how did *you feel*?" she persisted.

"I felt ripped in two. Betrayed by my father." A great heaviness settled over me.

In my trancelike state, I did not cry, although Ursula did.

"Is that your last link to Brody, your *very* last memory of him?" Madame Sweeper asked.

"Yes." Behind me, a window overlooked the sea. How I longed to swivel in the chair and look northwest.

"You will no longer . . ." while the old woman's voice slowed, she swung the pendulum faster—back and forth, back and forth, "remember Brody Hew, Corra, the Cashmere Hills, the Hew family, the sea, Daisy—your beloved pig, buttercups, Brody's siblings and family, the day you turned sixteen, the

Wacky cake, the lollyberry kiss, the fish and chips, the nangoonberry jelly…" Her voice droned on and on, while on the sidelines, the three sisters wept. Even Queen Mary sniffled while my memory emptied of all the treasures that I valued so dearly.

"And you will no longer remember tonight's pinwheel candy. Zip, zip, zip. May it never slip. Tonight's key word again is *Ugly Sisters*." Madame Sweeper completed her incantations, and then the women gathered around me.

"It's still there." Mary clamped both hands on her forehead, staring at me.

"When the love is deep, the stain is also," Madame Sweeper said.

"I promised Vincent it would be gone tonight. There are only two days until the Davenport Ball. Five hundred guests." Mary shook her head, unhappy.

"Then, tomorrow night, we'll simply have to empty her of all her *happy* memories." Madame Sweeper clicked closed her bag.

All of my happy memories? I questioned the cost. What becomes of a person when all of their happy memories are erased, and all that's left is an empty shell? Can the spirit flicker without the pearl?

Chapter Thirty

The three sisters paused near my chamber door while I folded back the covers and slid into bed. As I fluffed the pillow beneath my head, my hand brushed a piece of paper. *Was it a note of some kind? Who was it from?*

Ursula snapped her fingers and smiled.

Edith dimmed the lights.

"Goodnight, Wren, pleasant dreams," Mary said.

"Yes, Wren, try not to think about—Owh!" Ursula moaned. "That hurt."

Had she been about to say something she shouldn't have?

"Goodnight," Edith said, pulling the door closed.

"Goodnight." I smiled at their attentiveness.

Tired, I felt myself relax into the feather mattress like butter on a warm day. I was exhausted to the point of depletion. A good night's sleep would do me good. But, first, I wanted to read the note; if, indeed, it was a note.

In the top drawer of the bedside table, I found a match and flint and lit the resident tallow candle. I unfolded the fine linen paper and read:

Wren, this is from you… I'm worried about you. If, for some reason, you don't remember Brody, and who Brody Hew is, you must tell Father. He must be made aware that somehow, someway, someone is stealing your memories.

Love, Wren.

I stared at the note that I didn't remember writing. It was my cursive to a fault, but I didn't remember writing it or slipping it beneath my pillow. And, who was Brody Hew?

I stared into the darkness.

I had to find Father. I had to tell him. The giant and Pearl weren't the only people I'd forgotten. There was also a Brody Hew. Maybe I wasn't only losing people from my memory; maybe I was losing my mind.

I stayed beneath the covers and formulated a plan while I waited for the von Drake family to settle down for the night. After their voices eventually faded and the doors down the hallway clicked closed, I slipped out of bed and donned my robe. Several times I'd seen Edith walking the grounds after dinner—sometimes even along the bridge. I would pretend to be Edith and make my way to Father. I could barely go to my bedchamber alone without surveillance, much less for a walk outside, so it was best I disguised myself.

Downstairs in the large entry closet, I found a dark cloak similar to Edith's and an old wooden cane. Hunched over, I hobbled past some very tired, unobservant servants and then outside.

"Evening, Edith. It's late for you," said one of the guards as I passed through the postern.

"Evening. It is late," I said imitating her New World twang.

My heart thumped loudly as I neared the middle-aged guard who stood beside the entrance to the bridge.

"What'd you have for dinner *tonight*?" he asked.

"Swordfish and potatoes." I kept my shoulders hunched as I limped past, favoring my left side.

"It was probably the potatoes." He chuckled.

Was indigestion or flatulence the reason Edith strolled? Perhaps both. The long bridge was an ambitious distance to keep up this uncomfortable gait. Halfway across, I limped with my right instead of my left and hoped no one would notice.

The light of a campfire beckoned me toward the North Forty where Father's camp was arranged in a semi-circle over the rugged, uneven terrain. A gathering of men sat around the fire, and I knew from our travels here that it was routine for Father to sit amongst them.

My slow, elderly gait tired me, and I paused the last quarter of the way to peer over the side of the railing. At the bottom of the deep ravine, a silvery stream serpentined its way to the ocean. Lifting my gaze, I stared at the moon like it was God's representative.

"Please let things go well," I whispered to my heavenly Father regarding the conversation ahead of me with my earthly one. "Remember how You told Amy that You have a plan for me," I reminded God. "I'm going to hold You to it." I swallowed deep emotion. "Please tell me it wasn't only freeing the giants. Please tell me there's more." I waited in the fog-shrouded air for His whisper, but the wind carried no words. "I don't think this is what You've planned for me." Over my shoulder, I regarded Davenport Castle, its turrets gloomy in the moonlight.

"When You plan things, I'd like to think there's a little more love, and a little more of Heaven put into it than Father's style of planning. For You are my *loving* Heavenly Father." Eyes wide, I let him see my tears. "I truly believe that. Please strengthen me for what is ahead." With that, I inhaled deeply and prepared myself for Father.

ΦΦΦ

At the entrance to Father's camp, one of his men stopped me.

"Who are you and what business do you have here?" the gruff older guard asked.

"I would like to speak with King Francis," I said, keeping my gaze on the ground. "Tell him it's his daughter in disguise."

The guard leaned his head down to peer in my eyes. I did not recognize his pointy, unshaven face. There were over two hundred of our men here, and I apparently did not know them all.

"What are your siblings' names?" he asked.

It was a test of entry. "Alia, Odessa, Edwin…" It was best I not mention Elaina.

"Does your father have a mole on the left side or the right side of his nose?"

"The right side."

"James, go get King Francis. Tell him his daughter's here to see him." The guard stiffened his hand for me to remain where I was.

I had remembered all of my siblings. That was a good sign.

I watched Father rise from the circle of the fire. His back was to the moonlight, so his features were not visible until he was only a few feet away from me. He was weary. Perhaps the months of trying to find me had finally caught up with him.

"What is it, Wren?" he asked, recognizing me, even though I still wore my hood.

"May we step away?" I asked, wanting privacy.

He nodded and then followed me to a grouping of shrubs, a distance of about thirty feet away.

"Why are you dressed like an old woman?" Father was not in the best of moods.

"I was afraid Queen Mary wouldn't let me venture here on my own, and I wanted to speak with you in private."

"About what?"

I straightened my posture and looked up into his tired eyes. "I'm afraid. I'm afraid I'm losing my memory. Helmer. Pearl…" I shook my head. "I left a note for myself under my pillow that if I don't remember who *Brody Hew* is, that I had to tell you." I inhaled deeply. "And now, Father, I don't know who he is. Should I?"

His eyes narrowed and then drifted to my cheek; most likely the nangoonberry stain was visible in the moonlight. His cheeks bunched as he exhaled a chuckle. "You're a very clever girl, Wren, but you forget who you're dealing with."

As I stared at him, years of disappointment flooded me.

"I thought I was dealing with my father," I said. Without my permission, the corners of my mouth twitched down. I did not want to break in front of him, so without saying even a *goodnight*, I hobbled toward the bridge.

"Wrrrr-en," he called after me. "Wren."

I wanted to know who the names belonged to and he was the only one who knew. Although I was close to tears, I forced myself to turn around and face him.

"Yes," I said, damming the tears.

"Edith walks with a limp on her left side. You were not convincing."

"You're right." I struggled for another breath. "I have not *yet* mastered artifice like you." I hardened myself to the pain of being my father's daughter.

"No, tonight, you look like an amateur."

I let his words sink in. He thought it all an act. Everything.

"Father . . ." I inhaled deeply, "only the old woman was artifice, not the daughter." For a moment, I gave him a chance to redeem himself, but his lean, chiseled face remained unmoved in the moonlight.

I hobbled across the bridge like an old woman with a crippled left leg. My father did not call after me or try to catch up. With each labored step, I wept for the earthly father I so longed for but knew I would never have.

Chapter Thirty-one

The following morning as I descended the stairwell for breakfast, I glanced over my shoulder. Several doors down the hallway, I spotted a young female servant slip into my bedchamber. Throughout the day, it was not uncommon to see servants flitting in and out of my room, but this particular one had golden hair.

Was it merely coincidence that Vincent preferred the color?

Curiosity sparked, I started back for my room. If she had a mole on her left cheek, circumstances would confirm that not only was Vincent terrible at artifice; he was most likely harboring a mistress in our future home.

I paused outside my door and thought of knocking. Then, I told myself that *I didn't need to; it was my room,* and I boldly entered.

With her back to me, a female servant in the usual black-and-white attire crouched in front of the floor-to-ceiling gold drapery, a pair of long scissors in her grip. She froze mid-snip. On the floor to her right lay a long swath of the beautiful brocaded material.

The drapery panel, three feet shorter than its twin, hung only a few inches below the bottom of the window.

I clicked the door closed behind me. "Are you the seamstress?" I strolled toward her.

"Yes." She rose to her full height and turned slightly to regard me. "Queen Mary sent me here."

"To hem the drapes?"

"Yes, and two of your gowns. She said the burgundy one will be an inch too long for you."

I found myself staring at the mole beneath her left cheek bone and the sprinkling of freckles across her nose. She was Vincent's wishes all rolled into one.

"Princess Wren. Why didn't you tell me who you are?" Her blue eyes locked on mine. I thought she knew. Wasn't she here in my room?

"I am Princess Wren Alexandria Vankern Wells. And you are?"

"Pearl . . . Pearl Bates."

Pearl. This beautiful young woman was Father's spy, and she was also one of the people or memories that I'd forgotten. Or… I suppose there was the chance we'd never met her, and she'd simply weaseled her way into Father's confidences. Perhaps, she was an opportunist.

"Queen Mary also wanted me to shorten your cream-colored gown before the ball." She glanced toward the armoire, where several gowns now resided, and then at me. "I believe it's time for breakfast."

In her own way, Pearl—the servant spy—was dismissing me.

"What have you found out?" I asked, informing her that I knew.

"About?" Her face paled.

"About my intended . . ." I left my answer vague on purpose.

"Vincent is…" She bit her lower lip at the mistake of a servant dropping a royal title. "He's quite decent." She nodded. "And in the end… I imagine there's the possibility… that you could be… happy together." It took everything that was in her to say this, because she was in love with my intended.

Vincent had been such an ogre to me because he was in love with her.

In a way, it almost made him redeemable.

ΦΦΦ

Later that evening, the three sisters and I gathered in the library for our after-dinner coffee. Father and the men were shooting at targets. A spring-loaded mechanism released clay discs over the cliffs toward the ocean and the men would raise their rifles and shoot at them. Without question, I knew that Father would enjoy it immensely.

I sipped my coffee with cream and settled the cup to the saucer beneath.

Ursula leaned forward in her chair and watched me.

My mouth felt oddly dry, and it took great focus to set the cup and saucer down on a nearby table. The room and all of its contents shifted with my gaze. *What was happening?* Chairs, the piano, the bookcases—everything in the room— slid while the Queen and her accomplices rolled a wooden wheelchair toward me.

While they wheeled me down the hallway, I saw sailing vessels with cannons in the toile wallpaper. I blinked. Had I seen correctly?

"She looks like she sees something in the wallpaper," Ursula said. "I've heard stories about the artist who painted the toile."

"What kind of stories?" Edith asked.

"That he painted hidden stories in the paper. I can't see them."

"Neither can I," Mary said. "The Queen Mother hired the best painter in the world to simply paint the wall to look like wallpaper. He was very upset with her."

In my drowsy state, stories in the paper jumped out at me: ships and cannons, men with peg legs, treasure chests full of gold and jewels... The faster they rolled me past, the faster the grievances were told.

I awoke a short while later, groggy. My arms and ankles were tied to the chair with strips of old dark stockings with frayed gold threads. The three sisters and I were in a small, stone room, far removed from their usual gatherings.

"This will be a longer session than usual, ladies. I have my orders." A plump, elderly woman smiled across an old wooden desk at me.

"The Sweeper Woman is early, for once," Edith said.

I tried to blink myself awake.

"Ma-dame Sweeper," said the woman with a very poor French accent.

Ursula loosened the bandana which bound my mouth.

Before I could yell for help, Edith closed the heavy door.

"What's happening?" I moistened my dry mouth. "Why am I here?"

One barely noticeable gray brow arched as the Sweeper Woman regarded me.

"I demand that you tell me." I sat up straighter in the chair.

"Queenie, did you hear that? Your little successor's becoming demanding." The Sweeper Woman laughed softly.

"I'm afraid we have our hands full," Mary said.

The Sweeper Woman studied me with half-opened eyes behind her wire spectacles and then leaned across the desk toward me. "Tonight, little Miss Queenie, each and every person linked to your happy memories will be wiped from your memory."

Could she do such a thing? Was it possible?

"I hate this." Ursula groaned and chewed on her fist. "I just hate it."

"Shhh! It's almost over." Mary elbowed her.

"She's heartless, unfeeling… evil," Ursula said.

"I will not tolerate another word. Get out!" The Sweeper Woman pointed toward the door. "All of you, except for the girl."

"Awh, Ursula. Now, look what you've done," Edith said.

The three sisters rose and like sheep exiting a lush pasture, they dawdled out of the cold, stone room.

"I told you, we shouldn't have brought her," Edith said, pulling the door closed behind them.

Hours later, Madame Sweeper yawned. Seated on the front of the desk, she swung a gold locket to-and-fro—to-and-fro. "Did you ever have three sisters, a mother, a Maid Kimberlee, Edwin, or a beloved teacher named Crauley?"

"No. Did I?" I searched the crawlspaces of my mind and heart, but there was nothing there.

The old woman smiled. "Now, tell me your happy memories of your father, Wren?"

"Father? Hmm . . ." I searched the shoreline of my memory for something shiny, but all I found were his war stories, memories of hiding in his study, and acts of family betrayal that he justified as being for the good of our country.

"Come, come, we don't have all day," Madame Sweeper rolled back her shoulders, frowning.

"I can't find one," I said as the pendulum swung to-and-fro, to-and-fro.

"You must have *one* happy memory."

Though I searched and sifted not *one* could I find.

"Not one," I whispered.

"Search every corner, every crevice of your soul." Madame Sweeper grew impatient.

"I'm searching." Although I felt certain that I loved my father in a paternal way, not one happy memory did I find. "There isn't one," I said, exhausted.

"How fitting." She chuckled as the pendulum swayed. "Are there any happy memories left in you, Wren?"

In my trance, the corner of my mouth twitched and betrayed me.

"What is it? I saw a memory."

Somehow the lovely memory had slipped her earlier exploration.

"When I was much younger than I am now, not old like you," I said, lacking my usual tactfulness, "someone used to call me *Ducky*."

"When you were younger—not old like me." Madame Sweeper inhaled deeply. "The key will be *Ducky*—your deepest buried sliver of happiness. Do you remember who it was that called you *Ducky*?"

"No. She is only a gray shadow with long hair."

"You're wrong, Wren; the shadow has no hair."

"Who is she?" I asked.

"You are so-oo blessed and such a mess." The old woman laughed. Though her sentiments were unpleasant, a smile warmed her voice. "The key to your happy memories is *Ducky*." The gold pendant continued swaying. "You will never remember any of your fond memories or those attached to them ever again. You won't remember tonight or anything about the nangoonberry stain or anyone who ever made your heart smile. Or me, of course. Wren, you won't remember me—Ma-dame Sweeper—unless someone makes the mistake of calling you *Ducky*. Zip. Zip. Zip. May no one ever slip.

"I am so good at what I do." She gave into a peppered laugh. While she held the pendulum in one hand, she took a list of notes in her other and held them over a nearby candle.

While the paper burned, its tall flame reflected off the pendulum and arched into my eyes, sparking a memory.

"Awh . . . I remember something else," I said.

"You awful girl. What is it now?" Gripping her left arm, the woman grimaced in pain.

"There's a paper hidden away in my case. Words I've written down. Memories. Happy ones." I smiled brightly.

The old woman's face contorted in pain while she swayed the gold locket in front of my eyes. "Forget the paper. It's not in your case. It does not exist. You will not remember any of your happy memories or me. Not one drop. *Ducky* is the key. Zip. Zip. Zip. May no one ever slip." Her plump body shuddered as she slipped off the side of the desk, and fell to the floor like a ball of soft dough.

Who is she? I stared down at the body in front of me. *And why was I tied to this chair?* I tried to yank my arms free, but they were tied too tightly.

"Help! Help! Guards!" I yelled at the top of my lungs. "Help! Guards!"

The door burst open. Instead of men in uniform, Edith, Mary and Ursula barged inside the small, stone room.

"What's happened?" Edith glanced toward the body on the floor and then to me.

"I don't know. She grabbed her left arm and then she fell." I shook my head. "I don't know. Why am I here?"

"Oh, Wren! We didn't know where you were." Mary hugged me to her. Kissing my forehead, she showered me with concern.

Edith's and Ursula's knees cracked as they crouched down to examine the woman in front of me.

"She's gone. She died of a bad heart," Edith said, rising to her feet. She handed something to Mary, and in their exchange, I saw the shimmer of gold.

"She always had a bad heart," Ursula mumbled.

Mary tucked the item into her pocket; then she gazed softly at me and stroked the curve of my cheek. "You're all right, Wren," her sweet voice whispered. "We're here now. The nightmare is over."

Chapter Thirty-two

The next morning, Flora, my middle-aged lady-in-waiting, fashioned my hair. I was seated in front of the vanity table mirror, wearing another birdcage creation—a heavy, burgundy-colored dress with gold brocade that Pearl had masterfully shortened.

"Awh! . . . The stain is gone, Princess Wren!" Flora exclaimed. Eyes wide, she bit her lip.

"The stain?" I didn't quite follow her. Perhaps, I'd dribbled something on my garment the day before. I tried to remember what I'd worn.

"Aye." She piled my hair high atop my head and rolled a swath of it in a hot iron rod. "Master Vincent won't be able to take his eyes off of you."

"And why is that?"

"Because you look more beautiful than ever." She released the iron, producing a long spiral curl.

I gazed in the mirror. Flora was quite skilled at hairdressing. I turned, peering at both sides of my profile in the vanity table mirror.

Would Vincent like the style? Though my hair was still a coppery-red, would he find me more attractive?

"This is how you should wear your hair tonight. It's very becoming on you." Flora patted softly at her creation.

Tonight. I inhaled deeply. Tonight at the ball, Vincent would announce me as his bride. Although he was in love with

Pearl, we would be united in holy matrimony in less than six days.

I joined Vincent and his parents at the breakfast table. Everyone in attendance was unusually quiet, including the servants. My father breakfasted with his men as was routine for him. He'd dine with us later for the midday meal.

I unfolded the serviette in my lap.

"You're looking well today, Wren," Mary said, breaking the silence.

"Thank you, Queen Mary."

"Is she not looking well, Vincent?" she prodded.

Across the table, his dark eyes gazed at me with less interest then when he'd earlier reached for the salt shaker. "Yes, Mother," he said.

My future was void of happiness.

The plate that one of the servants slid in front of me contained five quail eggs fried in browned butter, two pork sausage patties, two scones dotted with golden sultanas, and a dish of muskmelon. I was going to be as portly as the Queen if I continued to eat like her.

"The balmy sea gale has cleared in time for the ball." Mary appeared to be in the best of spirits. "Everything is coming together beautifully." She glanced at her son. "No more excuses."

As Vincent regarded me, he looked like he could still come up with one or two.

I recalled the first time we'd met when he'd told me his favorite hair color. While I remembered his rude remark, I didn't remember my own. A swirly gray fog had replaced my half of our conversation.

I was certainly going mad. I looked around the table at my future family members. If I continued to lose my memory, would the von Drakes be loving toward me, or would they lock me away in a room upstairs?

ΦΦΦ

After breakfast, Vincent and his father adjourned to discuss business, and the three sisters and I made our way up the stairwell. In the library, the ladies sat down with their embroidery while I stood on tiptoe to select a plain leatherbound book from an upper shelf.

"Wrr-een!" Mary's voice was unusually shrill. Her gaze rose from the book in my possession to my eyes. "Please… play piano for us."

While I strolled toward the piano, I flipped to the book's title page. *Grievances of our Fathers – The Von Drake Family.* My pulse quickened. I understood Mary's concern. It was not quite the reading material she'd select for her future daughter-in-law.

I slowed my gait and continued reading on my way to the piano.

Piracy and looting will always be in a von Drake's blood. One must master it and make his life one of servitude to his fellow man. The future generations must make up for the past. Aim for noble deeds so the generational curse of plundering does not continue. I bumped into the corner of the painfully solid piano.

"Wren, that is not reading material for a young woman. Return it at once."

"I'm sorry, Queen Mary." Though the book was extremely hard to put down, I rerouted myself and continued my slow gait toward the bookcase from which I had found it.

"Wren, close that book at once!" Mary ordered.

Family rule number one: When asked about the von Drake family wealth, stick with this basic truth: We have always been in the business of international trade.

"Wree-en!"

I took a moment to collect myself and then reached up to slide the book onto the upper shelf. It was exactly six books in, and on the same shelf as the stuffed white and black eider duck. I'd retrieve the book later this evening and show it to Father.

"I still can't believe she's gone." Ursula said, jabbing her needle into the dark fabric of her stitchery.

"We are not to talk about her," Mary whispered while I strolled empty-handed toward the piano.

"I never liked when she called us the ugly sis—"

"Ursula!" Mary's hands froze mid-stitch as she stared at me.

Wide-eyed, Edith turned to stare at me, also.

I paused mid-stride and smiled softly at them. "I don't think you're ugly." I could see their anxious concern and dug deeper for the right words. "In your own way, you're all quite pleasant to look at."

Their shoulders slackened, and they sighed like my compliment had brought profound relief. They'd needed my encouragement, the poor dears.

I smoothed my heavy dress behind me and sat down at the rosewood grand piano.

"Play something pretty, Wren. None of your dark music," Mary said.

"You forget, she plays from memory," said Edith.

"Play about the lollyberry kiss and the night you turned sixteen." Ursula smiled, pulling her needle high into the air.

What did she mean? I'd never been kissed. I stared at her.

"Urs-ula!" Mary's embroidery arm dropped to her side. "Have you gone mad?"

"No." The large woman's beefy shoulders sunk and she gazed at me with a pitifully sad look.

"Nothing dark," Mary said and nodded for me to play.

I set my fingers to the keys and tried to play only the white, flat ones. Through the windows, the sky was a light gray. The rocky cliffs rolled down to the sea. If I were outside, I'd take down my high, pinned hair and let the wind weave its fingers through my curls and flap my dress, exposing my knee-high boots. Then, I thought of the decadent breakfast and how satiated I felt. My music waned as I continued searching my heart, that was all the light, pretty thoughts I could find.

From there, I drove the tips of my fingers deep into the sharp, black keys and recalled the first time I'd met my betrothed. I dwelled on Vincent's look of disappointment; and realized there had also been disgust.

"Nothing dark," Mary said.

My betrothed was in love with my seamstress. My future would not be a pretty one.

The library door swung open, and I could tell by the voices that Milton, Vincent, and my father had entered.

"Play something light. Nothing dreary," Mary said.

While I faced the window, several birds soared into view. Wings spread, they floated on the salt nipped breeze. I could drum up very few light memories, so I tried to imagine what flight must feel like for a bird. The beauty of flying over the ocean, the rocky cliffs, the untouched sandy shorelines...

Though it had been years since I'd played the piano, my fingers had not forgotten. I remembered sitting at our piano back home, my legs—not long enough to reach the pedals—had swung beneath the bench and a gray shadowy figure had sat nearby. "I thought she didn't play piano," Vincent said behind me.

"Wren!" Father sounded more surprised than pleased.

"Yes?" I paused, placed my hands in my lap, and waited for him to explain his outburst.

"Keep playing. It's . . . lovely," he said.

In all of my years, I'd never heard Father say the word *lovely* in the same sentence as me. His rare compliment was a gift.

"Nothing dark. Something light." Mary's words made me think of a white butterfly.

I tried to play something light like crepes, and despite Father's compliment, it soon began to feel heavy like this morning's breakfast.

Father strolled over to stand near the left side of the piano and with his back to the window, he gazed at me.

I glanced at him, smiling. While my music fluttered between dark and light, Father's chest inflated like the masts of a ship in a strong north gale.

After the final cadence, I remained seated and clasped my hands together in my lap with perfect piano posture. I didn't understand why I had taken such a long absence from it.

Father's soft gaze continued and locked on mine. As he looked at me, a love-lit tenderness filled his amber-colored eyes. Then a tear slid down his cheek. My gaze followed the droplet's course as it rolled past the line of his jaw.

He'd missed my playing, too.

"Wren . . ." He rested his arms on the lid of the piano and leaned toward me as if he were about to tell me something that was only for my ears. "We are going to go home now," he whispered. "We're going to go home."

Chapter Thirty-three

As I pulled the library door closed behind me, I averted my gaze from everyone—Mary, Edith, Vincent... Then, I took several steps down the hallway and paused. I would only eavesdrop for three sentences.

"This is morally unforgivable, inexcusable . . ." Father said. "Despicable."

"She will love me now," Vincent said.

"I told you not to do this!" Father's voice traveled back and forth across the room as he paced.

No wonder I rarely played the piano; it had put him in a very foul mood.

"Do what?" Milton asked.

"The stain is gone! When you take away a person's memories, you take away their ability to love, to grow, and appreciate who you are."

What stain? Who was Father talking about? Could it possibly be me? Had they taken away my memory? I forced myself to continue down the corridor toward my bedchamber. I was glad we were leaving. Though I would miss the three sisters, I cared very little for Vincent—or the wallpaper, for that matter. In its depths, I saw sailing vessels on lofty seas. Each time I strolled past, I saw something new. This trip was no different.

Happy to reach the sanctity of my room and its celestial wallpaper, I locked the door behind me. I packed my things into my case and then I sat on my bed and waited patiently for Father's knock upon the door. After what felt like a very long time, I grew tired and lay back on the bed to stare at the ceiling medallion overhead.

Had I misunderstood Father? Or had something gone very wrong?

I grew tired of waiting, and climbed down the steps of my bed and unlocked the door. For some reason, it had been bolted closed on the other side and would not budge.

Not a good sign.

Would the von Drakes allow Father to change his mind? Perhaps cold feet were not an option once an alliance was formed.

I cranked open my chamber window. From the second story, there was no balcony or ivy to climb down. But there was one of Father's messenger birds. The gray pigeon hopped along the stone ledge toward me, a piece of paper wrapped around its leg. I untwisted what might very well be a message from Father.

The strip of paper read: *Tonight at the ball, do not drink the punch.* Something had gone askew, and we were leaving from the ballroom instead of my room.

I put the dry, little strip of paper in my mouth and chewed, trying to destroy all evidence of its content.

Two servants entered my chamber. Gertrude carried a tray with my lunch and a pot of tea, and Flora toted a magnificent ivory-colored gown, weighing at least five stones.

I swallowed the round, little wad of paper.

"Pearl finished hemming it," Flora said. The skirt's five-tiered layers were hand stitched with gold thread. Like Queen Mary's wardrobe, the dress was heavy decadence, including the ruffled petticoats and of course, the steel hooped crinoline cage.

"Have you seen my father?" I asked the young women.

"No, Princess Wren," they said with lowered eyes.

ΦΦΦ

From the ballroom, the afternoon view of the harbor was quite the sight—sailing ships, dinghies, tuna boats and even a tug boat were anchored. Every slip of their extensive moorage appeared to be occupied. Guests in their finery walked the rough-hewn planks of the docks. The annual Davenport Ball appeared to be a boat-in-only party. Instead of the front door, it was the elevator that opened repeatedly.

The guests were as varied in dress as the boats in which they'd come. Eye-patches were in fashion. Several lovely, middle-aged women even wore the trendy, dark eye covering. Some of their garments had patches, as well.

Pearl was the only person in the room that I knew—besides the von Drakes, that is. I made my way towards her, surprised that Mary allowed her seamstress to attend parties dressed like royalty. Most likely, Pearl's attendance was on account of Vincent.

The young woman was not only beautiful but clever. From the gold brocade drapery, she'd sewn and now wore a magnificent gown with at least five tiers to its skirt. The bodice was a triangle of sky blue material that matched her reticule. She wore both the colors of Davenport and Blue Sky.

But, whose side was she really on?

I paused beside her. Though our crinoline cages touched, we were at least six feet apart. "You match my room," I regarded her over my shoulder.

"You sound surprised." About her slim neck, she wore a three-strand, lustrous pearl necklace. Each pearl was exceptionally round. She lifted a hand to her mouth as if to cough. "You are not to drink the punch," she whispered.

"I know." Had Father somehow tainted the punch with the milky chalk plant?

I was about to ask Pearl if she knew Father's whereabouts when I saw Vincent stroll across the ballroom toward us, his gaze fixed on the woman beside me.

Overhead the chandelier swung, and a slight rumble shook the expansive room.

Was it an earthquake or . . . ?

The orchestra stopped playing. The last note was a viola's.

From across the width of the ballroom, I recognized Lambert's frame and posture. His curly hair was now gray. He was indeed the violist of Davenport.

"Milton! What was that?" Queen Mary's voice trembled as she raised a white-gloved hand.

"Just a viola." He grinned. "And a slight quake. Nothing to worry about," he said on his way to the punch table.

"Father," Vincent bobbed a finger into the air, "there's something I need to speak with you about."

"Now is not the time." Milton lifted a crystal goblet with a bubbly liquid high into the air and cleared his throat. "A toast," he said, loudly.

Where was Father? I peered around the ballroom. Even though I'd received the little note, I couldn't help worrying about him. Had he made it to the safety of his men? Or had they hidden him away in a dungeon somewhere? Was he even alive?

The noise in the crowded room dimmed, and all five-hundred of their guests turned to give King Milton their undivided attention. Servants carried trays about the room until each and every person held up a glass of the punch, including the members of the orchestra.

"A toast, my good friends and family," said the King.

Family? I recalled the sentiments that I'd read only that morning: *Piracy and looting will always be in a von Drake's blood.* If Father was dead, this might very well be my future.

A plump, elderly guard marched through the double doors and into the center of the room. "King Milton, there's been a disturbance—"

"Now is not the time." Milton pointed toward the punch table. "Get a glass."

The guard reached for a goblet from a nearby tray and held it high like those in attendance.

"It is with great ceremony, that I pronounce Vincent's future bride and our reliance with Blue Sky Kingdom."

Milton was far too relaxed for as poor of a public speaker as he was.

". . . the industrious Princess Wren of Blue Sky." He held out his arm toward me.

I swallowed a large lump in my throat and managed to smile as my gaze scanned many of the faces of those in attendance. Was my father guised among them?

"The merger will expand our territories. Our future railway will reach the inferior of the continent." Milton carried the goblet high as he walked a very straight line toward us. "To Vincent and Wren, a toast." He paused beside us. In unison, he and everyone in the room lowered their glasses to take a sip.

I tipped my goblet and made sure the frothy liquid did not reach my lips.

"Father . . . I'm in love with Pearl," Vincent uttered quite loudly.

I told myself to blink as I took in all the implications.

"No, no, no." Milton shook his head. Under his breath, he added, "You'll do as I say or remember..."

"Your Lordship . . ." the elderly guard started toward us.

Milton held out a stiff hand. "Now, is not the time."

"I'm going to take you up on the cottage up the coast and marry Pearl, the woman I love," Vincent said.

Over my shoulder, I regarded Pearl.

She cast me an apologetic smile.

"The seamstress?" Milton yawned.

"Yes." Vincent yawned, too.

And so did a large percentage of their guests.

Around us, women swayed this way and that.

Men swayed as they tried to catch them.

"Your Lordship," the elderly guard stumbled forward, "King Francis' men have taken out the briii—dge." The guard stumbled sideways taking out one of the dessert tables.

"What the devil?" Milton collapsed backward, landing in a padded chair before rolling to the floor.

Everyone swayed, except, that is, for Pearl and me. We sat down on nearby slipper chairs and waited for the chaos in the room to still.

Guests stumbled, and crystal goblets crashed to the floor.

On stage, the viola in Lambert's grip emitted the ugliest, most piercing sound imaginable.

I suppressed a smile.

The pianist planted his forehead in the keys and played one, long poorly chosen cadence. Chairs and tables overturned and crinoline cages exposed far too many unmentionables, Queen Mary's being one of them.

"You are quite gifted." I admired Pearl's gown. The lovely pearl buttons adorning the shoulder of each sleeve tied in beautifully with the pearls strung about her neck.

"Thank you, Princess Wren. I may have to support my future husband with my gift. It seems he's been raised with no skills of any kind. But I'm told the cottage is quite nice."

"Yes, and you're fortunate that it's along the sea." I pictured Vincent on a ship picking up the trade of his forefathers.

My own father's frame filled the nearest doorway, and behind him, the chest of a giant before Helmer bent down and entered.

Father was alive. My heart soared.

He waved a hand for us to join him in the corridor.

Pearl led the way, stepping around and sometimes over the guests littering the dance floor. Near the punch table, we stepped over great Aunt Edith's arm, extended in a toast, most likely to Aunt Ursula who was only a few feet away.

Helmer, the giant, appeared to have accompanied my father as a bodyguard.

"Thank you for all you've done," Father addressed Pearl. "Now, you should return to the ballroom and pretend that you've also partaken of the punch. Unless, of course, you'd prefer to return with us to Blue Sky?"

"I will stay on here. Thank you for everything." She glanced at me. "Bye, Ennie."

"Goodbye." I was tempted to tell Father the news of Pearl's and Vincent's engagement, but from the tight way that he carried his mouth, I knew that now was not the time.

ΦΦΦ

The Davenport guards, who were on duty on the bridge, had also drunk the punch. Some slept upright, while others lay sleeping on their sides.

"We have a problem, Wren," Father informed me as we started across the bridge. "Herbert was supposed to blow the north end of the bridge up after our return, but... he blew it up before."

"What?" I suppressed a laugh. "Milton said it was an earthquake." I shook my head. "Herbert! You really shouldn't give him any more chances."

"You're right. Things go wrong on his watch. But, we're in luck. There's still enough of the bridge left for us to cross."

Off in the distance, the bridge looked like a giant diving board over the abyss.

"It looks gone to me," I said, trying to keep pace with Father and the giant.

As we drew closer to the edge, my earlier vision was correct. A narrow swath of the bridge, a remnant piece, was still attached at about a forty-five-degree angle. It had parked itself on a ledge on the other side of the ravine. The long, steel cable hung ten feet above it like a tightrope. The distance separating us from the other side was a mere thirty feet; but, the terrifying drop below made it feel like a mile.

"Once we reach the other side, our men will pull us up," Father said.

"The other side?" I heard myself whisper. My gaze narrowed to our men across the way. A dozen or so of them held onto a large braided rope that was tied to a towering spruce tree behind them.

"Yes, we'll wrap the rope around the steel cable above us. Though, there is a chance it might fray. We'll walk the old road down."

"Fray?" I stared below. The old road down wasn't even a foot wide. I could picture the wind grabbing a hold of my crinoline and sailing me off like a balloon.

My crinoline!

"But... you needn't worry. If worst comes to worse, we will have another rope tied around us," Father added.

"I have an idea," I said.

"What, Ennie?" Helmer asked with enthusiasm.

"Wha-at?" Father asked. I could tell he was short on patience.

Turning my back to our men, I lifted up my ivory ball gown and then the ruffled petticoat layers underneath and began unfastening the hook-and-eye closure of the crinoline cage.

"What are you doing, Wren? Have you gone mad?" Father glared at me.

"No. You'll see." I slid the hoop skirt down over my hips. It fell to the ground, and I stepped out of the wide contraption. "The crinoline cage is made up of steel hoops." I smiled up at him. "We can each have our own hoops to bend around the steel cable."

He was following me now; I could see it in his wide eyes.

"Ennie!" Helmer was, too.

"You are ingenious," Father breathed.

"No, not really." I smiled and for a moment, I let his compliment sink in. "I hate this thing. I can't bear to wear it another minute."

Helmer went first, tied off with a rope to our men. He bent five of the hoops in half, into the shape of a letter "C" and wrapped them over the top of the steel cable above him. With this hand-hold, he took a slow step out toward the road below.

Across the cavern, the men who weren't holding onto the rope bent to one knee. I'd always known we were a praying country, but seeing it firsthand meant a great deal to me.

Only the ball of Helmer's foot touched down before the speed of steel on steel took over, and he slid through the air, whooping. He made the terrifying ride look easy, almost fun.

His feet met the road, slowing his advance, and then he stepped off onto the ledge on the other side.

Father wanted to go last, so it was my turn next.

I glanced over my shoulder toward the sleeping castle. If Herbert hadn't blasted the bridge, we could have walked right out. Vincent was marrying Pearl.

My heart pounded as a rope was tied snugly about my middle. I stepped closer to the edge of the bridge and stared at the abyss below. A feather could take a month to float down.

Boom. Ba ba boom. Ba ba boom. My heart hammered in my chest.

Maybe I should go back and marry Vincent if he'd have me.

"Courage, my girl," Father said.

I sucked air deep into my lungs.

"Wren . . ."

"Yes." I glanced over my shoulder at him.

"There are times in life when we're scared enough that we don't realize it's a grand adventure. Try and enjoy this moment; it will be over before you know it."

My father was crazy.

"I'll try," I breathed.

"Good. Now, I'm going to give you a push, and you won't even have to worry about the road."

"Oh?" I'd liked the idea of having something solid beneath my feet. But... perhaps this was one of those times that Father knew best.

On tiptoe, I reached up and looped the bent hoops over the top of the cable. I took a deep breath and holding on tightly, stepped off. I dangled in the air, not tall enough to touch the road before Father gently pushed me.

Steel on steel was like ice on marble. I soared through the air, the wind in my face and not once did I look down. Helmer caught me in his arms before I could hit the wall on the other side.

The ledge was not large enough to comfortably accommodate the three of us, so Helmer prepared the rope for my ascent. He formed two large knots, one for me to hold onto with my hands overhead, and one for me to stand on with my feet.

"She's ready." He called up to our men.

I bumped against the rock wall as the rope lifted me, several feet at a time. I glanced down at Helmer, who waved up at me, smiling. Then I made the mistake of letting my gaze drift slightly to the left. *Down* is only a four-letter word; it really should be much longer. It should be one of the longest, hardest to spell words in the English language.

I couldn't seem to tear my gaze away from the terrifying drop below when several pairs of arms lifted me over the side to safety.

"Thank you," I breathed to the men around me.

Doctor Larkin pulled me several meters away from the edge and wrapped a blanket around me. From there, we waited for Father and Helmer's arrival.

I was shaking terribly now and feared my knees would crumple if I peered over the side to watch. I kept telling myself that when Father was safely on top, we would kiss the ground together like Christopher Columbus had done when he'd first landed on Cat Island.

A few minutes later, the soldiers on their bellies reached and pulled Father over the side.

Helmer was next.

Father dusted himself off and strode toward me, extending his arms.

Gone was any bravery I might have had, I simply burst into tears.

ΦΦΦ

In the carriage, Father held me and stroked my wet hair away from my cheeks. "I'm proud of you, Wren. Never have I been so proud," he whispered. "Not even when you were a little girl playing your viola."

Chapter Thirty-four

"**A** part of your daughter's mind appears to be locked, trapping her memories. In this case, her memories of loved ones." Dr. Larkin studied my complexion. I was seated on a stump in our camp several hours from Davenport.

"But, I remember Father," I said.

"Yes, but you don't remember your mother, your siblings, your governess…"

It was a puzzle. Despite our differences, I felt quite certain that I loved my father.

"What about Crauley? Wren, do you remember Crauley, your teacher?" Father's eyes narrowed as he studied me.

I stared toward the dark silhouette of the tall trees in the distance. I had no memory of the name. I shifted my gaze to Father's. "Who is he?"

He closed his eyes and folded his arms in front of him. "She's always been clever, Doctor; is there any chance, whatsoever?"

"None. Absolutely none." Dr. Larkin, a skinny man with a bowed back, set his hands on his narrow hips and studied me. "The hypnotist had to go deep into her memory to get rid of the stain. Whoever did this locked the memory with a key— either a word or a phrase. Something that was significant or important to your daughter."

"Wre-en." Father's voice cracked.

"It's simple," Dr. Larkin said. "We'll go back, find the hypnotist who did this. She has the key. They always do. But, she'll want to charge you for it."

"She died. Holding the only key to my daughter's memory, the old woman had the gall to die."

"I'm very sorry," Dr. Larkin whispered.

The old woman who'd lain at my feet must have been the hypnotist, the stealer of my memories.

"Why did she do it?" I asked.

"Vincent was behind this. You will not be marrying him." Father's mouth tightened.

"No, I most certainly won't," I said with a little laugh. "At the ball, he told Milton that he was in love with Pearl; that he'd rather marry her and live in the cottage up the coast than…" I shook my head.

"Pearl! She failed to tell me that." Father heaved a weary sigh. "Had I known that would have changed everything. We blew the bridge up when we could have just walked away."

Had Vincent stolen my memories to win my Father's disapproval? If that had indeed been his plan, he was much better at artifice than I had given him credit. I hoped he and the fabric stealer would be very unhappy together.

ΦΦΦ

Eleven days later . . .

I remembered home. The old woman may have locked people that I loved behind a dark curtain in my mind, but I had not forgotten the coppery red turrets, the weeping cherry trees that lined the drive, or the distant hills which patterned the landscape of Blue Sky.

Following Father's instructions, the driver parked our carriage in the livery stables. Our guards unstrapped our things from the back while Father and I stepped out of the shadows of the moss riddled stone building into the bright sunlight.

Off in the distance, a woman ran across the sweeping lawns toward us. Her gown was long, and her hair was gray. Was she Maid Kimberlee?

"Run to her! Run to your mother!" Father's deep voice wavered.

"I thought you said her hair is like mine?" I cupped a hand over my eyes.

"It used to be. Run, Wren, or you'll break her heart."

I lifted the heavy skirts of my Davenport ball gown and began running toward my mother.

"Wren," Father called after me, "tell her that you're sorry. Tell her…"

I waved back at him and continued running. Though she was still a great distance from me, my mother held her arms out wide for our embrace, and then she stopped running altogether, perhaps to catch her breath. But I kept on, narrowing the distance between us. As I grew closer, I saw that she was crying. Holding her hands over her chest, my mother, a beautiful woman with long, gray hair, was sobbing.

Her apparent love for me prompted tears to stream down my cheeks, as well.

She continued running towards me, bridging the distance. With the strength of a young woman, she threw her arms around my neck and gripped me tightly to her. "Wren… Wren…" Her voice broke. "We didn't know." Her warm tears spilled onto my neck. "We didn't know."

"I'm so sorry, Mother, so very, very sorry," I said over and over and found myself aware of the subtle scent of lavender perfume.

She held me away from her and, beaming, smoothed my hair from my face. My mother's features—her blue-green eyes, her clear skin, and the contours of her face—were like looking in a mirror of my future self.

A child had joined us—a girl with long, kinky auburn hair and pert-apple cheeks; trailing behind her was a blond boy. Odessa and Edwin—the twins. I held out an arm to embrace them as well; and we stood, the four of us, in a huddle of love and reunion.

Why in the world had I left? What had I pursued that could have possibly pulled me away from so much love?

ΦΦΦ

Eleven months later . . .

Father held out his hand to me. He was seated in his large wing-backed chair by the fire in the study. "Sit down," he said. There was no place to sit close enough to retain his hand, so I knelt near his feet.

"I've heard stories, Wren, and I would like you to tell me what you remember of the months when you worked in Gruel Kitchen." His jaw muscle twitched in his cheek.

"From who?" I asked, stalling. I did not want to remember Gruel Kitchen.

"Helmer has told me numerous stories."

And Father obviously believed him.

"I've heard Helmer's side; now I'd like to hear yours." He regarded me with a sheen in his eyes.

I gazed into the fire and wondered what good could come of it. Then for Father's sake, I began with the auction and told him every detail that I could remember about Stockford and the injustices there.

"A new governing body has been in place for almost a year." He nodded for me to continue.

"Good." That made me feel better. I nodded and continued. "I was a bad cook and the giants, especially Gid, wanted a cook who could sing." I told him about the gruel cakes and the cello.

He chuckled. "I'd like to hear you play the cello."

I smiled and in my retelling, I tried to work past patches of gray fog. "I'd lay awake in the middle of the night, hearing your voice."

I could tell by the knit of his brows that this surprised him.

"Snippets from my childhood. Things I'd overheard you say when I wasn't supposed to be in your study." I smiled at him. "Attack in the evening. Attack with swiftness. Never let your soldiers know your plans."

"We missed out on some good years, you and me." His gaze was soft.

"But, we are making up for them."

He nodded. "I want you to tell me the difficult part of your time in Gruel Kitchen."

Gruel Kitchen was my Misery Hill—my most painful battle. Would my retelling bring healing?

"After the giants fled, I hid in the pig pen from Remford, Blaird's giant. I was *locked* in there with the pigs—locked out of Gruel Kitchen." Though I tried to keep my voice steady, it reached a higher pitch. "For several days, Remford did not feed or water the pigs, and I could hear him through the door, laughing. He was the Devil himself, wasn't he?" I stared at Father.

"Yes, but you need not worry about him anymore. Over a year ago, now, Vincent and his men took care of him."

"Yes, I heard." It was a detail that I'd almost forgotten.

A gray-blue fog of emptiness wove its way in and out of my recollections. "When I was at my lowest, I recalled a verse that a woman in Hampershire had told me was just for me, *to knock and keep on knocking.*

"I began to knock, and I kept knocking on the door to the kitchen. I was no longer afraid of Remford; I was afraid of dying." I cried a little while Father softly rubbed my shoulder.

"There, there, now. Try and finish."

"I can't. There's an empty, gray fog." I shook my head. "But, I know this: Someone must have heard me, for here I am telling you."

He cradled my chin in his strong hand and gazed at me again with fierce, yet tender emotion. "And we praise God that you are. You are brave, Wren, and smart. But we are now in another battle. There are still people in your life that we must fight for. We are still at war.

"We want you with us. We want you home."

ΦΦΦ

Father and I often enjoyed our morning coffee on the terrace overlooking Mother's roses; but this particular morning, he wanted us to enjoy our coffee on the settee upstairs in the corridor near his study, across from the portraits of Alia and me.

"Why are you so dressed up?" he asked before taking a sip of his dark coffee.

"Mother's bridge party is today." For her ladies' engagement, Mother had selected a floor-length mint-colored chiffon, fitted at the waist for me to wear. My hair was rolled tight into a high, smooth bun with one vibrant peacock feather poking out of the top. I looked very out-of-the-ordinary, but it was the latest fashion. Mother was showing me off in her own way.

"Cook's pastries were exceptional this morning." Father patted my hand. "He asked if you remember the *brioche* rolls he often packed for your visits to *Crauley's*?" As he'd done of late, Father added a lilt to certain words.

"I remember the brioche rolls, but I don't remember Crauley. "I remember the brioche rolls, but I don't remember Crauley. That means I cared for him a great deal, doesn't it?"

"Yes." He nodded. "There were several times that you did not want to come home after visiting your beloved viola teacher."

I marveled at both my loss and my lack of grief.

"Father . . ." I stared into his love-filled eyes. "Why do I remember you? I mean . . . of course, I've always loved you."

He turned his profile to me, and the corner of his mouth pinched as he studied my portrait. "You were seven when I returned home from war, and you were very close to your mother. The next eight years, we were often at odds. But…" He shook his head and leaned forward to glance past the potted ficus tree toward the stairwell like he half expected someone.

"Do you think I blamed you when Alia left home? Mother said I was very lonely." I studied the beautiful portrait of my sister. "I hope I didn't."

"Most likely. But, we don't know for sure. You rarely confided in anyone." Rising to his feet, he strode to the mahogany sideboard, where he picked up a pile of mail.

I peered down in the mirror of my coffee. His abruptness made me think that I'd touched a nerve.

"You're right on time, Brody," Father said.

Off to my left, one of our guards had reached the top of the stairs.

"Good. I got lost in the ballroom, took the wrong hallway." While the young guard approached, his gaze was drawn to Alia's portrait, and I had an open view of him. In his blue and white uniform, he was quite good-looking, with thick, slightly wavy auburn hair and a sturdy build.

"Is this your oldest daughter, Princess Alia?" He halted a few feet to the left of the portrait of her. "I remember hearing about her."

"Yes. Alia and Wren were both painted six months before they turned sixteen."

The young man's attention drifted from Alia's portrait to the one of me. For an awkwardly long moment, his gaze locked on my own that George had so masterfully captured in the oil.

His Adam's apple bobbed in his neck.

Father cleared his throat. "I've just been enjoying coffee with my daughter," he said, then he continued sorting through the pile of letters or grievances as he often referred to them.

The young man slowly turned and his somber gaze regarded me over his shoulder.

I smiled politely.

"Wren . . ." he breathed my name.

Did I know him? I glanced at Father for a clue; but, head bent, he sorted through the letters.

"Princess Wren." The young guard appeared to collect himself and briefly bowed his head.

I nodded and took a sip of the lukewarm coffee, cradling the cup with the saucer beneath to protect my dress. Had it been empathy or commiseration that I'd heard in his voice? Perhaps he was aware of my condition.

"Wren, Brody is Edwin's younger brother," Father said.

"Edwin?" I smiled, more relaxed now with the young man. "My father is very fond of your brother."

"The feeling is mutual." Brody returned his gaze to my portrait, and his chest expanded. "The painter captured a distinct keenness in your gaze, Princess Wren."

"Yes." Even though he was not the first to notice, I found the guard's boldness, unsettling. "How would you describe my sister's gaze in her portrait?" It was easy to see that Alia held a dreamy, faraway expression.

With his hands clasped behind his back, he regarded the painting. "She looks like she doesn't have a care in the world like she's only thinking about shoes."

Maybe he was right.

Father chuckled and waved a hand. "Come along; we have much to discuss."

The guard bowed ever so slightly before following Father into his study, and the door latched behind them.

I regarded my portrait. Curious at what the young guard had seen, I rose to my feet and stopped within arm's reach of the canvas. While a soft, dreamy look waltzed in Alia's gaze, romance did not dance in mine.

I strode down the hallway to my chamber to stand in front of the cheval mirror. I lifted my chin slightly and then one brow until my expression was similar to the one that I had just beheld. Gazing at my reflection, I tried to understand the girl in the portrait.

Even though I recalled standing idle for long sessions while George had painted me, I didn't remember my thoughts. Yet, the quirk of my brow was proof that I'd been contemplating something far more important to me than shoes.

Chapter Thirty-five

September, one month later . . .

The moon, full and bright, shone through the parted drapes and across my coverlet into my eyes. I climbed out of bed and grabbed handfuls of the heavy drapes. While I pulled them closed, I spotted a guard on a large, white horse across the lawn—on this side of the labyrinth hedge. Beside the guard's horse sat a pig on its hind haunches, and a raven stood on the young man's shoulder.

I retracted one of the drapery panels to see if I'd imagined it all; and peeked around the side of it for a glimpse of them.

Illuminated by moonlight, Father's young guard—Brody Hew—and his pets appeared to be keeping watch… and of my room at that. Since Davenport, Father worried more about my safety.

The guard held the bird out to his side, and it flew in my direction, landing on the ledge outside of my window. A small scrap of paper was attached to the dark bird's leg with a piece of twine.

I cranked open the window a few inches, reached through the narrow expanse, and untied the knot.

By moonlight, I unfolded and read the little slip of paper: *The pig's name is Daisy.*

That was all.

Why in the world did he want me to know his pig's name? He was still watching my room, still watching me. The young guard was obviously a simpleton.

I strolled to my writing desk and wrote on the other side of the paper: *Daisy Bacon?* I returned to the window and wrapped my response around the patient bird's leg.

I very much doubted if the guard had permission to send me notes. I would ask Father in the morning. I drew the drapes closed and then returned to bed. My last thoughts were of the pig in the moonlight. I hoped Ogden, our cook, made bacon for breakfast.

I could almost smell it.

ΦΦΦ

Mid-morning, Father and I sat alone with our cups of coffee on the terrace, and I addressed the previous night's odd incident.

"He is not a stranger. You met Brody Hew outside of my study, a few weeks ago, and he has my permission."

"Am I not to think it strange that one of your guards is sending me notes in the middle of the night?"

"How many has he sent?"

"One." I was allowing myself to get ruffled over one little note, but I didn't know the man.

"I have also given permission for others to send you notes." He stirred his coffee with a small spoon, studying me. "And, you are to read the notes aloud."

"Who else? Ogden?" I asked. Only yesterday, our cook had sent a note with my afternoon cup of tea. It had read: *Do you remember your love for fruit butter? You loved the purple plum most.*

"Yes, Ogden."

"Well, of course, I remember Ogden and Wooten." Wooten, our scribe, had also sent a note. "But, it's very unsettling to be sent notes in the middle of the night by a stranger." Everyone was treating me like an oddity, a child. "Remind them that I have lost only my memories, not my mind." I sighed heavily. I felt like a tightly strung bow, ready to snap.

"You cannot get frustrated with us for trying. We all need to be patient, Wren, including you."

Of course, this was very easy for him to say. He had not been the one vexed with odd greetings for the past year. Instead of commonalities, such as *how are you today, Princess Wren?* I encountered: *the pig's name is Daisy.*

Did Daisy have something to do with my past? If so, what? There were pigs in Gruel Kitchen, but I did not have one as a pet. I'd remember. Wouldn't I? Surely, I had not gotten so close to a pig to tell the old woman about one.

"Wren . . ." Father wanted my full attention.

"Yes." I met his gaze.

"Your mother received a letter from Queen Mary. Vincent and Pearl are expecting their first child. Mary conveyed her apologies. And, her postscript was: the hypnotist—the Sweeper Woman—made you tell her all of your *happy* memories."

Father watched me closely.

The old woman hadn't simply stolen loved ones; she'd stolen my happy memories. That's why I still remembered Father.

"It makes sense, for I've always loved you," I said.

We gazed softly at one another.

"Mary also said to try this phrase…" He cleared his throat trying to prepare me. "Ugly sisters," he said very clearly.

I listened deeply and waited.

Nothing changed.

I shrugged a heavy sigh. "I'm glad that we're on speaking terms with her again," I said.

"Yes, though she conveyed that Milton is still very upset with me about the bridge."

Most likely he was also upset about the railroad, but I wouldn't bring it up.

ΦΦΦ

Moonlight did not stream through my parted drapes that night for I'd drawn them fully closed. I fell into a blissful sleep.

Tap-tap-tap. Tap.

I awakened for some reason and stared into the darkness. Tap-tap-tap. Yes, there it was again, a rhythmic tapping coming from the windows.

If Brody Hew had climbed the ivy to knock on the leaded glass, I would give him a tongue lashing, maybe even a push. I descended the steps from my bed and donned my house robe before I drew back the drapes. Illuminated by moonlight, the young guard on horseback and his well-trained pig were again on duty.

The raven pecked his beak against my window.

The guard should not be allowed to wake me, keep me up all hours of the night with his incessant little notes. I untied the scrap of paper from the bird's leg and unrolled it in the moonlight.

The note read *Buttercups*.

"Buttercups," I said with great annoyance. They were a poisonous, flowering weed. Perhaps pretty to the untrained eye, but like Father, I would never let any of my horses graze on them.

I sat at my writing desk and wrote in tiny print: *I am aware that they are poisonous. Please, no more "late" notes.*

I attached the note to the bird's leg and swished the raven away. Then, without giving the guard the pleasure of a glance, I drew the heavy drapery closed.

ΦΦΦ

Several days later, Mother and I were seated in the blue drawing room. She was reading one of her novels, *A Tale of Two Cities,* while I stared out the window at the distant hills. I felt listless, with little to do.

"Mother, why was I named Wren?" I asked while she turned the page.

"Well . . . my older brother used to call me *Wren.* It was a term of endearment, a nickname." She lowered the book to her lap and appeared thoughtful. "I loved Teddy's nickname for me. Your father, as you know, was away at war, so it was up to me to name you. With your coppery-red hair, I thought you looked like me."

"Irene and Wren," I said, noting the similarity.

"Yes, Teddy called me Wren just like Alia used to call—"

"Mother! Mother!" Odessa's voice carried down the corridor before she raced into the room. The apples of her cheeks were flushed with excitement. "Look at what I found!" She waved a fine linen letter in her grip. "It was in Wren's viola case behind the velvet."

Even though I held my hand out for it, Odessa handed the paper to Mother.

"Words I need to remember," Mother said, skimming the top of the page. "Wren, this might hold the key." She covered her mouth with one hand and continued reading.

"What did I write?" I asked.

She shook her head, holding the paper closer to her.

"What were you doing in my case, Odessa?" I turned my frustration on my younger sister. Several times of late, I'd caught her alone with my viola, running a hand over the wood, fingering the carved hearts.

"I was looking for rosin." Her head spun as Father entered the room. "Father! Father!" She ran to him and entwined one of her arms in his.

"What is all the excitement about?" He glanced over at me.

"I found a letter in Wren's viola case, tucked behind the velvet. Hidden. Just the edge of it was peeking out," Odessa said, breathlessly.

"Brody Hew's name is on the top line." Mother's curious gaze locked on Father's as she handed him the stationary.

"Brody Hew?" I shook my head. "The guard? Why would I write about him?"

Father glanced at me.

I began to feel uneasy. Perhaps, I had not written the letter. Perhaps someone else had hidden it in my viola case?

"I remember Brody Hew—Edwin's younger brother," Mother said, an airy quality to her voice. "Two summers ago, when we were at the lake house, Wren tried to go to town for candy all by herself. Brody later informed you of it; remember, Francis?" She regarded Father, smiling. "The two of you had such a fine laugh." Her gaze returned to me. "Your father loves Brody."

Father read the top line, then folded the letter, before sliding it into the pocket of his long blazer. "We'll go over it later, after dinner." He regarded me.

I was surprised he could wait. I couldn't wait. What if it held the key? And why would I go to town by myself for candy? Somehow Brody Hew had stopped me. I must have been upset with him. Maybe that's why I'd written his name at the top of the list. But, no, the woman had locked away my happy memories, not my unhappy ones. Could it be that she'd made an exception with Brody Hew?

"I remember now." Mother held up her pointer finger. "Brody thought you might be trying to leave to meet Vincent, your betrothed, before the wedding. But, I told your father that you were probably hoping to see Alia. You were very close." She sighed, meeting my gaze. "It was all very odd for us, you know. You never asked. We would have given you anything, Wren. But you never asked for a thing."

The past year—what I'd done and why—was like putting together a difficult puzzle of a thousand tiny pieces. And, in my case, many of the pieces were missing. Maybe I wasn't alone; maybe it was this way for others when they looked back on their teenage years.

"*Lollyberry* was the next word she wrote," Odessa said. "What is a *lollyberry*?"

"Perhaps it grows on the West Coast," Father said.

"I've never heard of such a berry." Mother shook her head. Odessa glanced at me.

I shrugged. The word was new to me, as well.

"Knowing you, it's some kind of candy." Mother giggled, hope heavy in her eyes.

ΦΦΦ

After dinner, I joined Father in his study. I closed the dark wood paneled door behind me and quickly made my way to where he was seated in his dark upholstered chair by the fire.

Although the chairs were grouped closely together, I knelt at his feet, content to be near him.

Father was touched by my choice, and I marveled at the warmth in his hazel eyes. Before the loss of my memory, there had always been this tug-of-war between us.

"Do you remember hiding this in your viola case?" He pulled the fine linen paper from his dinner jacket.

"No." I held no recollection.

"For some reason, you also hid this in your case." He held up a much smaller slip of paper and unfolding it, read, "No, I do not regret my decision. I must say your music is as dreary as ever, but I understand why. Y-H-S."

"Y-H-S?" I whispered.

"Yes, your humble servant."

"Oh."

"I believe you wrote this letter," Father unfolded the fine paper, "while we were in Davenport when you sensed you were losing your memory." As he held the paper off to his side, the firelight lit the page.

"Words I Need to Remember. Memories I Cannot Forget." Father turned to grip my nearest hand. "Wren, over the years, Dr. Duggan has dealt with three different cases of the nangoonberry stain."

I nodded. Dr. Duggan was our royal physician.

"He said when we find the key, which is also known as the trigger word, the sudden surge of memories may prove painful. He also said that they are often in an order that does not make sense. And that memories buried the deepest will prove the most painful for you." His voice trailed off.

Memories could often prove painful. Father could still not talk about the Misery Hill without adrenaline in his voice and mannerisms.

"I am going to take my time saying each word or phrase very carefully." He briefly squeezed my hand in his.

I nodded, trying to be brave.

"Buttercups," he whispered.

"What in the world?" I giggled, recalling the young guard's note from a few nights back. How could *buttercups* possibly be a trigger word for me?

Father waited for my giggling to subside before continuing. "He slid buttercups into my hair."

"Who am I talking about, Father?" I asked without lifting my gaze.

"Brody Hew."

Stunned, I stared at the carpet. "The young guard? Edwin's brother?"

"Yes."

Father had allowed him into our home, into his study.

"He's the guard who rescued you from the pig pen. That's why your memory is gray there."

I shook my head. "I have no recollection of him. None."

"You would know if you did." Holding the paper off to his side, he continued. "I love the Hew family. Brody's family. I love his burly arms." Father lowered the stationery to view me. "Dr. Duggan said that I need to prepare you."

Father paused as if simply pausing was enough to prepare me. He'd shocked me to the core. "I fell in love with one of our guards?" How in the world? I couldn't imagine.

"Yes. You loved Brody very much, Wren."

A guard? I'd fallen in love with a guard? It was too much to take in. "He's the one who found me in the pig pen. That right there is reason for me to love him." I'd figured that much out.

"Yes, I suppose it is."

"Did I go straight from Gruel Kitchen to Davenport?" I asked. I remembered nothing between the pig pen and meeting Vincent, except for the awful road.

"No, after Gruel Kitchen, you were with Brody and his family in *Corra*." Father's voice lilted on the word. "Now, listen carefully. It's very important that I read each word aloud." He held the paper closer to the fire's light. "Our walk up the Cashmere Hills." He paused, watching my reaction.

"The lollyberry. Brody's love for the salty sea air. The sunsets like a fireball on the horizon." He paused between each string of words. "Fish and chips fresh from the sea." In spite of what sounded like nonsense to me, tears ebbed in my Father's eyes. "Margaret's Wacky Cake."

"Who's Margaret?" I patted his knee.

"Brody's mother." He smiled softly and returned his gaze to the paper. "Diamonds before babies." Father glanced at me.

I wouldn't meet his gaze. I was so embarrassed. I never wanted to see Brody Hew again.

"And darest I forget the nangoonberry jelly." Without taking his gaze from the paper, Father reached for and gripped my hand in his. "I love this man whom they, whoever they are, might soon take away from me."

I stared sadly at the stationery in his grip. Father was almost done. Perhaps my letter to myself did not contain the key.

"Margaret's desire to see if I truly loved her son might cost my father an empire," he said and his Adam's apple bobbed in his neck. "And you ended with *I cannot forget Brody Hew*."

My love for this man had indeed cost Father an empire. "I'm sorry." The thought greatly saddened me. "So very, very sorry." I'd broken my parents' hearts, ruined the alliance for our country, and fallen in love with a guard.

"No, Wren." He gazed softly at me. "I'm the one who's sorry." His chin always so firm, wobbled. "You've always been such a clever girl; and in Davenport, I thought you were playing games with me. Almost to the end, I thought... no, I feared that there was a strategy to your madness.

"But when I saw you playing the piano without tears..." His cheeks bunched as he swallowed. "And that the stain was gone... I knew they'd stolen her from you." He lowered his chin as he spoke. "I knew then that you needed me in a way that you have never needed me."

"You're so wrong," I marveled. "I've always needed you."

My letter to myself did not contain the key to my memories. Yet, my fragile, broken thoughts, so often unspoken, had unlocked my father's heart for me. He'd wanted me to need him, and my letter helped him to understand how greatly I did.

ΦΦΦ

For several nights in a row, Brody Hew plagued me with his slips of paper. One read: *Wacky cake*. Another: *chewy lollies*. The last was the most ridiculous: *lollyberry*. Was food the only thing he thought about?

I yanked the drapes closed and returned to bed with a huff.

Why did my father allow a guard I had once been in love with to watch over me and send little slips of paper in the middle of the night?

Three nights of silence passed with no little tap, tap, taps on the window.

On the fourth night, I was simply too curious. I slipped out of bed and parted the drapes slightly to peer out.

Brody Hew was no longer on duty. A heavy-set, middle-aged guard on a dark horse had replaced him.

The young guard had already given up. I wasn't quite sure how to feel about the situation.

ΦΦΦ

During breakfast the next morning, I seized the first opening in Father and Mother's conversation.

"I noticed there has been a change of guard," I said.

Father looked up from his poached eggs.

"Brody Hew was not on duty last night," I said.

He nodded. "His father, a cabinet maker, broke his arm and sent word, requesting that Brody return home. He needs him to help with the family business."

"I see." I would no longer need to worry about the guard's presence.

"Wren . . ." Father drummed his fingers on the table. "What do you think of going to Yonder to see your sister?"

"Alia?" I asked.

"Yes."

I glanced at mother. "How long of a journey will it be?"

"About three weeks . . ." Father bobbed his head, "or so to get there."

Nothing was on my calendar except to play piano for two of Mother's little parties. "Do you think we should?" I asked.

"Can I go, too?" Odessa asked.

"No!" Mother said her voice unusually stern.

"After the new road is finished," Father attempted to soften Mother's immediacy. "Right now it is still a difficult trip."

Mother pressed a palm to her heart and breathed easier.

"During our travels from Corra to Davenport, Wren, you told me that Alia was the reason you ran away." Father took a sip of coffee and then lowered the cup to the table.

"I'm sorry, I don't remember."

"Of course, you don't; but, I do. You wanted to see her before you were married." He gazed lovingly at me as he often did nowadays. "Before he left, Brody and I spoke. He confirmed how very important it is that you see Alia again; that it was your heart's desire.

"So, in answer to your question, Wren: yes, we should go to Yonder to see her." With that, Father reached over and gripped my mother's hand.

Chapter Thirty-six

Yonder, one month later . . .

We traveled the new road to Yonder for two weeks. Small villages had cropped up along the way with shops and markets. We then hit a long, difficult stretch in the middle that added more than a week to our plans. Even though the journey was long, it was good for Father to see more of our country. Vast amounts of land and people were joined in Yonder and Blue Sky's merger.

After another five days of travel on a road built by Yonder, my sister's kingdom came into view. No red turrets or brightly colored flags brightened the sky. From the distance, the castle and grounds appeared purely military in scope.

Would my older sister recognize me? My stomach knotted.

Our carriage and men halted outside of the gatehouse. While Father spoke with Yonder guards, I couldn't help but feel apprehensive about meeting someone I'd once loved so very much. What if we'd come all this way and I never remembered her?

Father extended his hand, assisting me out of the carriage. With Helmer in front and three guards behind us, we strode past the gatehouse.

"It's been far too many years since I saw Alia and I have yet to meet my grandchildren," Father said.

I did not need to feel pressure in our circumstances. Our long journey here served him, as well.

Inside the fortress's thick walls, the grounds were pleasant. Numerous plantings—topiaries, roses and hollyhocks softened the courtyard.

Yonder guards led us through a postern, down a winding, slate-lined corridor—so unlike home, and into a Great Hall where black and gray flags hung from the wall and one royal blue and white flag representing their alliance with Blue Sky. A fire blazed in the hearth, adding warmth to the large stone room.

"It is only your company I desire in attendance now, Helmer," Father said, dismissing the other guards.

They returned to the corridor.

A lovely grand piano sat in the alcove of the Great Hall. Only a handful of servants were in view. A dignified, older woman strolled toward us. Her hair was fashioned in three white snowballs high atop her head

"Eunice, I know we are a surprise for you," Father said.

"I should say you are, Francis." She chuckled, patting at a brooch pinned in the V of her dress and regarded Helmer with a quizzical eye. "Don't tell me you're at war again?"

"No, not officially. Although, we are entertaining the idea." He inhaled deeply and held a hand out toward me. "This is my daughter, Wren."

"And so like her mother." Queen Eunice lifted the wire spectacles hung about her neck to study me. "I've heard about you for years. Like Alia, you have beautiful clear skin and wavy hair. Other than that, the two of you look nothing alike."

"Is Alia here?" Father searched the expansive room.

"No. They're in Delfrey today, the whole family. Oh-hh, Francis, you'll finally meet the children. Franklin is the spitting image of you."

"I've greatly looked forward to it." He inhaled deeply. "Another reason we are here, Eunice, is that Wren desires to see her sister."

"Awh . . . what a beautiful gift you've given her." Tears collected in the older woman's eyes. "That was once my heart's desire, too, to see my older brother. But, it was not to be." Her gaze lowered, and a sweeping sadness set her back for a moment.

I nodded, gripping Father's arm.

"Your timing couldn't be more perfect." the Queen blinked, summoning a smile. "Our annual reunion at The Bell Tower is only a few hours away. It'll be the perfect way to surprise Alia and the children."

Although a tad hesitant, I nodded.

"In the meantime, Roger will escort you to The Cottages for your stay." The Queen fluttered her fingers for a middle-aged guard's attention. "We'll see you at seven o'clock at The Bell Tower. It's on the north side of town and is clearly marked."

Even though the Queen was dismissing us, Father didn't move.

"Wren is not entirely herself, Eunice. It's a long story, but all of her happy memories have been locked away in a part of her brain. She does not remember those dearest to her, including Alia." There was a surprising break in his voice. "It is our greatest hope that we'll find the key while we're here."

"I see it now." The Queen lifted her spectacles for a closer look at me. Behind the thick glass, her eyes appeared twice their normal size. "She has lost her essence." Lowering her glasses, she thoughtfully regarded me.

"Wren, when you see your sister tonight, remember this: She has missed you, thought about you, and prayed for you all of your years apart. She loves you. And, whether or not you recall your memories, tonight will still be a very special *new* one for you."

Her sentiments were so moving that I brushed a tear from my eye. "Thank you, Your Highness."

Father turned to leave, and I followed his lead.

Eight feet away stood Helmer. Tears glistened in his eyes. The giant was clearly a dear soul, a man of great empathy.

I couldn't help but smile at him.

ΦΦΦ

For the occasion of meeting my sister, I wore my hair down and the green taffeta gown with its crinolette cage that I'd worn for my portrait. Father said that I looked very much like Mother when she was young.

The Bell Tower, a stone building on the edge of town, was crowded, dimly lit, and packed with rowdy commoners.

Why would Queen Eunice want us to meet Alia here?

A large-bellied man sitting in front of us leaned back in the captain's chair. "Tonight is our favorite show of the season," he informed Father and me. "It is the annual reenactment of Long's reunion with his wife on the day of his release from prison many years ago."

"Ten years ago to be exact," Queen Eunice said from her table slightly ahead and to the right of ours. "They'll soon see for themselves. Don't tell them any more than that."

We might see, but that didn't mean we'd understand. Yonder was an odd country. I hoped my sister liked it here.

Men carried long-handled snuffers about the room and extinguished sconces until only the stage area remained lit.

I sighed, all too aware of my nerves.

Father patted my hand.

Near the front door, our waitress sang an unfamiliar tune in a high, nasal voice.

"Keep your appetites, folks, and keep your eyes on Gerdie," announced a frizzy, gray-haired woman.

"Princess Alia is the one in the cloak," the man in front informed us.

"Oh, thank you!" I sat up taller in my chair.

The play was about an elderly blind man, being reunited with his wife after he'd been imprisoned for many years. Unfortunately for me, Alia wore a hooded cloak, and with the dim lighting in the room, I could see very little of her.

I had a hard time following the storyline.

While Long, the blind man, peered into the darkness reciting poetry, I remembered Queen Eunice's earlier sentiments: *She has missed you, thought about you and prayed for you all of these years. She loves you. And, whether or not you remember your memories, tonight will still be a very special new one.*

I closed my eyes. *Please, allow me to remember.*

Following Long's poetry, the audience clapped unreservedly. So unlike the ladies at Mother's parties.

Long leaned his head toward Alia and—when the crowd noise dimmed—asked, "Do you see my Molly?"

With a hand cupped over her eyes, she scanned the entrance area. Everyone turned in their chairs to look.

"It won't be long, Long," she said.

Father glanced over his shoulder at me.

I smiled, finally caught up in the show.

"Little, old woman, where are you?" Long's voice carried through the warm room.

The wiry built man who'd left earlier looking for Long's wife returned. A deep hush fell as Molly, wearing a soiled apron and windblown cheeks, entered The Bell Tower, her gaze riveted on Long.

"Long . . . a beautiful woman with flowing white hair is slowly walking toward us." Alia's voice rose a pitch as we turned in our chairs.

"Does she look like she's forgiven me?" Long asked.

"There is no doubt," she whispered. And then raising her voice added: "She looks like a bride, there is so much love in her eyes."

"Little old woman . . ." Long held out his hands and turned slightly toward the stairs. "I'm so blessed…"

His wife lifted her skirt at the knee, and slowly climbed the steps, her knees cracking with age.

"Words cannot express . . ."

Molly took that final step toward him and then pressed her cheek to his chest, wrapping her arms around his long waist.

"Awh . . . my Molly." He kissed the top of her hair.

Tears glistened on my father's cheeks before he brushed them aside.

The three thespians remained onstage together and bowed. And then without warning, Alia flipped back her hood, exposing her long, curly auburn hair and clear complexion. With an intake of air, I saw that my sister—the girl in the portrait—was now a beautiful woman.

Everyone who'd participated joined the trio onstage. There were cheers and sniffles as the group of eight took their final bow.

I watched, enthralled.

Father grinned and squeezed my hand.

"Play something, Princess Alia." The requests began. "Princess Alia, play."

She sat down on a stool in front of a squatty, odd looking piano and—with perfect posture— set her fingers to the keys. Her memories were lovely, and her playing was the most beautiful piano music I'd ever heard.

In spite of the entrancing melody, my gut knotted with unease.

What if Alia didn't hold the key? What if she, like everyone else, spoke oddities of times and things I didn't remember?

I briefly closed my eyes. *Please, help us find the key.*

Alia's music was so moving, so full of love and remembrance, that I felt convinced she relived the time she and her husband had first met or first believed they were in love.

From the nearby table, Queen Eunice looked over at me and curled two fingers, bidding me to her.

She wanted me to go on stage.

Panic zig-zagged through me. This isn't how I'd imagined meeting her: onstage, with an audience, who might hear me say: *I'm your sister, Wren, and I'm sorry, I don't remember you.*

A thousand worries pinned me to the chair.

Queen Eunice now implored me with her wide eyes.

"Wren . . ." Chin low, Father whispered. "Where is my brave girl who faced the giants? I know she's in there somewhere."

I inhaled deeply. He was right. I had to find Wren—the girl in the portrait who I didn't understand.

Heart thumping in my chest, I bent low trying not to block the audience's view as I made my way toward the Queen's table.

"Go up there," Eunice whispered, nodding toward the stage. "Alia doesn't know you're here; I wanted it to be a surprise. Stop near her on this side of the piano and look back at her." Cupping one hand, she pointed with the other to the front of the stage. "The audience will have a full view of her

face when she first sees you. They will only see your profile."
She took my hand in her soft, smooth one.

"For many years, Alia has dreamed of visiting Blue Sky with her family to see all of you. The road has taken longer than we foresaw. But know this, dear girl," Queen Eunice's large eyes implored mine, "your sister loves you very much. It is a love worth facing."

Even as she said it, my limbs began to tremble. I glanced back at Father.

Closing his eyes, he nodded.

While my sister played another moving melody, I took much the same route through the room as Long's Molly. *It is a love worth facing,* I repeated as I lifted my dress at the knee and climbed the steps of the stage.

Murmurings rippled through the crowd.

"It is with my permission," said the Queen.

In my long evening gown with its sloped in the back crinolette cage, I was dressed more like royalty than most of the people here. Perhaps Alia would know me by my gown. I kept my gaze fastened on the edge of the stage, not on the nearby dimly lit sea of faces. My heart pounded like a gong as I moved past my sister to stand where the Queen had instructed, near the right side of the piano.

Alia did not look up from her playing. Eyes closed, she was lost in the memory of it all. After a lovely cadence, she rested her hands in her lap.

Instead of applause, there was simply silence.

Like our audience, I waited for her to open her eyes.

Aware of my presence now, her head turned slightly toward me, and then her gaze lifted to mine.

My sister had the most beautiful hazel eyes; up close, she was even lovelier than her portrait. I gazed at her with awe, and although I felt I knew her from all of the stories I'd heard about her, I remembered nothing of my own.

Brows gathered, she shook her head. Tears misted her gaze, and then her face contorted in pain before she covered her mouth with one hand.

"…key," she murmured. Something I hadn't quite heard, even with my gift of listening.

I didn't have my wits about me. I should have just informed her *I am your sister, Wren*. But, I'd hoped her memory was larger than my own.

"I'm sorry, I didn't hear you," I murmured.

"Ducky . . ." she breathed, "I know it's you." She reached for my hands, and gripping them tightly, wept into them.

Zip. Zip. Zip. May it never slip. In her black high heels, the old women had fallen in front of the desk. The key to my memory was *Ducky*. Tears rolled down my cheeks as I remembered sharing with the old woman my last sliver of happiness.

Onstage, Alia and I held each other tightly. No longer were we children; we were grown, and I was even an inch taller than her.

"I have so much to tell you," I said, smiling into her eyes. "Tonight, you'll tell me about everything, and I'll tell you."

"No, Ducky." She laughed, moving her hand briefly to wipe at tears. "Tomorrow morning, after a good night's sleep, we'll talk."

She was my long lost love remembered.

Father strolled across the stage toward us, his gaze fixed on me. With the reunion at hand—Alia and her children, I didn't understand why I'd be the focus of his attention.

Alia must have seen his concern because she stepped back away from me.

Father pressed me snugly against him, wrapping one hand about my head and the other around my back.

I didn't understand, but in his tight embrace, I recalled Dr. Larkin saying *it takes a very special love for the nangoonberry stain, and her stain is very deep.*

Then, there was such a radiant shimmer of memories; it was as if someone had flipped back the lid of the treasure chest of my heart.

Me sitting on Mother's lap, her beautiful coppery-red hair; Maid Kimberlee tucking me into bed and kissing my cheek; Crauley lifting his arm to point out an oriole and then lowering it to pat my hand; Odessa sitting beside me on the settee as I told her stories; Pearl mending my dress in the cornfield; Helmer holding his hands over his heart while I played the cello. And then a hazy memory became heart-wrenchingly clear as Brody Hew climbed the Cashmere Hills to say goodbye.

I felt like someone had stabbed me in the center of my chest.

I cried out in great pain and would have doubled over if Father had not been holding me up.

"Everything is all right," he whispered. "Everything is all right." Through the spinning and the pain, my father's arms held me fast until I relaxed against him at last.

"You're home now," he whispered. "My dear, dear girl, you're finally home."

Chapter Thirty-seven

We were still on stage when Father held me away from him in his arms.

Under his gaze, I felt the all too familiar discomfort as the nangoonberry stain crept up my neck, over my jawbone, to settle in the hollow of my cheek.

"It's back, Wren. I think you know that," he said.

"It hurt, but the sting is over now." I smiled bravely.

"I've heard . . ." Father paused to weigh his words, "that the only remedy that works is marriage."

"Marriage?" I inhaled sharply.

"Yes, to the man you made the jelly for." He traced his fingers along the curve of the stain, smiling.

I pressed my cheek against his chest and held onto him tightly.

ΦΦΦ

After one week in Yonder, it was time to say goodbye to my sister.

Alia, her husband, Wron, their son, Franklin, and daughters, Olivia and Violet, walked us to the gate. It was time to say the goodbye that was never said.

Holding hands, Alia and I smiled at each other.

"I'll see you again, dear sister," she said. For a moment we just stared at one another.

It was my turn. "Next time we won't wait so long." My voice climbed an octave.

"I promise to write, Ducky."

"I do, too."

Instead of goodbyes, we said promises.

"We will plan a trip to Corra, and you and Brody will plan a trip here." She wiped aside her tears.

I nodded, smiling. "I promise."

ΦΦΦ

After ten days of travel, we could see the ocean and smell the salt nipped air. As we drew close to Corra, I recalled one of the pathways that led down to the beach and knew my joy would not be complete if I did not take it.

"Father, I need a moment to myself," I said.

He nodded, but I could tell by the lines that gathered in his forehead that he didn't fully understand.

I left our two hundred soldiers and Father and strode down the sandy trail to the ocean that I loved. I walked until I was ankle-deep in the surf. There, I looked out at the infinite view and marveled at our Creator.

"You know," I whispered, "You know everything." Salty tears rolled down my cheeks. "It wasn't as easy as I would have chosen… if you'd given me a choice. But…You took the mess I'd made," I lifted my face heavenward as tears rolled down my cheeks, "and You made everything right."

ΦΦΦ

Our legion of horsemen, clad in their blue and white, lined the Cashmere Hills overlooking the town of Corra. Thanks to Mr. Sutharlan and his pair of binoculars, the townspeople gathered in the village square. Perhaps they feared an invasion.

I stood between my father and Helmer, and watched below as Brody and his father strode out of the cabinet shop behind their home. They must have called for Margaret, for the front door swung open, and she hurried down the walk, untying her apron.

I waited until they joined their neighbors in the street before I started down the hillside, alone.

Just me—a girl of seventeen in a long white gown, wearing a garland of buttercups that Father and Helmer had helped to pin in my hair.

My future countrymen continued to gather outside of their homes and shops.

Even though my heart wanted to run ahead of me, I walked toward my beloved. I breathed in the salty air and tried to take in every detail.

Remember this moment . . . Never forget.

Long of gait, wearing an expression of both shock and jubilance, Brody made his way toward me. As we bridged the distance, my future etched in front of me. I would marry a carpenter. We would have carved hearts in the top of our kitchen cabinets. I would simply be a wife, someday a mother if God should grant it so. I would gladly give up my title to marry the man I loved.

Before I'd even had a chance to tell Brody that I remembered him, that I loved him, he crushed me to him. His chest and shoulders quaked as he held me.

He spun me around and around, squeezing the tears out of me before he finally set me down.

"Are ya here to marry me, Ennie? Is that why yer here?" His sparkling gaze searched mine.

"I can't very well marry anyone else with this on my face. Now, can I?"

"It came back." He grinned, eyeing the stain.

I nodded. "As soon as I remembered you."

He cupped my chin in his strong hand and gazed at me.

Remember this moment, I told myself. *Never forget.* I clung to memories tighter now. *Never let it go.*

ΦΦΦ

"Are ya Brody's, Ennie? Are ya?" Margaret breathed.

Before I had a chance to tell her, she crushed me to her, spilling my tears.

"I knew ya loved my son." Her wiry frame quaked as she gripped me. "Forgive me, Ennie…" She held me away from her. "A mother wants to feel certain. Ya might not understand it now, but someday when ya have a wee bairn of yer own, ya will.

"Are ya home to marry our Brody?" Margaret asked with the pride of a queen.

I nodded, too emotional for words.

"She's ours. Trev, did ya hear that?" Margaret sobbed into her hand. "She's ours."

"I heard, Mum." Trev hugged me with his good arm.

ΦΦΦ

The entire village of Corra and my beloved pig, Daisy, attended our wedding, which took place on the Cashmere Hills overlooking the sea. My future husband was now Sir Brody. Father knighted him for his exceptional code of conduct and commitment to servitude in saving my life.

At the start of our ceremony, Father stood up and addressed the village. "You, who have been so faithful to Blue Sky, and yet so dependent, will become your own kingdom now and a port city like no other."

I loved Corra as it was, with its quaint simplicity and its traditions, including the nangoonberry jelly. I vowed that we would retain this tradition.

"And you will always have the protection of your ally— Blue Sky Kingdom. For you are marrying one of our own, my beloved daughter, Wren," Father's voice quaked, and so did my heart.

Margaret had chosen twenty young girls from Corra, three of whom were her daughters, to hold my bridal train. My train stretched twenty meters wide across the green velvet hills and was a sight to remember.

Brody and I faced the sea while we said our vows.

And my Father gave me away one last time.

"I now pronounce you man and wife," the minister said.

Brody gripped my chin; his gaze soft on mine, and then he kissed me for the second time.

"I'm so happy, Ennie," he whispered.

I nodded, too emotional for words.

We simply smiled at one another for a moment before we remembered our audience. And then, we turned toward our witnesses—our friends, our family, and our country.

"It's a labor of love, it is," Margaret's whisper reached me in the gentle wind.

As she had warned, the nangoonberry stain followed the age-old tradition and inched its way down my cheek. It hurt a little; I won't lie. All of my countrymen watched as I, their future queen, tried to be brave at the unfamiliarity of it all. Tears pricked my eyes as the stain made its way down my neck and then deep into the chambers of my heart.

"It's gone, Ennie," Brody marveled. He bent and gently kissed my cheek, where the stain had been. "It's gone."

The people of Corra cheered.

With my father and my husband by my side, we turned to watch the sun set like a ball of fire into the horizon. And deep in my soul, I knew I would endure it all again—*everything*—for the love of these two men.

The end

Wacky Cake

Margaret Hew makes this cake for all seven of her children's birthdays. She's too busy to ask if they like chocolate or not. It's a great easy recipe. The cake is surprisingly moist and delicious.

Preheat oven to 375'.
In an ungreased 9 X 13 glass pan, sift the following:
3 cups flour
2 teaspoons baking soda
2 cups sugar
6 tablespoons cocoa
$\frac{3}{4}$ teaspoon salt

Make three holes in the center of the dry ingredients (use the back of a spoon)

Put $\frac{3}{4}$ cup vegetable oil in the center hole.
2 teaspoons vanilla in one hole.
2 tablespoons vinegar in the last hole.

Pour 2 cups water over the top and **stir with a fork,** reaching into the corners, until the batter shows no traces of flour. This is why it's nice to use the glass pan, so you can see every last drop.
Bake for 25 to 30 minutes, or until a toothpick inserted in the center comes out dry.
Cool completely before frosting.
See Frosting recipe on next page.

Chocolate Frosting

$\frac{1}{2}$ cup butter
2/3 cups cocoa
3 cups powdered sugar
1/3 cup milk
1 teaspoon vanilla

Melt butter in a medium-sized saucepan over medium heat. As soon as it is completely melted, remove from heat. Stir in cocoa. Alternately add powdered sugar and milk, beating to spreading consistency. Add additional milk, if needed. Stir in vanilla.

Makes about 2 cups frosting.

Books by Sherri Schoenborn Murray

Counterfeit Princess Series
The Piano Girl – Part One
The Piano Girl – Part Two
The Viola Girl

Christian romances
Fried Chicken and Gravy
Sticky Notes
A Wife and a River

Sherri's audiobooks are available
at www.audible.com

About the Author

Sherri Schoenborn Murray plans for at least two more stories in the Counterfeit Princess series. She lives with her husband Dave and two of their four children in Vancouver, Washington. (Two of their children have already escaped for their adulthood adventures.) They have three chickens, two cats, and one pesky dog.

If you have a favorite character you want her to write more about or simply want to touch base, Sherri enjoys hearing from her readers.

Sign up for Sherri's newsletter on her website:
www.christianromances.com

Email her at: christianromances@gmail.com

Acknowledgements

Sun Tzu's book: *The Art of War* was very helpful for Wren's giant war.

www.allaboutbirds.org for Crauley's scenes;

Katy Kauffman and her book: *2 Timothy: Winning the Victory* which inspired me in my early plotting.

And my husband, Dave, and his sentiments for Brody's description of the sea.

Thank you to Beacock Music in Vancouver, Washington, for lending me the beautiful viola for the cover art/shoot.

Cover photo of Wren by Clari Noel Photography.
Cover art by Steven Novak Illustrations

And to my editors: fellow writer Patty Slack – thank you for all the questions you asked; Jean Hall, thank you for all the encouragement you gave; and final editor, Kristi Weber, thank you for rewriting my wrongs. Also, my moral compasses, editors and proofreaders: my mother, Ethel Schoenborn, and, my daughter, Cori Murray.

Made in United States
North Haven, CT
09 December 2023

45444356R10200